The First-Year Experience Monograph Series No. 5

Residence Life Programs & The New Student Experience
3rd edition

William J. Zeller, Editor

Association of College & University Housing Officers – International

National Resource Center for The First-Year Experience® & Students in Transition, University of South Carolina, 2008

Cite as:

Zeller, W. J. (Ed.). (2008). *Residence life and the new student experience* (Monograph No. 5, 3rd ed.). Columbia, SC: University of South Carolina, National Resource Center for The First-Year Experience and Students in Transition.

Sample chapter citation:

Benjamin, M., & Chatriand, C. M. (2008). The role of residence life programs in recruitment, retention, and transition. In W. J. Zeller (Ed.), *Residence life programs and the new student experience* (Monograph No. 5, 3rd ed., pp. 7-14). Columbia, SC: University of South Carolina, National Resource Center for The First-Year Experience and Students in Transition.

ISBN 978-1-889-27165-1

The First-Year Experience® is a service mark of the University of South Carolina. A license may be granted upon written request to use the term "The First-Year Experience." This license is not transferable without written approval of the University of South Carolina.

Special thanks to Tracy L. Skipper, Editorial Projects Coordinator, and Dottie Weigel, Graduate Assistant, for copyediting and proofing; and to Erin Morris, Graphic Artist for design and layout.

Additional copies of this monograph may be obtained from the National Resource Center for The First-Year Experience and Students in Transition, University of South Carolina, 1728 College Street, Columbia, SC 29208. Telephone (803) 777-6229. Fax (803) 777-4699.

Library of Congress Cataloging-in-Publication Data

Residence life programs and the new student experience / William J. Zeller, editor. -- 3rd ed.
    p. cm. -- (First-year experience monograph series ; no. 5)
 ISBN 978-1-889271-65-1
 1. College student orientation--United States. 2. College student development programs--United States. I. Zeller, William J. II. National Resource Center for the First-Year Experience & Students in Transition (University of South Carolina)
 LB2343.32.R47 2008
 378.1'98--dc22
           2008031074

Contents

List of Tables and Figures..v

Foreword.. 1
Mary Stuart Hunter, Tracy L. Skipper, & Sallie Traxler

Introduction & Overview 3
William J. Zeller

Chapter 1... 7
The Role of Residence Life Programs in Recruitment, Transition, and Retention
Mimi Benjamin & Craig M. Chatriand

Chapter 2... 15
Student Learning and Development: Applications for First-Year Residence Halls
Brad V. Harmon & Merrily S. Dunn

Chapter 3 31
New Students, Emerging Technologies, Virtual Communities, and the College Residential Experience
Richard Holeton

Chapter 4... 53
Living-Learning Programs for First-Year Students
Karen Kurotsuchi Inkelas, Matthew Soldner, & Katalin Szelényi

Chapter 5 67
Social Justice as a Strategy for Residence Hall Community Development
Mary L. Hummel

Chapter 6... 75
Residential Programs Promoting Students' Academic Success
Gene Luna

Chapter 7 83
Faculty Involvement in Residence Halls: Bridging Faculty and Staff Cultures Through Residential Learning Communities
Calvin J. Bergman & Aaron M. Brower

Chapter 8 97
Leadership Development and Advising First-Year Student Leaders
Norbert W. Dunkel and Mary Kay Schneider Carodine

Chapter 9 107
Current Staffing Patterns Supporting First-Year Students
Joel Johnson & James Parker

Chapter 10 121
Residence Hall Architectural Design and the First-Year Experience
Bradford L. Angelini

Chapter 11 137
Safety and Security: An Important Element of First-Year Residence Education
James C. Grimm, Jim Day, and Leslie Atchley

Chapter 12 149
**Residential Programs for Other New Students: Serving Graduate and Transfer
Students**
William J. Zeller

Chapter 13 159
Assessing First-Year Residential Programs
Andrew Beckett and John R. Purdie, II

Chapter 14 173
**Concluding Thoughts: Residence Life's Impact on the First-Year Experience Today
and in the Future**
Beth M. McCuskey

About the Contributors 183

List of Tables and Figures

Table 3.1	Net Generation Traits and Learning and Developmental Principles	33
Table 3.2	Web 2.0: The Social Web	36
Table 3.3	Web 2.0 and Learning Principles	37
Table 4.1	Demographic Characteristics of First-Year National Study of Living-Learning Programs Respondents	57
Table 4.2	Significant Differences by Race Within Living-Learning Programs	60
Table 4.3	Predictors of Four Student Outcomes in Living-Learning Programs	61
Figure 10.1	Honors Hall, University of South Carolina	123
Figure 10.2	Typical Residence Floor, Honors Hall, University of South Carolina	124
Figure 10.3	Learning Resource Center at the University of Michigan's West Quad Housing Complex	125
Figure 10. 4	A Traditional Double Room Completed in 2006 at the University of Oregon	126
Figure 10.5	Adjoining Suite-Style Construction Completed in 2006 at Arizona State University	127
Figure 10.6	Grouping of Four Single Rooms in a Suite Designed for the University of Missouri, College Avenue Housing	127
Figure 10.7	Two-Bedroom Apartment Designed for Northern Arizona University as Part of a Housing Master Plan	128
Figure 10.8	Four-Bedroom Apartment Designed for Northern Arizona University as Part of a Housing Master Plan	128
Figure 10.9	Union Drive Neighborhood, Iowa State University	131
Figure 10.10	Lower Level of Dining/Community Center, Iowa State University	132
Figure 10.11	Ground Level of Dining/Community Center, Iowa State University	132
Figure 10.12	Ground Floor of a Residence Hall in the Bader Snyder Complex, Fort Lewis College in Colorado	134
Figure 13.1	Example of a Logic Model	161
Figure 14.1	Student Learning in Residence Halls	178

Foreword

It is with great pleasure that the staffs of the National Resource Center for The First-Year Experience and Students in Transition and the Association of College & University Housing Officers – International (ACUHO-I) present the third edition of *Residence Life and the New Student Experience*. The long-standing partnership between our two organizations personifies collaborative efforts that are also inherent in successful initiatives created and implemented for new students in residence life settings on our college and university campuses.

The National Resource Center has long served as an organizing structure for those in higher education who advocate improving student learning and transitions into and through higher education. The many outstanding faculty and staff in our international network are well aware of the critically important transition experience students face as they begin their undergraduate experience. The Center's research, publications, conferences, and institutes facilitate the efforts of higher educators worldwide to advance the knowledge, information, and resources that make the first-year experience a better one for students on campuses of all types.

ACUHO-I and its members recognize that a campus's residence halls provide far more than just shelter. These halls are vital environments for student education, development, socialization, and growth. Residence life programs—particularly those designed for the critically important first year—are essential for making that experience a productive one for the students, both individually and collectively, and are proof that learning doesn't end at the classroom door. These innovative programs are incredible opportunities for student affairs professionals, faculty, and academic officers to work together to advance the campus's educational mission. That is why, through the years, a number of ACUHO-I publications, professional development events, and conference sessions have explored the hows and whys of challenging and supporting students as they experience that transitional first year.

This monograph serves as a visible reminder of the mission and purpose of our two organizations and how our work has evolved over the years. As William Zeller notes in the Introduction to this volume, much has changed in higher education and residence life programs since the first edition of this monograph was published in 1991. A quick comparison of the tables of contents, however, suggests that many of the topics of importance to residence life professionals have remained the same—staff training and development, education for diversity, leadership development, academic success, living-learning programs, and assessment. Yet, the treatment of these topics has changed dramatically. While programming and paraprofessional training were concerned largely with social adjustment issues in the past, the authors of this edition discuss the evolving nature of residence life staffs' responsibilities given the current focus on student learning and academic success. Diversity and leadership education are now situated within the larger frameworks of social justice and civic engagement, respectively. The earlier editions of this monograph offered a handful of model living-learning programs to illustrate ways to bridge the in-class and out-of-class learning environments in the residential setting; the current edition draws on the results of national survey research—both illustrating the expansion of these programs over the last two decades and providing a breadth of understanding not possible before. Informed by the larger accountability and assessment movements, the chapter on assessment has moved beyond needs assessment and program evaluation to discuss strategies for measuring learning and developmental outcomes.

Other topics were clearly present in the earlier editions of this monograph and are now more completely developed, with full chapters being devoted to them. These include theories of learning and development, the impact of emerging technologies, faculty involvement, and architectural design to support learning and community development outcomes.

Finally, since the National Resource Center's founding in the mid-1980s, its mission has evolved to consider a range of significant transitions into and through higher education. Similarly, the authors of this volume acknowledge that first-year students are not the only new students on our campuses. A chapter new to this edition addresses the needs of incoming transfer and graduate students and discusses model programs designed to serve them.

The commitment to providing environments that foster student development is why the National Resource Center and ACUHO-I formed a partnership for the first edition of this monograph almost 20 years ago. Our commitment spans the years and is as strong today as it was in 1991. With a mixture of practice and theory, we are confident that the information and resources in this monograph will prove valuable to ACUHO-I's members, educators in the National Resource Center's network, and all higher educators concerned about student success. Finally, we would like to thank all the readers who will apply the lessons of this monograph to their everyday work for the good work they do on behalf of students in their first college year and beyond.

Mary Stuart Hunter
Assistant Vice Provost and Executive Director
National Resource Center for The First-Year Experience and Students in Transition
University of South Carolina

Tracy L. Skipper
Editorial Projects Coordinator
National Resource Center for The First-Year Experience and Students in Transition
University of South Carolina

Sallie Traxler
Executive Director
Association of College & University Housing Officers – International

Introduction & Overview

William J. Zeller

Much has happened in higher education and residential life since the first edition of this monograph was published in 1991. The early nineties marked the end of an era, which had embraced a "sink or swim" philosophy toward new first-year students, and a campus experience that was generally designed to weed out those who did not belong. First-year students were often assigned to the least attractive and least popular residence halls on campus and had to wait their turn for priority accommodations until their sophomore or junior years. New residential programs specifically designed to support new student transitions and academic success were just beginning to emerge.

Student learning as an overarching construct for curricular and cocurricular reform had not yet been introduced, and certainly not in residential life. In response to a renewed emphasis being placed on student learning over the past decade, many components of first-year residential programs have been transformed: The services, staffing patterns, programs, facilities, and use of technologies have all been significantly influenced by the student learning and first-year experience movements. Teaching and learning is no longer confined to the classroom; rather, our campuses are now being designed to provide seamless learning environments in all areas of the campus, especially in the residence halls.

Although residence hall safety was a priority, the context and importance of safe and secure residential facilities has changed dramatically. The Clery Act had just been adopted in 1990. Since then, 9-11 and the Virginia Tech and Northern Illinois shootings have dramatically altered our concerns about campus safety. Higher expectations, higher scrutiny and accountability, and higher stakes are entrenched in the planning and administration of residence hall safety systems—particularly for incoming first-year students. Even the lexicon has changed. In 1991, Gen X, the Millennials, the Baby Boom Echo, and helicopter parents had not yet become part of our vocabulary.

The new wave of living-learning programs and residential learning communities were in their infancy in 1991, and on most campuses they did not exist. The thought of faculty teaching classes and meeting with students in first-year residence halls was generally unheard of. Students typically studied alone in their residence hall rooms, and the thought of collaborating with other students on homework and test preparation was most likely viewed as inappropriate by many faculty members.

Of most importance, the use of technology was just beginning to blossom. (The first edition was stored on a "floppy disc" that Betsy Barefoot and I mailed back and forth to each other). In-room connectivity, computer labs, wireless zones and instructional technology, cell phones, laptops, iPods, music downloading, video-streaming, podcasting, Facebook, MySpace, blogging, wikis, and Google were, of course, not created yet. Many students still used typewriters, kept written notes and notebooks, used "land-line" telephones in their rooms, and listened to radios, cassette tapes, and records on their stereos.

Today, the role of residence life programs in supporting institutional goals for recruiting, retaining, and supporting the transitions of new students to our campuses is universally recognized as one of the most important elements of a quality campus first-year experience program. This was not the case in the early nineties. The expansion and enhancement of first-year living-learning programs, new staffing patterns, residential technology resources, and enhanced residential facilities with new types of spaces and amenities have come about through the common acknowledgement of the importance of a quality, residential experience for first-year students.

We have attempted to bring to this third edition of the monograph a collection of authors who have described the current state of the residential first-year experience and who will shape our thinking about the future.

In chapter 1, Mimi Benjamin and Craig Chatriand begin by exploring the role that first-year residential programs play in supporting the initial phase of the first-year experience—the recruitment and initial transitions of new students to the campus, and ultimately their retention at the institution. The authors discuss increasing expectations among students and their families regarding the quality of the residential facilities, programs, and services that campuses offer to students.

Brad Harmon and Merrily Dunn follow in chapter 2 with a discussion of how student development and student learning theory should shape program and service design in first-year residential communities. Ensuring that the developmental and learning needs of new students are fully supported requires a comprehensive program model. It is imperative that residence life professionals draw from both developmental and learning theories to shape a program that uniquely fits the needs of first-year students who live on campus.

In chapter 3, Richard Holeton provides an insightful review of how new technologies are shaping the curricular and cocurricular residential student experience in the 21st Century. He discusses the traits of the Millennial or Net Generation, key technology trends, new kinds of residential learning spaces, the importance of virtual communities in our student residences, and new media literacy for first-year students.

Karen Kurotsuchi Inkelas, Matthew Soldner, and Katalin Szelényi (chapter 4) provide an overview of living-learning experiences and the important roles they play in enhancing the first-year residential experience on our campuses. They report specifically on the results of the National Study of Living-Learning Programs and the key findings pertaining to first-year students. This ACUHO-I-sponsored study has assessed the impact of living-learning programs on campuses across the country, and their findings on the first-year experience, as reflected in this chapter, will allow us to continue to enhance such initiatives.

In chapter 5, Mary Hummel addresses social justice and community development, reviews current trends in diversity education, and conveys the importance of incorporating social justice education within first-year residential communities. For many of our students, living in a multicultural residential environment is the first opportunity they have had to intensively interact with people of different cultural backgrounds and ethnicities. Effectively designed programs and environments can greatly enhance understanding and skill development and the overall undergraduate experience.

Gene Luna, in chapter 6, highlights current trends in incorporating academic and transitional support services within residential settings. First-year programs must be designed to offer convenient "front-loaded" access to important support programs and services. On many campuses, the residence community has been designated as the place for providing front-line support connections to new students. These new initiatives have implications for space design, staffing patterns, budgeting, and ultimately the forging of partnerships with academic and student affairs colleagues across campus.

Calvin Bergman and Aaron Brower follow in chapter 7 and explore the important, yet complex issue of meaningful involvement of faculty in residential first-year programs. The authors offer an extensive overview of the issues, barriers, and strategies for building bridges with faculty and provide us with a first-hand understanding of what really occurs when faculty and student affairs staff come together to create a first-year residential program.

In chapter 8, Norb Dunkel and Mary Kay Schneider Carodine describe the role that first-year residence halls play in the development of leadership skills for first-year students and explain why residential environments are perhaps the best settings for introducing new students to leadership and community service. For many student leaders, their first leadership experiences occurred in a residence hall position, which ultimately served as a springboard to broader leadership service on campus and ultimately within career and community settings.

In chapter 9, Joel Johnson and James Parker offer an insightful description of how first-year residence hall staffing patterns have changed since the advent of the first-year experience movement. The goals of supporting and enhancing the transitions of new students and promoting learning and academic success have brought new staff members into the residential setting and have increased collaboration across campus. This chapter gives us a glimpse of the past and explains how new staffing models have emerged on campuses.

Architect Brad Angelini stresses the importance of facility design in shaping the first-year experience throughout chapter 10. More than ever, creating facilities which promote community and facilitate interactions between students and between students and faculty, while still providing privacy and spaces for individual and group study are essential for ensuring students have a successful first year at college.

In chapter 11, Jim Day and Leslie Atchley build on the work of the late James Grimm to heighten our awareness of the important role residential environments and programs play in ensuring that first-year students are safe as they arrive on campus, and ultimately become contributing members of an overall safe campus community. I am very pleased that the work of Jim Grimm in the second edition of the monograph could carry forward into this newest edition.

In chapter 12, I introduce two populations of new students who also need specialized programs and services from residential life. Graduate and transfer students are being given increased national attention, and calls for reform to better support their adjustment and academic success are coming from many directions. Residence hall communities can play an important role in supporting campus initiatives to better serve these students and ensure their success and engagement on campus.

The key to successful programs for new students is assessment. In chapter 13, Andrew Beckett and John Purdie provide an overview of current trends in the assessment of the first-year experience and student learning. Their framework for creating an assessment model for first-year residential programs is in full alignment with national trends in this area.

Finally, in chapter 14, Beth McCuskey uses her expertise to help us think about the residential first year for the next decade and beyond. McCuskey's dissertation research focused on future trends in the student housing profession, and applying her insights to the residential first year has proven to be very valuable.

As we look ahead to the next decade of higher education, exciting challenges and opportunities await us. Accountability, possible loss of funding, the infusion of new technologies to support teaching and learning, globalization, and social diversity will have significant implications for the higher education landscape.

Through the efforts of organizations like ACUHO-I and the National Resource Center for The First-Year Experience and Students in Transition, educators concerned with the transition of new students to our campuses will continue to have the resources they need to effectively do their work. I hope this monograph will serve as a resource for residence life and student affairs administrators, faculty, and other stakeholders involved in the residential first-year experience. It has been a pleasure working with the authors, the staff of the National Resource Center, and ACUHO-I to create this newest edition of this monograph. In particular, I would like to thank Tracy Skipper for her support, leadership, and expertise in the creation of this document.

Chapter One

The Role of Residence Life Programs in Recruitment, Transition, and Retention

Mimi Benjamin and Craig M. Chatriand

The transition into higher education may be influenced by many factors, including the experience of living on campus. Residential programs offer structures and supports that typically assist traditional-aged students in moving from their high school experiences and home environments to life on campus within a community of their peers. The opportunities available through residence hall living may impact students' decisions to enroll in a particular institution, their ability to make a successful transition, and their likelihood of remaining at the institution through graduation.

This chapter outlines some initiatives in residential programs that may influence the recruitment, transition, and retention of students who live in residence halls. It is important to note that the focus of this chapter is primarily on traditional-aged students, the student population most likely to live on campus.

Recruitment

Students choose to live on campus for a variety of reasons. In a review of the literature, Luzzo, Twale, Pattillo, and Harris (1999) noted that factors influencing this decision included gender, physical attractiveness of facilities, distance of the institution from home/parents, and the personality of the living unit. However, Luzzo and colleagues concluded that "the primary deciding factor was convenience in attending classes" (p. 19). Other influential factors included the opportunity to meet new people, have the "whole college experience," satisfy parental expectations of living on campus, and make new friends.

For students who plan to live on campus, residence life programs and initiatives can be key factors in the recruitment process, especially when residence life units partner with other units on campus. For example, partnerships with the Office of Admissions can be used to create consistent messages and provide prospective students (and their families) with information that makes the institution more appealing. At Iowa State University, a committee consisting of staff from admissions and the Department of Residence began meeting regularly in order to brainstorm ideas, determine how each unit's processes impact the other, and ensure that their messages are consistent (G. Arthur, personal communication, November 7, 2006). Another example of partnerships is at the University of Oregon where resident assistants serve as tour guides during Preview Days that are co-sponsored by orientation and residence hall staff (J. Vianden, personal communication, November 20, 2006).

Schroeder (1993) makes several specific recommendations about the role of residence life in recruiting new students. These include using residence hall students as telemarketers to potential students, awarding "housing grants" based on need and/or merit, and hosting summer institutes for underrepresented student populations (p. 526). He also recommends including overnight stays in the residence hall with campus visits. The Women in Science and Engineering (WiSE) program at Iowa State University has used this approach to recruit students who have been admitted to the institution but have yet to finalize their acceptance. In the "WiSE Getaway" program, visiting students are paired with volunteer WiSE participants in the residence halls and experience both the academic and residential aspects of the campus.

Today's students expect to find information about available programs in readily accessible online formats. As such, many institutions use web sites, chat rooms, and blogs to recruit students to the institution and to the residential system. Oregon State University asks two first-year students to track their transitions to college for prospective students to read. The blogs are posted on the university housing and dining services web site and touch on many issues including homesickness and transition, academic challenges, multicultural organizations, and major events on campus (Oregon State University, 2007). The blogs are an honest overview of the successes and challenges of a student's first year.

Virtual tours are another way technology can also be used to market the residential experience to prospective students. Housing departments have moved visual displays of their facilities from paper brochures to online formats, where a greater amount of information can be communicated to prospective students. Virtual tours, such as the one on Vanderbilt University's web site (http://www.vanderbilt.edu/ResEd/main/HallTour.php), can offer still pictures with captions, showcasing a residence hall room, customer service desk, and other hall amenities such as computer labs and laundry rooms. More advanced tours allow viewers to get a 360-degree view of a typical room. Utah State University takes this format one step further and gives prospective students 360-degree views of study lounges and the outside of buildings, as well.

At institutions with residency requirements, the housing office may not have to recruit new students to live on campus. However, the institution can use this requirement in recruitment by demonstrating the benefits of campus living to potential students and their families. Virtual or actual tours of rooms are especially helpful for students who are required to live on campus. Some institutions provide rationales for their residency requirements on their web sites. For example, the University of San Francisco (2007) explains why living on campus is considered important: "Research has shown that students who live on campus generally have a higher grade point average than students who live off campus. In addition, they are more likely to graduate within four years and have a positive college experience." Other institutions, such as the University of Massachusetts at Amherst and Marshall University have residency requirements for full-time students and offer information on exemptions to these requirements on their web sites, which can be helpful to students who may have a need for such an exception.

While residency requirements have been challenged on the basis of gender bias, Fourteenth Amendment issues, religious freedom, and institutions' alleged attempts to remove competing commerce in the housing market, Jones (1998) concludes, "The literature appears to offer educational support for a parietal rule supportive of the institution's mission" (p. 32). Citing DeCoster, Jones also notes that "making the campus more attractive to prospective students, increasing student retention, and increasing control over student behaviors" (p. 32) are additional reasons for having an on-campus residency requirement.

Many campuses require first-year students to live on campus despite having more demand for housing than they have available space. It is very important for institutions to communicate to new students and their parents how space is allocated, and who has priority. Thus, all new students will be able to effectively plan for their housing arrangements well in advance of their matriculation. When upper-level students are not allowed to stay in housing, the university should support their transitions into the off-campus market as much as possible, and new students should be aware that these services will be available to them when they are needed. An example of this model is St. Edwards University, a small Catholic liberal arts university in Austin, Texas, that requires first-year students to live on campus unless they commute from home. The institution established increased enrollment goals for 2000-2010, resulting in new residence halls being built. However, even with the new halls, the institution cannot house all students. Their intentional approach to housing students involves working toward the original cohort goal of reserving space for 90% of their first-year students (first-year cohort), 50% of their sophomores (second-year cohort), 25% of their juniors (third-year cohort), and 20% of their seniors (fourth-year cohort). As a result, they have implemented workshops and publications for juniors and seniors who are transitioning to off-campus living. Topics for the workshops include availability of off-campus housing, costs, advice on signing leases, and information about apartment complexes. They also offer information about a private company that helps students identify off-campus apartments of interest.

From the basic elements of residential living, such as the appearance of the buildings to the technological aspects of providing students with high-tech virtual tours and easy online processes, recruitment requires a great deal of attention and effort. Maintaining attractive living spaces is a priority for all institutions, despite the challenges that accompany upkeep. The technological aspects of recruitment require highly skilled staff members to create and maintain web sites, virtual tours, and online processes, while always attending to what is creative and new in the presentation of online information. Yet, it is also important to remember that not all students will have easy access to computers. Maintaining some "paper" presence, through brochures and forms may be necessary in order to reach all students.

Transition

Goodman, Schlossberg, and Anderson (2006) define a transition as "any event or non-event that results in changed relationships, routines, assumptions, and roles" (p. 33). Moreover, they identify four factors that must be considered for successful transitions: self, situation, support, and strategies. These four factors affect an individual's ability to cope with change and can be viewed as assets and/or liabilities. In a given situation, such as the transition to college, "[a]ssets may outweigh liabilities, making adjustment relatively easy, or liabilities may now outweigh assets so assimilation of the transition becomes correspondingly more difficult" (p. 57). What students bring, in the form of "self," and the situation of making the move to college cannot be controlled by the staff. However, residence life programs can create supportive strategies that lead to successful transitions for students.

Students experience the transition to college, and the transition to residential living, in a number of ways. Tinto (1988) noted that the shift from home to college may be experienced as a minor transition for some students and a major one for others. He stated that students who leave home for college need to disassociate both physically and socially from their previous communities to become part of their new communities: "In a very real sense, their staying in college depends on their becoming leavers from their former communities" (p. 443). However, this separation may not be desirable or appropriate for all students. According to Jones (2001), "Research has only begun to examine the subtle effects of disjunction on the success of multicultural students as they separate from, yet try to maintain connection with, their cultural heritage and identity" (p. 8). Staff and services can assist students in shifting from their original community to their new one at college, while also being knowledgeable about and respectful of the differing needs of various student populations. For example, some institutions offer a siblings' weekend that includes a residential component for siblings, creating structured opportunities for students to bring their familial support systems to campus.

In a study of first-time, full-time, first-semester students in a Canadian institution, Birnie-Lefcovitch (2000) determined that issues regarding changing interpersonal relationships, length of time for adjustment, and general first-semester stresses were of particular concern for the students. One recommendation involved creating orientation-type programs to assist students in meeting new people, something that can be facilitated through the residence life program. Also recommended was the use of early identification systems to identify those students who experience the university as more stressful than expected (Birnie-Lefcovitch), which would require staff training and planning. Schuh (1999b) recommended that staff be educated on the transition experience that students will face, specifically identifying the unique environmental challenges that students from underrepresented populations may experience.

The transition from high school to college may have similarities to the experience of transitioning to a new country, with the experience of "culture shock" being part of both experiences (Hoffenberger, Mosier, & Stokes, 1999; Zeller & Mosier, 1993). At the same time, Herndon (1984) hypothesized that "on-campus housing generally serves a valuable and positive socialization function that facilitates a student's adjustment and consequent satisfaction with the institution" (p. 29). The socialization and acculturation of new students to the campus and the residence halls is a process that can be enhanced by intentional efforts as described below.

In their study of colleges and universities in the Documenting Effective Educational Practice (DEEP) project, Kuh, Kinzie, Schuh, Whitt, and associates (2005) found that many institutions in their study front-loaded resources to assist students in understanding how to be successful. Similarly, front-loading activities focused on building community in the residence halls is a common practice and is usually helpful to students who are trying to create new identities in a new place. Meeting other students who are having similar experiences can be helpful. Whether they attend a floor meeting or an all-hall gathering, students can benefit from social interactions and start to establish personal communities within the institution. Other initiatives that may help students acclimate to college include programming focused on the first-year transition; encouraging students' involvement in residential leadership activities; and creating connections between students and faculty through events such as mentoring programs, invited lectures, and informal meetings (Hoffenberger et al., 1999).

Residence life units can also be involved with other initiatives designed to address new-student transition issues. At Indiana University, resident assistants (RAs) serve as guides for their students during Welcome Week programming provided through a partnership between Orientation and Residential Programs and Services. As part of their job responsibilities, RAs take their residents to prescribed orientation programs, such as tours of the school in which their majors are located and meetings with academic advisors who are housed in the residence halls. This type of collaboration between offices may also help students see the connections between the various aspects of their student experience.

In addition to the programmatic efforts, community and roommate agreements can be helpful in the transition process. The Community Standards Model at the University of Nevada, Las Vegas, serves as a model for other institutions in establishing behavioral guidelines for students in residence halls. According to Piper (1997), "Community standards are shared agreements that define mutual expectations for how the community will function on an interpersonal level, that is, how the members will relate to and treat one another" (p. 22). Such agreements create opportunities for dialogue about important elements of the living environment that can be revisited as needed and bring to light situations that new students may not have been able to anticipate.

Today's students may begin making the transition to their new living environment through social networking sites by seeking out new roommates and hallmates through Facebook and MySpace. Some students are very familiar with these sites, while others are new to "facebooking." In preparation for their arrival on campus, Mercyhurst College students receive information about social networking sites, specifically Facebook. The Residence Life and Student Conduct Office takes this opportunity to inform students about responsible conduct online during their transition to the institution. New students receive a letter and brochure entitled "FacetheFacts" that encourages them to make good choices regarding information they make available on such networking sites. A comparable letter and copy of the brochure are sent to faculty and staff to alert them to this use of technology by current students.

Special programming and activities also can help ease the adjustment process. The University of Wisconsin-Stevens Point created their "ARC to Success" program, in which first-year students and upper-division residential peer staff are paired and focus on study skills and transitional issues (Hoffenberger et al., 1999). At Bemidji State University, peer academic assistants live on the residence hall floors; staff an Academic Resource Center; and provide such services as topic-based study tables, tutoring, and referrals. Other programs that typically assist students with their transition to college are academic programs housed in the residential system such as leadership opportunities, learning communities, residential colleges, and first-year seminars taught in residence halls. These programs are discussed in detail in subsequent chapters of this monograph.

Students experience some transition issues that can be anticipated by residence life staff. These issues might include homesickness, interpersonal challenges, and the developmental growth that students may find uncomfortable but from which they learn a great deal. Residence life staff, both professional and paraprofessional, must have appropriate training in order to assist students as they become members of their new communities. Staff may also be challenged to identify appealing activities that aid in the transition process. Allowing residents to identify and coordinate events is one way to learn what activities are appealing to them and to create a sense of ownership for programs. For example, creating community standards/expectations can help new (and returning) students begin to recognize the elements of community life and their responsibilities to make that community successful.

Retention

An intentional focus on retention by all units within institutions, including residence life programs, typically is necessary to meet enrollment management goals. To be effective in this regard, Schroeder (1993) notes that staff in residence life programs must understand the rates of persistence and attrition within their housing systems and how these rates contribute to larger enrollment patterns. In fact, simply having on-campus housing available can decrease attrition. Numerous studies have indicated that residence hall living has a positive impact on persistence and graduation (Pascarella & Terenzini, 2005; Pascarella, Terenzini, & Blimling, 1994; Schuh, 1999a). Referencing Upcraft (1989), Schuh (1999a) "observed that there is an inherent goodness in living in residence halls if staying in college, graduating, and achieving personal development are inherently good" (p. 4).

One reason living on campus may promote retention is that it leads to greater investment in the college experience. Defined as "the amount of physical and psychological energy that the student devotes to the academic experience" (Astin, 1984, p. 297), student involvement, or participation in college beyond the minimum, results in positive gains, including increased retention. The opportunity for social and possibly academic involvement with peers, faculty members, and the institution appear to impact student success (Pascarella & Terenzini, 2005), and those opportunities are an inherent part of the residential experience. In addition, research has shown that student satisfaction with their residential experience has an influence on retention (Li, McCoy, Shelley, & Whalen, 2005). Finding their place within the residential system may be the first step for integration into the larger college/university system for some students.

Leadership opportunities in the residence halls provide immediate opportunities for involvement for many students and serve as a training ground for later campus-wide leadership roles. Many halls provide hall government roles that students can assume. Some institutions employ the "house system," referring to floors/floor sections as "houses" that have their own house government, financial resources, and activities. The house system is especially helpful in establishing leadership opportunities at a local level for students. Student staff roles, such as resident assistants (or those with similar titles), peer mentors, and other live-in student staff positions offer leadership opportunities to which new students may aspire. These and other on-campus work experiences in the residence halls may have positive results for students, including increased persistence (Pascarella & Terenzini, 2005). Chapter 8 in this monograph provides a more complete discussion of leadership development and civic engagement.

Some institutions offer courses (e.g., first-year seminars) that help students become acclimated to both the institution and college-level work. Assessment results of many of these courses suggest that they have a positive impact on retention (Barefoot, 1993; Barefoot, Warnock, Dickinson, Richardson, & Roberts, 1998; Tobolowsky, Cox, & Wagner, 2005). These courses may be taught in the residence hall where the students live, providing another opportunity for students to create bonds with their peers while learning more about navigating the institution and life as a college student. Having courses taught in the residence halls or by residence hall staff suggests to students that their living environment is not completely separate from their academic activities and that there is a connection between their in- and out-of-class experiences on campus.

Schroeder (1993) noted that residence programs involving diverse living arrangements tend to lead to persistence and retention. Living-learning communities, in their different forms, attempt to address retention as well as transition. Living-learning communities may include floors or housing units where all students share a major or an academic area of interest (e.g., foreign language, community service). Academic programs such as learning communities and residential colleges can create strong bonds between participants, offer a solid academic foundation for students, and may help students become more connected to the institution, thus impacting retention. Residence-based learning communities provide a link between the students' living and academic environments, integrating curricular with cocurricular experiences (Shapiro & Levine, 1999).

Cornell University offers a number of living-learning options for students, such as subject-oriented theme houses (e.g., Ecology House), foreign language houses, and cross-cultural living units (e.g., Latino Living Center). Residential colleges, where faculty members typically reside with the students, are available at institutions such as Princeton University, the University of Michigan, Rice University, and Murray State University. More detailed information about these types of programs is provided in later chapters of this monograph.

Many institutions indicate on their housing web sites that retention is a goal of their programs, and they include academic programming in their residence halls to enhance students' success and help them achieve their goals. Assessment of these efforts is critical to determining their impact on retention. Effective programs can also be adapted to fit the cultures of other institutions as they attempt to increase retention.

The residence hall experience may mitigate some of the other forces that lead to student departure. The literature indicates that student involvement is critical, yet getting students involved can be a challenge. It is often tempting to continue using programs and events simply because they have worked in the past. However, students change as do their interests. What was appealing to students years ago may not be interesting currently. It is important that staff understand the changing student population and acknowledge those changes when they design activities intended to foster connections between the students and the institution. Programs such as learning communities and first-year seminar courses taught in the residence halls create connections for students between their academics and their "student life" experiences—an essential element of effective retention initiatives. Continuing to identify ways to marry the academic and student life experiences, thus creating a holistic experience, is something that residence life staff are well-positioned to address.

Conclusion

Residence life programs clearly have important contributions to make to the recruitment, transition, and retention of students in higher education. The literature suggests that the residential experience has a positive impact, and the opportunities for creative approaches to all areas abound. Partnerships are a key element to success, as different units throughout campus have these three purposes in mind as they create initiatives. Finding ways to connect those initiatives not only makes sense but also creates a more seamless and interconnected learning experience for students. In addition, providing opportunities for students to see the connections between their in- and out-of-class experiences may also lead to a more holistic college experience.

References

Astin, A. W. (1984). Student involvement: A developmental theory for higher education. *The Journal of College Student Development, 25,* 297-308.

Barefoot, B. O. (Ed.). (1993). *Exploring the evidence: Reporting outcomes of freshman seminars* (Monograph No. 11). Columbia, SC: University of South Carolina, National Resource Center for The Freshman Experience and Students in Transition.

Barefoot, B. O., Warnock, C. L., Dickinson, M. P., Richardson, S. E., & Roberts, M. R. (Eds.). (1998). *Exploring the evidence: Reporting outcomes of first-year seminars, Vol. II* (Monograph No. 25). Columbia, SC: University of South Carolina, National Resource Center for The First-Year Experience and Students in Transition.

Birnie-Lefcovitch, S. (2000). Student perceptions of the transition from high school to university: Implications for prevention programming. *Journal of The First-Year Experience & Students in Transition, 12*(2), 61-88.

Goodman, J., Schlossberg, N. K., & Anderson, M. L. (2006). *Counseling adults in transition: Linking practice with theory* (3rd ed.). New York: Springer Publishing Company.

Herndon, S. (1984). Recent findings concerning the relative importance of housing to student retention. *The Journal of College and University Student Housing, 14*(1), 27-31.

Hoffenberger, K., Mosier, R., & Stokes, B. (1999). Transition experience. In J. H. Schuh (Ed.), *Educational programming and student learning in college and university residence halls* (pp. 34-49). Columbus, OH: Association of College & University Housing Officers – International.

Jones, D. P. (1998). On campus residency requirements. *The Journal of College and University Student Housing, 27*(2), 32-35.

Jones, L. (2001). Creating an affirming culture to retain African-American students during the postaffirmative action era in higher education. In L. Jones (Ed.), *Retaining African Americans in higher education* (pp. 3-20). Sterling, VA: Stylus.

Kuh, G. D., Kinzie, J., Schuh, J. H., Whitt, E. J., & Associates. (2005). *Student success in college: Creating conditions that matter*. San Francisco: Jossey-Bass.

Li, Y., McCoy, E., Shelley, M. C., II., & Whalen, D. F. (2005). Contributors to student satisfaction with special program (Fresh Start) residence halls. *The Journal of College Student Development, 46*(2), 176-192.

Luzzo, D. A., Twale, D. J., Pattillo, K. L., & Harris, J. Jr. (1999). Evaluating factors that contribute to undergraduates' decisions to live on campus. *The Journal of College and University Student Housing, 28*(1), 16-26.

Oregon State University. (2007). *University housing and dining services: UHDS blogs*. Retrieved January 26, 2007, from http://oregonstate.edu/uhds/future_students/blog.php

Pascarella, E. T., & Terenzini, P. T. (2005). Educational attainment and persistence. In *How college affects students: A third decade of research, Vol. 2* (pp. 373-444). San Francisco: Jossey-Bass.

Pascarella, E. T., Terenzini, P. T., & Blimling, G. S. (1994). The impact of residential life on students. In C. C. Schroeder, P. Mable, & Associates (Eds.) *Realizing the educational potential of residence halls* (pp. 22-52). San Francisco: Jossey-Bass.

Piper, T. D. (1997, July/August). Empowering students to create community standards. *About Campus, 2*(3), 22-24.

Schroeder, C. C. (1993). Conclusion: Creating residence life programs with student development goals. In R. B. Winston, Jr., S. Anchors, & Associates (Eds.), *Student housing and residential life* (pp. 517-534). San Francisco: Jossey-Bass.

Schuh, J. (1999a). Student learning in college residence halls: What the research shows. In J. H. Schuh (Ed.), *Educational programming and student learning in college and university residence halls* (pp. 1-20). Columbus, OH: Association of College & University Housing Officers – International.

Schuh, J. (1999b). Conclusions and recommendations. In J. H. Schuh (Ed.), *Educational programming and student learning in college and university residence halls* (pp. 171-179). Columbus, OH: Association of College & University Housing Officers – International.

Shapiro, N. S., & Levine, J. H. (1999). *Creating learning communities: A practical guide to winning support, organizing for change, and implementing programs*. San Francisco, CA: Jossey-Bass.

Tinto, V. (1988). Stages of student departure: Reflections on the longitudinal character of student leaving. *The Journal of Higher Education, 59*(4), 438-455.

Tobolowsky, B. F., Cox, B. E., & Wagner, M. T. (Eds.). (2005). *Exploring the evidence: reporting research on first-year seminars, volume III* (Monograph No. 42). Columbia, SC: University of South Carolina, National Resource Center for The First-Year Experience and Students in Transition.

University of San Francisco. (2007). *University life: Residency requirements*. Retrieved January 26, 2007, from http://www.usfca.edu/residence_life/international/RESIDENCY.html

Zeller, W., & Mosier, R. (1993). Culture shock and the first-year experience. *The Journal of College and University Student Housing, 23,* 19-23.

Chapter Two

Student Learning and Development: Applications for First-Year Residence Halls

Brad V. Harmon and Merrily S. Dunn

While learning and development are often considered separately, many educators writing about these concepts acknowledge that these domains are largely integrated (Arnold & Kuh, 1999; King & Baxter Magolda, 1996). These researchers note that college students experience learning and development not just within the context of the classroom but also beyond its confines, especially within the residential setting. As a result, each person working in a college or university setting should be intentionally focused on creating conditions that empower college students to become engaged in their own learning and development (Evans, Forney, & Guido-DiBrito, 1998). Residence life professionals have a special role to play in this regard, especially in providing first-year students the guidance, support, and resources they need to persist to graduation. Yet, if residence life professionals are to design effective programs and services, they must have a comprehensive understanding of the development and learning styles of first-year students. The application of developmental theories to the design of first-year living-learning environments also allows for greater cohesion between academic affairs and residence life professionals and affords living-learning initiatives greater centrality in regard to the overall institutional mission and curricular goals (Baxter Magolda, 1999).

The purpose of this chapter is to give an overview of the relationship between the first-year experience and residential programs, discuss the relationship of theory to the goals of first-year residential programs, and provide an understanding of how theories might be most useful as a tool for structuring and grounding programmatic efforts and pedagogical practices in first-year residential programs. While the chapter introduces a number of theories, it is impossible in a format such as this to do justice to their full significance and complexity. Thus, readers are encouraged to consult the original works of each theorist as well as relevant secondary sources that discuss, critique, and offer suggestions for use in the residential setting.

The First-Year Experience and Residential Programs

The first year of college, and every subsequent year, offers an ever-changing set of transitions students must navigate. The process by which college students find their way through these transitions and integrate themselves into the collegiate environment significantly affects their persistence at the institution. Students are more likely to successfully integrate into the collegiate environment when they can readily identify with that environment. Further, the extent of a student's involvement in the life of the institution has an impact on his/her subsequent learning and development (Astin, 1996; 1999). The specific meanings college students assign to the transition experience, as well as their interactions with the collegiate environment, have a significant effect on whether or not they can successfully integrate the various aspects of college life. Students are more likely to leave college if they are insufficiently integrated into the collegiate experience. On the other hand, students who experience greater levels of academic and social integration are more likely to be more committed to the goal of graduation (Tinto, 1975; 1993). As a result, colleges and universities have a direct responsibility to create intentional learning environments and develop programs and initiatives that support such integration.

Developmental Goals That Support First-Year Student Success

The fundamental philosophy of the first-year experience is to intentionally create an institutional environment that supports students as they navigate the transition to college, in all its variants, and ensures their successful persistence to graduation. Yet "first-year student success," a broad concept proposed by Upcraft, Gardner, and Barefoot (2005), involves more than just ensuring retention to the second year. When intentionally designed, the first college year fosters an environment that is directly related to developmental goals facing entering students while also offering the support necessary for students to achieve these goals. Predominant among these developmental goals is that students establish intellectual skills, including an appreciation for what it means to be an educated individual. While this requires that students successfully complete their academic coursework, it also mandates that they develop abilities tied to critical thinking, problem solving, and reflective judgment. The concept of first-year student success is also tied to establishing positive interpersonal relationships and learning to effectively manage stress and maintain personal health and wellness. An effective first-year experience provides a means for students to examine and clarify their academic and career goals and objectives while helping them understand the importance of appreciating diversity in an increasingly global society. Most importantly, it ensures that students begin to explore their identity and learn how to become responsible citizens.

The first-year experience should also seek to facilitate learning and development both inside and outside the classroom. Residential communities for first-year students can be an important component of an intentional institutional environment focused on student success. For example, residence life programs ensure academic success by creating a physical environment that supports learning and development. The Association of College & University Housing Officers – International (ACUHO-I) (2007) provides a series of professional standards that offers guidance on the physical environment, such as computer laboratories, classroom space, or common areas, within residence halls that provide an atmosphere conducive to learning and development.

The ACUHO-I standards also include suggestions that can be used to support the developmental goals related to first-year student success discussed earlier. For example, the standards advocate that all residence life programs support the institutional mission while offering educational programs and services that help students learn how to become responsible community members. This involves the creation of educational programming that helps students become mature adults and achieve the respect for themselves and others necessary to live in a residential community. It also requires the development of opportunities for students to be exposed to new ideas and cultural differences that enable them to learn how to cooperate and live with those who are different from themselves. Residence life programs and services can also provide experiences for students that (a) engage their critical-thinking and problem-solving abilities, (b) help them to practice positive health and wellness behaviors, (c) assist them with clarification of personal and educational values, and (d) support their academic and career choices. As a result, residence life staff are responsible for not only providing educational programs but also serving in an advisory role that appropriately challenges and supports students in their curricular and cocurricular learning.

An important part of the ACUHO-I standards model also includes collaboration with academic counterparts to ensure that students are exposed to interactions with campus faculty beyond those found inside the classroom. In other words, residence life professionals must work with their academic counterparts to guarantee a solid connection between the curriculum and cocurriculum that further supports the developmental goals linked to first-year student success. Whatever physical structures, programs, or services housing professionals develop, they must be prepared to assess these efforts to make sure those efforts are having the desired effect on first-year student development and success.

Intentional Development of First-Year Learning Environments

The ACUHO-I standards also require residence life professionals to reconsider the manner in which educational programming is provided within the residence halls. The traditional model of residential programming has typically focused on important transitional topics such as "appreciating diversity, building healthy relationships, maintaining personal wellness, and developing leadership" (Kerr & Tweedy, 2006, p. 10). The success of such a model is often measured in the number of programs offered and in student attendance. While such an approach may support first-year student success, residence life professionals must expand their thinking to consider the ways in which students learn and develop individually (Kerr & Tweedy). They must also begin to consider alternate ways of measuring program effectiveness. An understanding of student learning and development will allow residence life professionals to design educational programming that more effectively promotes individual growth and development and to identify more meaningful assessment measures.

The creation and maintenance of learning environments within residence halls requires an understanding that new pedagogies must be considered and designed in order to better integrate the curriculum and cocurriculum. Furthermore, learning environments should be developed with a great deal of consideration given to how they support the institutional mission (Kerr & Tweedy, 2006). Residence life professionals are especially well equipped to collaborate with their academic counterparts on the creation of learning outcomes, taking both developmental theory and institutional mission into account. Learning experiences and environments must also be designed with consideration of how important institutional learning outcomes are related to the cocurriculum (Bloland, Stamatakos, & Rogers, 1996). While it is not expected that every aspect of residence life programming and services relate back to the curriculum, it is imperative that residence life professionals understand the importance of integrating cocurricular programming with curricular objectives and work collaboratively with their academic counterparts to develop learning environments that promote student success and persistence.

The discussion of how to successfully integrate curricular and cocurricular environments to support the unique needs of first-year students is not new. The development of learning communities in residence halls provides a structure for focusing programs and services on student learning (Zeller, 1996). Residence life professionals, faculty, and administrators on many campuses have already engaged in collaborative dialogues with the intention of creating living and learning environments that not only integrate the curriculum and cocurriculum but also more successfully connect students to the life of the institution by providing them with opportunities to actively participate in their learning and development where they live. This "residential nexus" is based on the idea that:

> Academic and student affairs colleagues recognize the value of the residential setting in providing opportunities for faculty-student interactions and developing a myriad of learning experiences...that allows student learning to become the focal point for the interactions that will occur in a residential setting. (Zeller, p. 2)

As part of this dialogue, residence life professionals must constantly consider how they can best design learning environments within the residence halls that assist students with managing and adapting to the various transitions they face, particularly during the first year of college. When learning environments are purposefully designed with consideration given to the integration of the academic content provided; the interpersonal interactions and relationships among students, faculty, and staff; and the physical space the environment occupies, they enhance learning and promote a sense of community that supports student engagement in the life of the institution. Students are then involved in an environment where academic and social experiences are intertwined to such a degree that students become more engaged (Brower & Dettinger, 1998). As a result, students are not only more engaged but are also more strongly connected to the institution, a factor that significantly increases the odds that they will successfully persist and obtain their educational goals and objectives (Astin, 1996; 1999; Tinto, 1975; 1993). For a more detailed discussion of living-learning environments, see chapter 4 in this monograph.

The successful development of first-year learning environments within the residence halls primarily depends upon residence life professionals understanding that they must provide appropriate levels of challenge and support for development and learning to occur. Too little challenge will lead to situations where students may feel safe and comfortable within their environment but may not actually experience learning and development; whereas, offering too much challenge will most certainly lead to situations where students feel overwhelmed and may not be able to adapt successfully to their new environment (Sanford, 1966). Developing first-year living and learning environments and educational programming based on this appropriate balance of challenge and support while also assisting first-year students with the various transitions they face involves the realization that learning and development are intertwined and that learning outcomes connected to the curriculum should be linked to the developmental goals of the cocurriculum (Dickson, Sorochty, & Thayer, 1998). In order for residence life professionals to effectively design programs and services that are focused on student learning and development, they must first consider who their college students are, the psychological and social processes that foster learning and development, and the factors associated with transition to the college environment that can either promote or inhibit learning and growth (Knefelkamp, Widick, & Parker, 1978). Having an understanding of the development of students, across an array of domains, can assist residence life professionals in creating programs and services to meet individual student needs in an environment where all students can grow and learn.

Relationship of Theory to the Goals of Residential Programs for First-Year Students

Since first-year programs in residence halls will typically house traditional-aged (17-23 years old) students, it is appropriate to ground residential programming in theoretical models most relevant to this age group. Theories related to student transitions, student persistence, psychosocial development, and cognitive-structural development offer useful vehicles for developing a greater understanding of this population. They also provide structure for programs designed to meet the goals of supporting students as they confront various transitions during the first year of college and assisting them with achieving the developmental objectives tied to first-year student success. Residence life professionals play an important role in facilitating student learning and engaging them in the life of a college or university. Whether residence life staff realize it or not, they are uniquely tied to whether students are retained from the first to the second year of college and whether they persist to graduation. As a result, it is important for them to remember that any programming they develop must be assessed for its commitment to the development of supportive academic and social communities that meet the unique needs of first-year students (Tinto, 1975; 1993).

Student Transitions Theory

Transitions are critical aspects of first-year students' lives. Schlossberg's transition theory (Schlossberg, Waters, & Goodman, 1995) delineates the components of these transitions making them more understandable and often more predictable, allowing residence life professionals to anticipate, plan for, and respond to them more fully. According to Schlossberg et al., transitions are simply continuous and changing situations that students face over time, to which they react, and by which they are changed to some degree. The meaning assigned to a specific transition is determined by the individual experiencing it and is affected by factors such as the type of transition being faced, the context of the transition, and the degree of impact it has on daily life. In addition to the individual student and specific situation surrounding the transition, Schlossberg et al. suggest that the amount of support the student receives in adjusting to the change and the strategies used by the student to process and adapt to the transition influences a student's ability to cope with a specific transition.

Because residence life professionals work where students live, they are in the unique position of being able to identify students who are confronting transitions and assess students' reactions to the transitions, as well as, the meaning they derive from them. They can also connect students to important support structures. This is an area where residence life professionals can collaborate with their academic counterparts, fellow student affairs professionals, and other key campus support staff, providing insight into how students experience and manage transitions and the kinds of services needed to support them in their efforts.

Student Persistence Theories

Another major theoretical perspective that requires attention is student persistence. Tinto's Interactionist Model (1975; 1993) focuses mainly on traditional-aged, residential students. He theorizes that student persistence is related to the meaning students assign to the interactions they have with the various aspects of a college or university. The basic concept is that when students fail to successfully integrate into the institutional environment, they are less likely to be engaged by it and are more likely to succumb to any number of factors that will increase the chance that they leave the institution without successful degree completion. Perhaps most important for residence life professionals to understand is that the characteristics of students upon entry to the institution (i.e., race, ethnicity, gender, social status, experiences in high school, financial resources, motivations for entering college, expectations of earning a degree) can provide a broader understanding of not only who students are but also the specific challenges they may have as they work toward integration into the institution, and ultimately, degree attainment. Such an understanding is particularly important in working with students who are not from the majority culture because they may have very different transition experiences than their peers, which will have a profound impact on their decision to remain at the institution (Torres, Howard-Hamilton, & Cooper, 2003).

Residence life professionals are in a unique position to provide programs and activities that offer opportunities for positive and supportive peer interactions. While many first-year students are probably well schooled in issues of diversity, they may not have as much exposure to topics such as oppression and various forms of privilege. Programs that engage students in conversations about how privilege structures and supports their college experience can help them understand not only their own world more fully but also that of those who are different from them. McIntosh's (1989) work on this topic is powerful, easily understood, and a great stimulus for dialogue with and among first-year students. Further, providing the opportunities for such dialogues may reduce negative peer interactions (e.g., racist or homophobic remarks) and create a more supportive environment for all learners, thus increasing the chances that students will remain at the institution.

Astin (1996; 1999) provides another model related to student persistence, suggesting that a student who is involved in the college or university environment is more likely to devote physical and psychological energies to the student experience and is therefore more likely to stay. However, the amount of learning and developmental growth that a student experiences is directly related to the level of involvement they achieve in college. Astin explains that students who live in residence halls are more likely to persist to graduation because living on campus facilitates certain forms of involvement such as interacting with faculty and participating in student organizations. As a result, those students who live on campus are more engaged in their educational pursuits. Astin also notes that peer interactions play a significant role in whether students identify with a college or university and serve as the single most significant factor in students' development and achievement of educational goals and objectives.

Whether in a more formal setting or as a natural consequence of the living environment, peer interactions are also likely to enhance critical-thinking skills (Twale & Sanders, 1999). An understanding of the importance of providing positive peer interactions within the residence halls should not only focus on programs promoting these types of interactions but should also have broader ramifications for the selection and training of paraprofessionals (e.g., resident assistants) who can provide a vitally important positive role model for first-year students. Residence life professionals must also consider the intentional design of facilities and spaces that promote engagement and positive peer interactions.

Because of their presence in the residence halls and increased contact with students, residence life professionals are in a unique position to support institutional retention efforts. They may more readily recognize those students who are not involved and have conversations with them, eventually facilitating involvement in the residence halls as well as the institution (Arboleda, Wang, Shelley, & Whalen, 2003). Yet, residence life professionals must consider the manner in which residence hall policies and programs encourage and actively support student involvement.

Psychosocial Theories

While having an understanding of theory related to student transitions and persistence in college is important, a working knowledge of psychosocial theories allows residence life professionals to design programs that support developmental goals for first-year students involving identity, relationships, and career exploration among other things. Some psychosocial theories address specific aspects of identity development such as race and ethnicity (e.g., Cross, 1995; Helms, 1993; Renn, 2003; Torres, 1999; 2003) or sexual orientation (Cass, 1984; D'Augelli, 1994). However, the work of Chickering (1969) and his collaborator Reisser (Chickering & Reisser, 1993) is arguably the most widely used and influential psychosocial theory (Pascarella & Terenzini, 2005).

Chickering and Reisser's (1993) seven vectors (i.e., the life tasks occupying young adults) provide a model for psychosocial development beyond identity alone. The tasks include developing a variety of forms of competence, managing emotions, moving through autonomy to interdependence, developing mature interpersonal relationships, establishing identity, developing purpose, and developing integrity (Chickering & Reisser). Chickering and Reisser argue that colleges and universities can intentionally create environments that significantly impact student development along the seven vectors. Specifically, the development and maintenance of these types of positive educational environments involve giving consideration to issues such as the institutional climate, the academic practices at work in the curriculum and cocurriculum, the involvement of faculty, the various academic and support services provided to students, and the physical design of facilities. In order to ensure that polices, practices, programs, and services produce an environment where student learning is valued and development along each of the seven vectors is supported, residential life professionals must consider both those factors that support or inhibit this form of growth.

First-year students are often engaged in developing competence, the first of Chickering and Reisser's (1993) vectors. Comprised of three components—intellectual, physical, and interpersonal—mastery of competence is a key element of a successful first year. There are numerous examples of how growth in this area can be encouraged. A book club during the academic year or summer reading program that assigns a common book can be facilitated in concert with faculty. It is important to choose a book that highlights an issue or theme relevant to the student while providing thought-provoking and stimulating content that will challenge and broaden student thinking. The commonality of experience bonds the group while the processing and discussion of the material demand critical-thinking skills, an important aspect of the development of intellectual competence (Chickering & Reisser). Residence life professionals can play an important role in this activity. Book clubs can meet in residence hall common areas and be led by staff members, reinforcing the idea that learning and the construction of knowledge happen in a variety of places with many participants learning together.

Life in a residence hall provides many opportunities for the development of interpersonal competence. Hallmarks of this aspect of development include listening skills, the ability to self-disclose, working well in groups (including the facilitation of group conversations in a productive fashion), and not monopolizing conversations (Chickering & Reisser, 1993). Residence hall student governments that are carefully and intentionally structured and advised by residence life professionals provide opportunities for the development of these characteristics. Well-designed training for hall government leaders that includes discussion of roles, communication, and group dynamics heightens the effectiveness of these programs in meeting developmental goals.

Cognitive-Structural Theories

Residence life professionals should also have a good understanding of cognitive-structural theories, which differ from psychosocial theories in that they focus on meaning-making structures rather than on the content of decisions and the completion of life tasks. These theories can help residence life professionals understand how students learn and how they make decisions, choices, and commitments.

William Perry spent many years studying Harvard undergraduates. Starting with the most basic question—"When you think back over the past year what stands out for you?"—he completed a longitudinal study leading to his scheme of intellectual and ethical development of college students (Perry, 1970). This elegant, complex theory details the ways in which individuals look at the world and make meaning from their experiences. Positions include (a) basic dualism, where all questions can be answered in terms such as "good" and "bad" or "right" and "wrong" and by looking to an authority who has all of the answers; (b) multiplicity, where right answers are not always known, all opinions are equally valid, and peers serve as more legitimate sources of knowledge; (c) relativism, where contextually defined and evidence-based opinions are valued over the unsupported opinions accepted in earlier positions; and (d) developing commitment, where decisions are based on a contextual world in which an individual comes to understand the potential consequences and implications of their commitments.

Analysis of the student interviews led Perry (1970) to conclude that the positions are stable places where students land as a result of the assimilation and accommodation inherent in development. The transitions between the positions involve significant developmental work and are, as Perry termed them, "the reorganization of personal investments" (Perry, p. 49). Residence life professionals can help first-year students move through some of these transitions by providing an appropriate balance of challenge and support (Perry; Sanford, 1966) and by creating situations that engage students in ways of thinking that are one level above their current position.

Since first-year students often enter college as dualists, exposure to multiple perspectives can be a useful strategy for moving them toward multiplicity. Programs designed around current issues that do not lend themselves to "right" answers are one vehicle to illustrate this thinking. Panel discussions among those holding differing viewpoints or student-led dialogues or debates expose students to a multiplicity of ideas and positions relative to complex problems and issues. Residence life professionals are present as they facilitate formal group discussions and make themselves available for informal conversations about politics, the environment, terrorism, or any number of other topics. Professionals versed in Perry's theory can see those places in conversations where a well-formed question may challenge students' ways of thinking and move students away from the stability of their current position.

Influenced by Perry's work, Baxter Magolda (1992; 2001) studied the intellectual development of both women and men during their undergraduate careers. Her qualitative research revealed gender-related patterns of thinking that roughly parallel Perry's positions. In her model, intellectual development culminates in self-authorship or the "ability to collect, interpret, and analyze information and reflect on one's own beliefs in order to form judgments" (Baxter Magolda, 1998, p. 143). Students who have achieved self-authorship internally define their own beliefs and the relationship of these beliefs to the world and are able to construct knowledge. Yet, Baxter Magolda notes that colleges and universities have not emphasized helping students achieve self-authorship. Residence life professionals are well positioned to advance the educational agenda in this respect. Baxter Magolda (2001) suggests three strategies for fostering cognitive development toward self-authorship: (a) validating the fact that students are capable of creating knowledge, (b) recognizing that learning should be situated in the learner's experience as an understanding of the self is essential to knowledge construction, and (c) sharing a mutual construction of knowledge where authority and expertise are shared among peers.

Baxter Magolda's study (1992) revealed that 68% of the first-year students interviewed were absolute knowers. This way of knowing is characterized by a certainty of knowledge, a reliance on instructors as absolute authority figures, and knowledge acquisition (i.e., collecting facts) rather than learning for understanding. Gender-related patterns emerged, revealing that female students were most likely to receive knowledge (record it when they see it and hear it) and that male students were most likely to master knowledge through participation with it. To help students move beyond absolute knowing, Baxter Magolda recommends creating opportunities for peers to have positive interactions and take responsibility for teaching and learning from each other. Community development initiatives may be one way to accomplish this in the residence halls. Initially, students will see residence life professionals as authority figures who are responsible for developing a community. When residence life professionals provide a framework outlining possible community roles, rights, and responsibilities and parameters and the process by which students can discuss these options, students may begin to see themselves as capable of creating the shared knowledge necessary for community building. Residence life professionals facilitate conversations that allow students to understand that they do know what they want. When students falter, residence life staff can provide the information students need to be able to work with others to create a supportive environment. Because men and women frequently approach knowing and knowledge construction differently, residence life professionals will want to take the gender-related differences Baxter Magolda noted into account when they design community development initiatives. In particular, they will want to make sure that a range of processes is available and used by students so that everyone feels supported.

Person-Environment Theories

A variety of theorists have written about the interaction between people and the environments in which they live as well as students' perceptions of the environments and their social climate (Moos, 1979; 1994; Pace, 1979; Pace & Stern; 1958; Stern, 1970). These works typically focus on the environment rather than the development of students within them, but these theories are especially applicable to students living in residence halls because "whether people are attracted to a particular environment or remain satisfied and stable within it is a function of how they perceive, construct, and evaluate that environment" (Strange, 1996, p. 256). It is important to remember when using these theories that while they do not address learning and developmental growth, they provide important applications for the intentional construction of residential environments that facilitate this type of change. Strange and Banning (2001) indicate that the physical environment of a college or university campus can significantly influence student behavior through the connection between its functional aspects, the actual aspects of the environment that are planned and constructed, and its symbolic aspects (i.e., the meanings students assign to an environment based on the intrinsic messages it may convey). As a result, the design of the physical environment can actually hinder or prohibit learning from occurring. The important lesson that residence life professionals can learn from this theory is that they play a central role in the intentional design and construction of physical environments that support the values and goals they have for student learning and development. Chapter 10 focuses on environmental design and offers a more detailed discussion of this concept.

New Conceptions of Living and Learning Environments for First-Year Students

Student learning and development often occur as the direct result of the way in which students respond to situations or tasks that challenge their current developmental capacities (Strange, 1999). The conceptualization of learning in a college or university setting requires a recognition that learning is an extremely complex process that can only be understood when "conversations across the institution and conversations across programs or departments can become the means for identifying the sets of educational practices that contribute to what students are expected to attain over time" (Maki, 2004, p. 3). With institutional goals focused on enhancing learning, ensuring the successful transition into the collegiate learning environment, and fostering growth in areas tied to developmental goals, it is useful to broaden the conceptualization of where learning can occur. The traditional idea that learning is wrapped in student achievement does not completely address this. More important is a thorough examination of the coherence between the curriculum and cocurriculum with consideration given to the academic courses and educational experiences beyond the classroom environment, which provides substantive opportunities for students to learn or build on previous knowledge (Maki). The goal is the creation of seamless learning environments for students, making them active participants in their learning and development, enabling them to make concrete connections between curricular content and cocurricular experiences (Kuh, 1996). This notion becomes the idea that learning can and should occur anywhere and everywhere. When this is the starting point, the world becomes the classroom. For residence life professionals it builds upon generations of traditional programming for students and takes on new expression of what intentional learning environments can be.

Learning Outside the Boundaries of the Classroom

The consideration of seamless learning environments, where students see the integrated connections that facilitate learning, has led to increasing collaborations between residence life professionals and their academic counterparts. The result is an important paradigm shift in the learning environment. No longer is learning solely confined to the traditional boundaries of the classroom. The emergent paradigm is that student learning and development are the joint responsibility of academic affairs and student affairs professionals and that a significant amount of learning takes place beyond the classroom as students informally interact with faculty, staff, and their peers (American Association of Higher Education, American College Personnel Association, & National Association of Student Personnel Administrators, 1998). In fact, by simply partnering with academic colleagues to intentionally design learning environments, residence life professionals create opportunities for students to make connections between their in- and out-of-class experiences, which will ultimately enable them to function better in an increasingly complex world (King & VanHecke, 2006). Learning now involves a more complex search for meaning by students including information acquisition, reflection, emotional engagement, and active application. As a result, learning has become a transformative process, fully considering the knowledge students have as well as their individual values and belief systems. New opportunities for collaboration emerge out of the necessity to develop more intentional learning environments, integrating the curricular and cocurricular experiences of students (Keeling, 2004; 2006).

Residential Learning Communities

There are many models of collaboration in residential programming, administration, and design that integrate learning and development as part of an intentional, transformational process. Residential learning communities are perhaps one of the most well known and increasingly well used collaborations designed to meet the needs of students and achieve developmental goals that are tied to first-year student success. The primary purpose of learning communities is to involve students in the learning process (Levine, 1998), and they support several major developmental goals related to first-year student success. Students are also more satisfied with residential living when the experience is intentionally designed to be intellectually stimulating, features quality social interactions, and offers programming that promotes a sense of comfort and encourages greater levels of involvement (Li, McCoy, Shelley, & Whalen, 2005). Such satisfaction may be the result of greater involvement in the life of their residential community and increased facility at studying and collaborating with their fellow students (Arboleda et al., 2003). This type of environment supports the developmental goals that are tied to establishing academic competence and positive interpersonal relationships while helping students respect their fellow community members and create a positive culture where living and learning are intertwined. Participation in residential learning communities, even when controlled for students who are motivated to self-select these types of living environments, is a significant predictor of academic success and intellectual engagement for students (Pasque & Murphy, 2005; Zheng, Saunders, Shelley, & Whalen, 2002). As a result, learning community students are more engaged than those who elected not to participate in learning community activities.

While learning communities are a good example of a residential first-year program that can support the developmental goals tied to first-year student success, the actual process of designing an effective learning community involves a precarious balance between the necessary academic interactions, social activities, and physical environment in order to best support the goals of the learning community (Inkelas & Weismann, 2003). It is not surprising to discover that learning communities have increasingly become a more common partnership between academic and student affairs. Residence life professionals have recognized the importance of building collaborations that integrate learning and have worked to develop dedicated residence hall spaces to promote academic and social interactions beyond the classroom environment. They have also collaborated with their academic counterparts to structure academic and social activities.

For faculty interested in collaborating with residence life professionals, developing an understanding of learning and development can greatly enhance students' success in the classroom. Levine (1998) has emphasized that collaborating in a learning community with residence life professionals involves the willingness of faculty to also become part of a unique faculty learning community around which they construct a learner-centered environment. Both faculty and residence life professionals work together to improve instruction and develop a learning community that supports first-year student success. Faculty regarded as outstanding teachers can present information related to classroom pedagogy, while residence life professionals can offer information related to student development issues that might impact pedagogical choices. The focus on student development provides approaches for faculty to support learning and growth beyond the classroom and encourages faculty to develop their own out-of-class activities that facilitate social interaction and engagement among their students. This not only builds a strong collaboration but also strengthens the intentionality behind the learning community while fully integrating learning and development between the curricular and cocurricular aspects of the program.

Involvement with Collaborative Teaching

Collaborative teaching is another way to bring the knowledge, skills, and talents of residence life professionals together with their faculty colleagues in ways that strengthen learning experiences for students. Living-learning advocates (Shapiro & Levine, 1999) and those studying the effects of such models attest to the effectiveness of team teaching (Kuh, Kinzie, Schuh, Whitt, & Associates, 2005). Locating classrooms in residence halls provides an important way for residence life professionals to collaborate with their academic counterparts because it situates teaching and learning where students live. However, there is often less emphasis on collaboration in terms of residence life professionals actually becoming instructional partners with discipline-specific faculty. Regardless of subject matter, residence life professionals can contribute significant expertise via student development and learning theories that enhances the effectiveness of classroom teaching. For instance, residence life professionals well schooled in developmental theory can describe for faculty how Perry's dualists and Baxter Magolda's absolute knowers learn best and are most effectively challenged, while highlighting situations that are most likely to overwhelm these students and inhibit learning. Conversations about these theories combined with learning outcomes for classes expose faculty to a greater understanding of how students learn while residence life professionals see what the goals of a given class are. Knowing this can help staff structure programs and activities within the residential environment in a way that is congruent with the goals of the course. It also enables them to make connections between the curricular and cocurricular aspects of student experience. This is also an acknowledgement of the strength that results from situating learning not only in a traditional classroom but also within the living environment (Shapiro & Levine; Kenney, Dumont, & Kenney, 2005).

Residence life professionals can also educate graduate teaching assistants about student development and learning theories in order to better prepare them for their role in the classroom. This is especially critical for graduate students who are in the process of mastering their disciplines and have had very little teaching experience. Rather than serving as the instructor of record, many graduate teaching assistants play a supporting role in the classroom, which limits the actual exposure they have to the unique responsibilities of the classroom environment. As a result, they have little experience with course preparation and instructional methods (Davis, 1993; Nilson, 1998). Being a new instructor at the college or university level can be a daunting experience, even for those teaching assistants who have worked closely with a faculty member in the classroom or who served as an instructor of record. Knowledge of the learning process as outlined by these theories, coupled with residence life professionals willing to work with graduate teaching assistants to help them be better prepared and more effective, is collaboration with both purpose and impact. Thus, collaborative teaching can begin with simply providing a place to hold classes and progress to collaboration in the training of graduate teaching assistants.

Conclusion

Oftentimes, fear of the ability to use student development and learning theories in any meaningful way can block consideration of their applicability. Questions about their effectiveness, ease of use, and assessment may deter educational professionals from using theory as a guide to practice. While these fears are legitimate and need to be considered carefully, there is another reality for the use of theories. Knowledge of them allows for greater understanding of how students learn, which can only improve the quality of residential programs designed to support the needs of first-year students. The development of a working knowledge of theories and a little time and space to discuss them with others illuminates the experience of learning in such a way that it can become second nature. These theories can, with time and some intentional study, become part of the lens through which students and the way they learn are experienced and understood. As a result, a more seamless learning experience can be created to ensure first-year student success.

References

American Association of Higher Education, American College Personnel Association, & National Association of Student Personnel Administrators. (1998). *Powerful partnerships: A shared responsibility for learning.* Washington, DC: Authors.

Arboleda, A., Wang, Y., Shelley, M. C., II, & Whalen, D. F. (2003). Predictors of residence hall involvement. *Journal of College Student Development, 44*(4), 517-531.

Arnold, K., & Kuh, G. D. (1999). What matters in undergraduate education? Mental models, student learning, and student affairs. In E. J. Whitt (Ed.), *Student learning as student affairs work: Responding to our imperative* (NASPA Monograph Series, Vol. 23, pp. 11-34). Washington, DC: National Association of Student Personnel Administrators.

Association of College & University Housing Officers – International. (2007). *ACUHO-I standards and ethical principles for college and university housing professionals.* Columbus, OH: Author. Retrieved March 25, 2008, from http://www.acuho-i.org/Portals/0/pdf/2007_EB_Approved_Standards_Revisions.pdf

Astin, A.W. (1996). Involvement in learning revisited: Lessons we have learned. *Journal of College Student Development, 37*(2), 123-134.

Astin, A.W. (1999). Student involvement: A developmental theory for higher education. *Journal of College Student Development, 40*(5), 518-529.

Baxter Magolda, M. B. (1992). *Knowing and reasoning in college: Gender related patterns in students' intellectual development.* San Francisco: Jossey-Bass.

Baxter Magolda, M. B. (1998). Developing self-authorship in young adult life. *Journal of College Student Development, 39*(2), 143-156.

Baxter Magolda, M. B. (1999). Defining and redefining student learning. In E. J. Whitt (Ed.), *Student learning as student affairs work: Responding to our imperative* (pp. 35-49). Washington, DC: National Association of Student Personnel Administrators.

Baxter Magolda, M. (2001). *Making their own way: Narratives for transforming higher education to promote self-development.* Sterling, VA: Stylus Publishing.

Bloland, P. A., Stamatakos, L. C., & Rogers, R. R. (1996). Redirecting the role of student affairs to focus on student learning. *Journal of College Student Development, 37*(2), 217-226.

Brower, A. M., & Dettinger, K. M. (1998). What is a learning community? *About Campus, 3*(5), 15-21.

Cass, V. (1984). Homosexual identity formation: Testing a theoretical model. *Journal of Sex Research, 20*(2), 143-167.

Chickering, A.W. (1969). *Education and identity.* San Francisco: Jossey-Bass.

Chickering, A.W., & Reisser, L. (1993). *Education and identity* (2nd ed.). San Francisco: Jossey-Bass.

Cross, W. E., Jr. (1995). The psychology of Nigrescence: Revising the Cross model. In J. G. Ponterotto, J. M. Casas, L. A. Suzuki, & C. M. Alexander (Eds.), *Handbook of multicultural counseling* (pp. 93-122). Thousand Oaks, CA: Sage.

D'Augelli, A. (1994). Identity development and sexual orientation: Toward a model of lesbian, gay, and bisexual development. In E. J. Trickett, R. J. Watts, & D. Birman (Eds.), *Human diversity: Perspectives on people in context* (pp. 312-333). San Francisco: Jossey-Bass.

Davis, B. G. (1993). *Tools for teaching.* San Francisco: Jossey-Bass.

Dickson, G. L., Sorochty, R. W., & Thayer, J. D. (1998). Theory to practice: Creating a student development curriculum using the developmental advising inventory. *NASPA Journal, 35*(2), 119-136.

Evans, N., Forney, D. S., & Guido-DiBrito, F. (1998). *Student development in college: Theory, research, and practice.* San Francisco: Jossey-Bass.

Helms, J. E. (1993). *Black and White racial identity: Theory, research, and practice.* Westport, CT: Praeger.

Inkelas, K. K., & Weisman, J. L. (2003). Different by design: An examination of student outcomes among participants in three types of living-learning programs. *Journal of College Student Development, 44*(3), 335-368.

Keeling, R. P. (Ed.). (2004). *Learning reconsidered: A campus-wide focus on the student experience.* Washington, DC: National Association of Student Personnel Administrators and American College Personnel Association.

Keeling, R. P. (Ed.). (2006). *Learning reconsidered 2: A practical guide to implementing a campus-wide focus on the student experience.* Washington, DC: American College Personnel Association, Association College & University Housing Officers – International, Association of College Unions International, National Association for Campus Activities, National Academic Advising Association, and National Association of Student Personnel Administrators.

Kenney, D. R., Dumont, R., & Kenney, G. (2005). *Mission and place: Strengthening learning and community through campus design.* Westport, CT: Praeger.

Kerr, K. G., & Tweedy, J. (2006). Beyond seat time and student satisfaction: A curricular approach to residential education. *About Campus, 2*(5), 9-15.

King, P. M., & Baxter Magolda, M. B. (1996). A developmental perspective on learning. *Journal of College Student Development, 37*(2), 163–173.

King, P. M., & VanHecke, J. R. (2006). Using skill theory to recognize how students build and rebuild understanding. *About Campus, 2*(1), 10-16.

Knefelkamp, L. L., Widick, C., & Parker, C. A. (Eds.). (1978). *Applying new developmental findings.* (New Directions in Student Services, No. 4). San Francisco: Jossey-Bass.

Kuh, G. D. (1996). Guiding principles for creating seamless learning environments for undergraduates. *Journal of College Student Development, 37*(2), 135-148.

Kuh, G. D., Kinzie, J., Schuh, J. H., Whitt, E. J., & Associates. (2005). *Student success in college: Creating conditions that matter.* San Francisco: Jossey-Bass.

Levine, J. H. (1998). Building learning communities for faculty. *About Campus, 2*(6), 22-24.

Li, Y., McCoy, E., Shelley, M. C., II, & Whalen, D. F. (2005). Contributors to student satisfaction with special program (Fresh Start) residence halls. *Journal of College Student Development, 46*(2), 176-192.

Maki, P. L. (2004). Maps and inventories: Anchoring efforts to track student learning. *About Campus, 9*(4), 2-9.

McIntosh, P. (1989, July/August). White privilege: Unpacking the invisible knapsack. *Peace and Freedom,* 10-12.

Moos, R. H. (1979). *Evaluating educational environments.* San Francisco: Jossey-Bass.

Moos, R. H. (1994). *Work environment scale manual: Development, applications, research* (3rd ed.). Palo Alto, CA: Consulting Psychologists Press, Inc.

Nilson, L. B. (1998). *Teaching at its best: A research-based resource for college instructors.* Bolton, MA: Anker Publishing Company, Inc.

Pace, C. R. (1979). *Measuring outcomes of college: Fifty years of findings and recommendations for the future.* San Francisco: Jossey-Bass.

Pace, C. R., & Stern, G. G. (1958). An approach to the measurement of psychological characteristics of college environments. *Journal of Educational Psychology, 49*(5), 269-277.

Pascarella, E. T., & Terenzini, P. T. (2005). *How college affects students: A third decade of research* (Vol. 2). San Francisco: Jossey-Bass.

Pasque, P. A., & Murphy, R. (2005). The intersections of living-learning programs and social identity as factors of academic achievement and intellectual engagement. *Journal of College Student Development, 46*(4), 429-411.

Perry, W. G., Jr. (1970). *Forms of intellectual and ethical development in the college years: A scheme.* New York: Harcourt Brace Jovanovich College Publishers.

Renn, K. A. (2003). Understanding the identities of mixed-race college students through a developmental ecology lens. *Journal of College Student Development, 44*(3), 404-419.

Sanford, N. (1966). *Self and society.* New York: Atherton.

Schlossberg, N. K., Waters, E. B., & Goodman, J. (1995). *Counseling adults in transition* (2nd ed.). New York: Springer Publishing Company.

Shapiro, N. S., & Levine, J. H. (1999). *Creating learning communities: A practical guide to winning support, organizing for change, and implementing programs.* San Francisco: Jossey-Bass.

Stern, G. G. (1970). *People in context: Measuring person-environment congruence in education and industry.* New York: John Wiley and Sons.

Strange, C. (1996). Dynamics of campus environments. In S. R. Komives, D. B. Woodard, Jr., & Associates (Eds.). *Student services: A handbook for the profession* (3rd ed., pp. 244-268). San Francisco: Jossey-Bass.

Strange, C. (1999). Student development: The evolution and status of an essential idea. *Journal of College Student Development, 40*(5), 570-586.

Strange, C. C., & Banning, J. H. (2001). *Educating by design: Creating campus learning environments that work.* San Francisco: Jossey-Bass.

Tinto, V. (1975). Dropout from higher education: A theoretical synthesis of recent research. *Review of Educational Research, 45*(1), 89-125.

Tinto, V. (1993). *Leaving college: Rethinking the causes and cures of student attrition* (2nd ed.). Chicago: University of Chicago Press.

Torres, V. (1999). Validation of a bicultural orientation model for Hispanic college students. *Journal of College Student Development, 44,* 532-547.

Torres, V. (2003). Influences on ethnic identity development of Latino college students in the first two years of college. *Journal of College Student Development, 44*(4), 532-547.

Torres, V., Howard-Hamilton, M. F., & Cooper, D. L. (2003). *Identity development of diverse populations: Implications for teaching and administration in higher education* (ASHE-ERIC Higher Education Report Vol. 29, No. 6). San Francisco: Jossey-Bass.

Twale, D., & Sanders, C. S. (1999). Impact of non-classroom experiences on critical thinking ability. *NASPA Journal, 36*(2), 133-146.

Upcraft, M. L., Gardner, J. N., & Barefoot, B. O. (2005). The first year of college revisited. In M. L. Upcraft, J. N. Gardner, & B. O. Barefoot (Eds.), *Challenging and supporting the first-year student: A handbook for improving the first year of college* (pp. 1-12). San Francisco: Jossey-Bass.

Zeller, W. (1996). The residential nexus: A focus on student learning. *Talking Stick, 13*(7), 6-10.

Zheng, J. L., Saunders, K. P., Shelley, M. C., II, & Whalen, D. F. (2002). Predictors of academic success for freshman residence hall students. *Journal of College Student Development, 43*(2), 267-283.

Chapter Three

New Students, Emerging Technologies, Virtual Communities, and the College Residential Experience

Richard Holeton

One Morning at 21st-Century University

Brenda is a first-year American college student living on campus at 21st-Century University (21CU). She awakes to her smartphone's alarm (a song from her iTunes) and rolls over to find her roommate gone for crew practice. She texts a message to Jill, down the hall, asking if she wants to meet for breakfast. Brenda and Jill met online, in 21CU Facebook groups, four months before arriving on campus, and they found they had a lot in common, sharing pictures, music, and movies. When they met face-to-face during orientation week, they felt they already knew each other. Jill says "okay" to breakfast. Brenda quickly checks Facebook on her smartphone, to see what her hallmates and other friends were up to overnight. She's been tagged in a couple new photos from orientation. She updates her status ("groggy this morning but will kick butt in Econ") and dashes off to meet Jill.

Returning to her room with a bagel, Brenda opens her laptop and checks her e-mail. Someone agreed with her idea, on the residence chatlist, about designing a dorm tee shirt, and she got an e-mail from her dad just checking in. On the Web, she logs in to the course management system to check her calendar and class announcements. Her Econ TA has posted material to read for their next section meeting; there are new messages in her Anthro course discussion board and from the peer-editing group in her first-year writing course—she'll have to reply later. Her calendar updates include a meeting of the 21CU Green Campus Club, a student organization she and her roommate plan to check out.

Brenda syncs her calendar and iTunes to her smartphone, then rides her bike to class listening to the podcast of a biology lecture that she had partially slept through. Arriving at Econ, Brenda silences her phone and unsleeps her laptop. Using both devices, she types notes during class and occasionally exchanges IMs and text messages with friends and hallmates. She Googles a few Econ terms that come up during the lecture. She texts a question to her TA, as he's encouraged students in her section to do. The TA collects the questions for their next meeting.

After class, Brenda has a latté at the student union. She updates her Facebook status again in case anyone she knows is nearby and wants to join her. Almost immediately, she receives a text message from Alex, a hallmate she's considered going out with, telling her that he's on his way. Before she forgets, Brenda logs on to the 21CU library course reserves to save a reading for her Anthro class.

Brenda and Alex make tentative plans for a group dinner off campus this weekend. They both like Mexican food, and they check out a couple local menus online, then use Google Street View to see what the restaurants look like. One offers a student discount so they print the coupon at a nearby kiosk in the student union. Then with Alex's phone they click a picture of themselves and attach it to a group invitation that they send to hallmates, to join them at the Mexican restaurant, with links to the menu and directions. It's already 10:30 a.m., time for Brenda's next class.

As 21st century learners and technology users, Brenda, Jill, and Alex are members of the "Net Generation." The chapter opens with a discussion of who they are. It also addresses key technology trends with wide impact in higher education; emerging ideas about physical learning spaces in residence halls; the impact of virtual communities on residential life; and, in the context of these emerging technologies and social issues, the need for new kinds of support and guidance for first-year residential students.

The Net Generation Comes to Campus

As noted above, Brenda is a member of the Net Generation, also known as the Keyboard Generation, Google Generation, iGeneration, Digital Natives, Millennials, and more recently, Neo-Millennials. Millennials are usually defined as those born from 1982-2000, and they comprise the largest American generation in history, eclipsing their Baby Boom parents in numbers and cultural impact (Howe & Strauss, 2003). If TV was the defining technology for Baby Boomers (born 1946-1964) and video games the defining technology for GenX (1964-1982), the Web defines Millennials (Dugdale & Long, 2007). Likewise, in affluent countries over these three generations, our essential communication tools have shifted from the typewriter, to the computer and to the smartphone; from the telephone, to e-mail, IM, and text messaging; and from library books, to CD-ROMs, online databases, and the Web.

Brenda and the technologies she uses at 21st Century University may not yet be the norm everywhere. Yet, research suggests that members of the Net Gen share notable characteristics. As a group, they

◇ Are heavily "deviced" and generally fluent in technology
◇ Have a strongly social orientation to technology and a bias for collaboration
◇ Crave and expect constant connectivity to maintain social networks
◇ Prefer to access information in hypertext, hypermedia, and multimedia modes
◇ Prefer instant gratification and "just-in-time learning"
◇ Are heavy multimedia content producers
◇ Are skilled multitaskers
◇ Switch media readily and change or combine communicative purposes (i.e., personal, social, academic) within any one medium (Fox & Madden, 2006; Jones & Madden, 2002; Kaiser Family Foundation Program, 2005; Lenhart & Madden, 2005a, 2005b; Oblinger, 2003; Oblinger & Oblinger 2005a, 2005b; Prensky, 2001)

What happens when these students come to our campuses? As Zeller (2008) notes,

To casual observers, students appear to be engaging in "traditional" undergraduate activities: going to class, living in residence halls, eating in campus dining venues, and working out in campus recreation centers. However, closer observations reveal that today's college experience is qualitatively different from that of a generation ago. (p. 67) Prensky (2001) goes further, contrasting "digital native" students with "digital immigrant" faculty and staff and arguing that "Today's students are no longer the people our educational system was designed to teach" (p. 1). Students like Brenda are still studying, learning, socializing, and exploring identity, as first-year college students have always done, but—even if Prensky's "natives" versus "immigrants" is an oversimplification—*how* they conduct these activities has changed radically. For students, even more so than for faculty and staff, recent changes associated with new technologies have been transformative.

These transformations bring, of course, challenges as well as opportunities. Many teachers and administrators have felt at sea in dealing with unfamiliar student behaviors around technology. Perhaps especially for student affairs staff, new kinds of problems have bubbled to the surface like online stalking and harassment, Internet-related plagiarism, and Digital Millennium Copyright Act (DMCA) copyright complaints. We will revisit some of these challenges below, but I want to suggest that such problems—to continue the oceanic metaphors—are only the most visible tip of the iceberg. The rest of the story, what's below the surface, comprises a confluence of changes with tremendous potential to reshape higher education and our residential campuses in constructive ways in the 21st century.

Perhaps most encouragingly, the proclivities of the Net Gen or Millennials parallel key learning and developmental principles. In the widely accepted social-cognitive models of how people learn, learning is contextual and situated (including in various learning styles); active and participatory; social and relational; holistic; and continuous (not bound by time or place) (Bransford, Brown, & Cocking, 2000; Pascarella & Terenzini, 2005). According to student affairs researchers, student development and success in college is facilitated by opportunities for active engagement and expression, the co-construction of values and norms, student involvement and shared responsibility, and the opportunity to participate in inclusive communities (Kuh, Schuh, Whitt, & Associates, 1991; Kuh, Kinzie, Schuh, Whitt, & Associates, 2005). (See chapter 2 in this monograph for an in-depth look at learning and development theories.) Table 3.1 suggests a simple mapping of Net Gen traits map onto such principles.

Table 3.1
Net Generation Traits and Learning and Developmental Principles

Net Gen trait	Learning or development principle
Collaboration bias	Social learning, social construction of knowledge
Preference for hypertext, hypermedia	Multiple intelligences, learning styles, blended learning
Just-in-time, action oriented, 24/7	Active, self-situated, holistic learning
Multimedia content production	Active learning, multiple learning styles and modalities
Social networking	Self-expression, identity construction, interpersonal competence, negotiating social norms

These parallels become even more compelling when we look at key technology trends and their impacts in residential learning environments in the next section.

Key Technology Trends: Online, Anytime/Anywhere, Interactive

Four key technology trends are helping to fundamentally transform the college campus experience:

◇ The movement of content online
◇ The increasing mobility and convergence of personal technologies
◇ The development of prosumer (i.e., professional/consumer or producer/consumer) devices and software
◇ The emergence of interactive and participatory Web applications known as "Web 2.0"

Not merely the flavors of the day, these trends appear sweeping and inexorable—and they are mutually reinforcing, in a kind of virtuous (some may say vicious) circle, with the Net Gen's proclivities. Together these trends are powerfully moving the locus of student learning and socializing from formal institutional spaces and technologies (i.e., library, classroom, computer lab) toward informal, personal, and virtual spaces and technologies (i.e., residence hall, online game world, smartphone).

Online Content

The explosion of digital content is familiar to most educators. Billions of books are freely available online. Libraries are rapidly digitizing their collections. The Internet archive grows by some two billion Web pages a month. Other so-called "born digital," new media materials are also growing exponentially. University libraries are grappling with how to describe, organize, store, and make all this information available to scholars. With inevitable improvements in discovery and search, nearly all digital content will become available on the Internet. And with fast-increasing storage capacities, it will not be long before our personal devices can hold (or easily access from the network "cloud"), for example, all the music ever recorded.

While some librarians lament the Google-ization of research, the movement of content online has fundamentally changed how scholars conduct their work. Students visit the physical library more frequently to study and less frequently to check out books. For research, they visit the online library (after they Google) from their residence halls. Like faculty scholars, students increasingly collaborate on research projects, and they integrate multiple media (web sites, databases, online articles, and multimedia artifacts along with traditional library materials) into their work.

Students need support for this 21st century scholarship in the residence halls, where they do most of their work at night, when the physical library may be closed. Many colleges and universities now offer "Ask a Librarian" services by both live chat/IM and e-mail, but most, so far, have limited hours. Some are supplementing these efforts with off-campus and regional consortiums. Two examples are L-net, a statewide digital reference service with 24/7 live chat for students at Oregon colleges and universities (Oregon Libraries Network, 2008); and Ask Us 24/7, offering virtual chat with librarians in the Western New York, Rochester, and Syracuse areas, including schools such as Buffalo State University and Medaille College (Western New York Library Resources Council, 2008).

Mobility and Convergence

Wireless networking, laptop computers, and multi-functional cell phones are fast becoming ubiquitous on our campuses. Most universities have a strategic plan for wireless (Campus Computing Project, 2007), and hundreds already have fully wireless residence halls, supplementing "port-per-pillow" wired Internet connections in student rooms. Reported laptop ownership among undergraduates nationally has risen to 74% in recent surveys (Caruso & Salaway, 2007) and often exceeds 90% on individual campuses. Typical of the growing number of colleges with a laptop requirement for first-year students, Lander University (2008) wishes "to prepare our students for a mobile technology workforce and to enhance the student's experience within the campus community." In addition, in 2006-07, 86% of undergraduates owned cell phones, 76% had music devices, and 24% had personal digital assistants or smartphones (Caruso & Salaway). Led by Apple's popular iPhone introduced in 2007, Mobile Internet Devices (MIDs) and dual-mode devices (which can use either cellular or WiFi networks) promise to proliferate quickly, along with new mobile applications to run on these devices.

With ever smaller, more mobile devices capable of voice communication, text messaging, Internet access, audio and video playback and recording, and global positioning, learning and socializing are becoming "anytime-anywhere" experiences. How to support and leverage all this mobile student-owned technology, and how to tie it in with university classroom and administrative systems, remain formidable challenges. In the wake of the tragic 2007 Virginia Tech shootings, many colleges have integrated student cell phones into emergency notification systems that send text-message alerts. But how can we leverage student devices in more proactive and constructive ways in our campus living-learning environments? Duke University's pioneering iPod First-Year Experience, which grew into the Duke Digital Initiative, provided iPods to all first-year students in 2004 and—in addition to inspiring curricular innovations—has been praised for providing "content that addressed dorm life, campus activities, community events, health and safety . . . and details about freshmen residence halls" (Duke Office of Information Technology, 2007). Milne (2007) predicts that "as the mobile experience continues to evolve, systems embedded in physical environments will provide richer interactive opportunities" and augmentations of personal devices (p. 14). He points to MIT's Steam Cafe, "where students can send SMS messages to a display system installed in the space and leave messages for other students" (Milne, p. 14). This "digital graffiti" is "a form of interactive digital art" (Milne, p. 26) that can engage Net Gen students, inspire interaction, and promote learning.

Abilene Christian University (ACU) (2008), the first university to provide iPhones to entering students, offers a compelling vision: "In the converged space where the Internet and telecommunications meet, new possibilities exist for the convergence of in-class and out-of-class activities, curricular and extra-curricular learning" (2008, ¶14). The university envisions a "new world of mobile learning" and "a wall-less, virtual environment that enables and empowers its communities for the future" (ACU, 2008, ¶46). For example, in Barret Living and Learning Hall, where 22 learning communities focus on various academic majors, community service, or social advocacy:

> Converged mobile technology like the iPhone or Blackberry would allow for greater connectedness among every member of the Barret community. Students could post to blogs instantly from a service project. Faculty could inform and affirm student work at flexible times. The ACU community would be able to get podcast updates from students and faculty who volunteer in all sorts of contexts, from weekend work-projects in Laredo to summer internships in China. While it's nearly impossible to gather all 180 Barret students and faculty mentors together for

a traditional meeting, a virtual meeting—where documents, audio, video, and web content are shared—could be more easily managed with this sort of technology. (2008, ¶45)

Prosumer Technologies

Related to mobility and convergence is the development of "prosumer" technologies, hardware and software with high-end capabilities but low barriers (in cost and usability) for non-professional use. Examples include affordable digital video (DV) cameras and free software like iMovie (for MacOS) and MovieMaker (for Windows). Prosumer technologies offer new ways to engage Net Gen students in campus and residential life and thus can enhance learning and social development. Students now routinely make videos not only for coursework but also for residence hall programs, student organizations, and personal uses. The familiar end-of-year slide show has become an elaborately edited and musically scored video available on DVD and the residence hall web site. Video contests held at many universities focus on student life. Colleges are now creating their own YouTube channels, some open to student productions. Besides running contests and integrating multimedia into residence life activities, we need to make prosumer resources easily available for students, ideally 24/7. Such resources include AV equipment to supplement student-owned devices, powerful multimedia computers with editing software, and abundant file storage for media projects.

Web 2.0 and Participatory Culture

Web 2.0 is not a sudden development but rather the collective name for a combination of new Web applications and evolving social uses of them. A useful metaphor for this phenomenon is the transition from a "read-only" to a "read-write" Internet—that is, from an emphasis on the *delivery* of information to *authoring, production, and interaction*—made possible by the new applications. Table 3.2 expands this metaphor for the "Social Web."

Table 3.2
Web 2.0: The Social Web

Web 1.0	Web 2.0
Read-only	Read-write
Consumer, passive reception	Producer, active participation
Information delivery, publishing	Authoring, interaction
Static Web pages	Dynamic content, user-generated content, shared content
Top-down taxonomies, gatekeepers, experts	User-tagging of information, folksonomies,[1] collective intelligence
Single work of art or software application	Collages, mashups[2]

Examples of Web 2.0 applications include wikis[3] (and *Wikipedia*); blogging; media-sharing sites such as Flickr and YouTube; social bookmarking[4] applications such as *del.icio.us*; collaborative document editing sites such as Google Docs; Massive Multiplayer Online Games (MMOGs), especially social or cooperative games, such as *World of Warcraft*; Multi-User Virtual Environments (MUVEs) such as Second Life; and, of course, social networking communities such as MySpace and Facebook.

If we think again about Millennial proclivities, and the parallels between those traits and key learning and development principles (Table 3.1), it is easy to see why Web 2.0 applications have achieved such overwhelming traction among our entering students. The parallels between Web 2.0 and those same learning and development principles, as suggested in Table 3.3, make many educators excited about the potential of these new technologies.

Table 3.3
Web 2.0 and Learning Principles

Web 2.0 applications	Learning or development principle
User-generated content, user tagging,[5] folksonomies	Active learning
Shared content, MUVEs, MMOGs	Social learning
MUVEs, mashups	Multiple intelligences, blended learning, active learning
Aggregated content, dynamic content, location tagging[6]	Active, self-situated, and holistic learning
Multimedia platforms, individualization, customization	Contextual learning, multiple learning styles and modalities
Social networking sites	Self-expression, peer negotiating of norms, constructing identity

Web 2.0 and prosumer tools may be seen as the technological manifestations of a larger social trend that Jenkins (1992, 2006a) calls "participatory culture" and "convergence culture," and that Lessig (2004) calls "read/write culture" and "free culture." Participatory cultures blur the lines between consumers and producers and have low barriers for involvement. Millennial students, as we have seen, are natural players in participatory cultures. The overall challenge of Web 2.0 for higher education, as articulated by Martin Weller (2008) of the UK's Open University, "is this—when learners have been accustomed to very facilitative, usable, personalizable and adaptive tools for both learning and socializing, why will they accept standardized, unintuitive, clumsy and out of date tools in formal education they are paying for?"

Residential Students Moving "Off Campus"

Mobile social networking (like Twitter, which broadcasts short updates to networks of friends on cell phones) and the use of mobile streaming media are examples of trends that combine online content, mobility, convergence, prosumer tools, and Web 2.0. The latter have been called "event blogging," "lifeblogging," or "lifecasting." These emerging technologies promise to further impact campus life, when, for example, both course lectures and student parties can be streamed live on the Web by almost anyone. Ironically, associated with all these trends is also a massive movement of students "off campus" in terms of their technology use. Whereas in the 1980s and 1990s, colleges and universities provided the vast majority of student information devices, software, and services, in the 2000s students increasingly use their own devices and off-campus commercial services like Google and Facebook. Among the resulting new dilemmas for student affairs professionals is how to handle behavior issues that arise on non-university hosted services—for example, a dispute between hallmates that occurs virtually "off campus" in Facebook or Second Life or offensive comments posted anonymously in college gossip sites (e.g., Young, 2008). Administrators must now juggle university acceptable-use policies and other campus policies (that may or may not apply) with commercial services' terms of use, free speech, and common sense. We are clearly on shifting ground here, sometimes working together with students to create new norms for unprecedented social situations.

Spaces for Learning and Community Building

In their study of student success in college, Kuh and colleagues (2005) found that physical environments were key to engaging students. Earlier, Strange and Banning (2001) suggested we create physical environments according to learning-needs priorities reflecting Maslow's (1943) hierarchy of psychological needs. Mobile Millennial learners—constantly accessing online content, equipped with converged devices and prosumer technologies, and interacting in virtual spaces—require us to rethink all the physical spaces in our residence halls as informal learning spaces. Student rooms, hallways, lounges, foyers, study spaces, dining halls, courtyards, and lawns are all, more than ever before, adjuncts to the formal learning spaces of classrooms and research labs. This anytime-anywhere learning-space mindset gives "living-learning community" an even deeper resonance in the 21st century.

Experience with formal learning spaces would suggest a list of residence hall "no-brainers": the need for robust wired and wireless networking; abundant electrical connections to recharge devices; plentiful natural light and good artificial lighting; comfortable, human-friendly spaces; and ergonomic, flexible, moveable furniture. Welcome almost anywhere are soft seating, comfortable chairs with tablet arms, other laptop-friendly furniture, and large displays that can be shared. Regarding the need for flexibility and adaptability, we should bear in mind that students use the same spaces in different ways depending on the time of day or night or the week of the academic term.

Despite all their laptops and other devices, at least for the near future, students continue to need university-provided computers, software, and other technology resources, ideally located in the residence halls where they do most of their work. The "myth" that "public labs are no longer needed" because most students have their own computers is debunked by Hawkins and Oblinger (2007). They point out that some students cannot afford and do not receive financial aid for the high-end hardware or software applications they need for coursework. Even well-equipped students do not carry their laptops everywhere. At Stanford University, where 99% of undergraduates own at least one computer, 70% still use the computer labs located in every residence, primarily for the availability of technology-enhanced study space away from their room, for the software and courseware provided on public computers, and for printing and production activities (Stanford Student Computing, 2008). Students also need multimedia production facilities in or convenient to their residence halls and available 24/7, so that they can digitize materials, edit audio and video, and do high-quality laser printing. As Zeller (2008) argues, we need "to ensure that the technological resources available within the living-learning programs support and complement the instructional technologies being utilized in the classroom," with the important goal of enhancing "seamless in-class and out-of-class student experiences" (p. 72).

Residential learning spaces are evolving, for both curricular and cocurricular purposes, from what Hawkins and Oblinger (2007) call the "room with technology" to the "multifaceted space utilized for collaboration, socialization, and computational research" (p. 11). They note:

> As faculty increase the number of software applications used and team projects required, students view labs as a logical place for group work. Public clusters provide more than just access to the technology. These are "social places" where students can collaborate and share expertise, both technical and disciplinary. Labs may even be used off-hours for entertainment (e.g., LAN parties or gaming tournaments). (p. 11)

The increasing classroom uses of collaborative pedagogies such as project-based and problem-based learning play well with the tendency of Net Gen students to use technology for social, extracurricular purposes. In what Milne (2007) calls the "Interaction Age" on the heels of the Information Age, many colleges have made technology-rich spaces for group work a high priority.

Following are some exemplary or innovative residential learning spaces that support academic, community, and social needs aimed at first-year students:

◇ At the University of Oregon, the Living-Learning Center (LLC) includes a variety of technology-rich learning spaces—a 2,700 square-foot performance hall, two classrooms, and a conference room. As described by assistant director of residence life and adjunct assistant professor Kevin Hatfield (personal communication, June 19, 2008), these rooms and similar spaces in the Earl International House are "used frequently by residential students and classes (e.g., first-year seminars, Freshman Interest Group (FIG) College Connections courses) for review/study sessions, mini-seminars, and group projects" as well as by "visiting scholars for living learning programs," for art installations, and for "co-curricular academic initiatives supporting international students, student cultural groups, and multicultural/ diversity education" (A. Bonamici, personal communication, June 19, 2008).

◇ At Morrisville (NY) State College, recent residential and dining spaces are designed with nooks to support "nomadic" students and student project groups of four to five using laptops, cell phones, and handheld devices needing multiple power outlets (M. Barber, personal communication, June 16, 2008).

◇ At Loyola Marymount University (Los Angeles), the Life Science Early Awareness Program (LEAP)—a living-learning community for first-year students in biology and natural science—integrates the intensive use of technology with team-taught multidisciplinary courses and cocurricular experiences (LEAP, 2008). LEAP provides similarly equipped group collaboration spaces in the residence hall, classroom, and open labs. Each space includes large shared displays and laptop collaboration software called TeamSpot® (J. Cevetello, personal communication, June 24, 2008). TeamSpot® allows groups of walk-up laptop users to work together on public displays in conjunction with their personal laptops by sharing files, screen views, and annotations (Tidebreak, Inc., 2008).

◇ At the Massachusetts Institute of Technology (MIT), group work spaces with 40" LCD displays and TeamSpot® software are deployed in four undergraduate residence halls. Along with other collaborative workspaces, they were created because "students have consistently expressed a need for computing spaces where they can work together, in addition to spaces where they can work individually. Cooperation and teamwork are an essential part of many MIT classes" (MIT, 2008).

◇ At the University of California (UC), Berkeley, "Academic Service Centers" in the five main residential units support living and learning programs with academic peer advising, tutoring, and faculty programs plus technology services like printing, copying, binding, and equipment such as headphones and voice recorders (UC Berkeley Office of Student Development, 2008).

◇ At Stanford University, the Florence Moore Hall "Smart Lounge" provides a state of the art audiovisual presentation space for lectures and section meetings of the Structured Liberal Education (SLE) program, in which first-year students take required courses in humanities and writing and receive tutoring in the residence. In the early evenings, the faculty Resident Fellow and student resident assistants host guest speakers, film discussions, and other residential programs in the Smart Lounge. At other times, students use the Smart Lounge casually for group study, gaming and Local Area Network (LAN) parties, music, movies, and social events. A similarly equipped residence lounge in the Chicano/Latino ethnic theme dorm, Casa Zapata, hosts campus-wide Latino community events as well as house programs and casual student use.

More examples of formal and informal learning spaces, plus a rich set of resources including podcasts, presentations, and case studies, are available from the EDUCAUSE Learning Initiative (ELI, 2008) and a recent EDUCAUSE eBook, *Learning Spaces* (Oblinger, 2006).

Intersections of Real-Space and Virtual Communities

Perhaps the most compelling story about residential life on college campuses today lies in the rich intersections between physical, real-space community and online, virtual community. Whereas large bodies of social science and group behavior research address real-space human communities, on the one hand, and virtual communities, on the other hand, little research has explored intersections between the two, when groups of people live together or are geographically bounded.[7] That dearth of research is particularly surprising given that it neglects what has been, for some two decades, a dominant experience at colleges and universities. The emergence of Facebook on college campuses—online networking based on real-space geographical communities—has inspired some researchers to begin filling that void. Groundbreaking work has been done at Michigan State University (Ellison, Steinfeld, & Lampe, 2006, 2007), in particular, about the role of Facebook in forming social capital among undergraduates. This work, discussed in more detail below, offers both immediately compelling results and a promising framework for future work about the overlapping of online and offline social networks in higher education. Also discussed below, at Stanford, we have begun examining the use of Facebook specifically in the context of residential life.

Group Formation and the Transition to College

In today's living-learning communities, both the "living" and "learning" activities have become dislodged from the time and space constraints of being co-located in the physical residence hall. Indeed—for better or for worse—class-year and residential community building begins, in virtual spaces, long before students arrive. As soon as they get their acceptance letters or e-mails, entering students form Facebook groups for their class-year, and, like Brenda and her classmates at 21CU, they begin active discussions and preparations for college. (This grass-roots phenomenon arose in the early 2000s, pre-Facebook, in Yahoo Groups.) Residence hall Facebook groups are formed as soon as entering students learn where they are living. By late summer 2007, 82% or more than 1,400 members of the incoming Stanford University first-year class had joined the Class of 2011 Facebook group (Ly & Schiller, 2008). *USA Today* reported that entering Syracuse University students created groups for "almost every residence hall on campus" in which they shared "room numbers, floor plans for their buildings and other tips they have heard about their new home" (Collura, 2007). Some colleges even use Facebook to help students select roommates (Collura; Zeller, 2008).

Historically, at some universities, students do not learn their residence hall assignment until late summer and do not find out who their roommate is until they arrive on campus. "From a group formation standpoint," explains Josh Schiller, associate director of Residential Education at Stanford University, "if students do not know each other or their roommates before they arrive, they do not have preconceptions" (personal communication, June 30, 2008). Such policies obviously face challenges today and need to be reexamined. Referring to Tuckman and Jensen's five-stage model of group formation (1977; Tuckman, 1965)—forming, storming, norming, performing, and adjourning—Schiller notes that the forming stage is most affected by Facebook usage, as students begin projecting their identity to the group much earlier than previous generations. The fact is, the horse is out of the barn, insofar as students do form preconceptions online before they arrive. To help manage those preconceptions, some administrators are adopting a "If you can't beat 'em, join 'em" strategy. The ("Official") Stanford Class of 2012 group—with nearly 1,400 members as of July, 2008—was formed by the Office of Admission and includes staff from Public Affairs, Undergraduate Education, and the Freshman Dean's office.

In their study of 286 Michigan State University (MSU) undergraduates, Ellison et al. (2006) examine what they call "high school social capital" or "maintained social capital" (Ellison et al., 2007) in order to gauge the impact of Facebook on the transition to college. Social capital is a measure of the value of social networks, the resources that individuals and groups accumulate through group relationships. At MSU, 90% of students formed connections with their new college friends and classmates, and 97% continued connections to high school friends through Facebook (Ellison et al., 2006). This "maintained social capital" was greater with more intensive use of Facebook, helping students avoid "friendsickness" (Ellison et al., 2007).

Wired Frosh: Electronic Community Building in First-Year Residences

Facebook continues to provide the dominant virtual community for students after they arrive on campus and enter Tuckman and Jensen's (1977) storming and norming stages of group formation. Entering students are also introduced to other online tools and rich media that residence life professionals can leverage as part of today's complex communication ecologies. In a preliminary study of Facebook in the residences by Student Computing and Residential Education, Stanford students said that their residence hall e-mail chatlists were about equally as useful as Facebook for "sharing interests and opinions" (Ly & Schiller, 2008), second only to face-to-face communication. This finding is consistent with an earlier study I conducted, while serving as the Resident Fellow in a first-year residence hall in the 1990s (Holeton, 1997). I analyzed the house e-mail discussion list and found that controversial topics on the list sometimes provoked heated reactions but often led to substantive discussion, both online and offline, that helped develop critical thinking skills, a key learning goal for first-year students. Second, I found that residents can successfully use online discussion to help construct shared values and norms by working through how to talk (or joke) together about sensitive issues like gender, sexuality, race, ethnicity, religion, and politics (Holeton,

1997). Third, as *Newsweek* reported, "the people who dominated dorm life in face-to-face encounters were not the same folks who ruled the e-mail debates. Electronic discourse, it seems, offered a voice to some students who might not otherwise be heard" (Branscum, 1997).

Just before MySpace ushered in the tidal wave of social networking, in 2003, I had the opportunity to teach a course for Stanford's Program in Writing and Rhetoric in which I asked 15 first-year students to study the "nexus of virtual and face-to-face community" (Holeton, 2003; in press). The students conducted fieldwork in their own residences, looking at their peers' online behaviors and uses of new media. One student who studied his residence hall e-mail list concluded that many students are more comfortable discussing controversial issues online than in large groups like house meetings, and that residence staff (even if silent) play an important moderating role on such lists (Andersen & Samagh, 2003). Many students in the class chose to study instant messaging (IM), at that time their "dominant and under-researched form of mediated communication" (Holeton, in press). Student researchers found that IM, while heavily used with peers living in the same house as well as elsewhere, was especially effective at strengthening social relationships across distant residences on a large campus (Cheung, 2003)—usually "weak ties" in terms of social capital. They also learned that students used IM extensively for flirting and that students used IM-away messages as a dynamic, sophisticated voice-mail-like system (Nachbaur, 2003).

Facebook, Social Capital, and Residential Life

The main affordances of Facebook are a user profile consisting of shared personal information, a user-constructed and user-defined audience of "friends," private messaging, and public commenting. Facebook groups facilitate various affiliations through group discussions, events, and shared media, and thousands of optional plug-in applications add various other social and networking tools. In their pioneering study, Ellison et al. (2006) note that Facebook "constitutes a newer form of virtual socializing in which connections are initially made offline and then migrated online" (p. 27) because of the way it serves spatially or geographically bound communities. The MSU students "overwhelmingly used Facebook to keep in touch with old friends and to maintain or intensify relationships characterized by some form of offline connection such as dormitory proximity or a shared class" (Ellison et al., 2006, p. 27). The researchers found that the use of Facebook facilitated "the maintenance and formation of social capital of all kinds" (Ellison et al., 2006, p. 30), not just the "high school social capital" associated with transition. Intensive Facebook usage increased both "bonding" and "bridging" social capital, that is, it strengthened relationships with both close friends and more distant "weak ties." Ellison (2007) adds that bridging social capital may be especially important during the "emerging adulthood" of ages 18-25. Intensity of Facebook usage was also associated with increased self-esteem and satisfaction with college life (Ellison et al., 2006; 2007).

In 2007-2008, partly inspired by the MSU work, Student Computing at Stanford partnered with Residential Education to study how students use Facebook in the context of residential life. Our work so far is only preliminary, but the tentative results are striking (Ly & Schiller, 2008). Nearly all Stanford undergraduates live on campus (99%) and use Facebook (94%) (Ly & Schiller). A majority participate in living-learning programs, including academic theme or focus houses, language and culture houses, ethnic theme dorms, and first-year houses. These programs are led by faculty resident fellows, associated with academic directors, and supported by student staff including resident assistants, resident computer consultants, peer academic coordinators, theme or focus associates, and resident tutors. We selected five different kinds of houses to study, including an all-first-year-student house, a four-class academic focus house, and a four-class ethnic theme house. Students in each house rated the most useful ways of communicating with people who do live in the same residence compared with those who do not from among these media: (a) face-to-face, (b) Facebook, (c) texting, (d) IM, (f) individual e-mail, (g) group (list) e-mail, (h) phone, and (i) Web (other than Facebook). They rated each medium for the following purposes: (a) "getting to know people" (i.e., making new friends); (b) "staying in touch" (i.e., maintaining relationships with people you already know); (c) "sharing interests and opinions"; (d) "flirting"; and (e) "arranging social life." Not surprisingly, we found that face-to-face is the preferred medium in nearly every context. However,

◇ Facebook ranked first (ahead of face-to-face) for "staying in touch" with people who do not live in the same residence.
◇ Facebook tied with face-to-face as the best way to "arrange social life" with people who do not live in the same residence.
◇ Facebook ranked a strong second to face-to-face for every other purpose, regardless of place of residence. As mentioned before, only group e-mail—the venerable and still useful residence hall chatlist—came close to Facebook for the purpose of "sharing interests and opinions" with fellow residents.
◇ First-year students found Facebook more useful for making new friends ("getting to know people") than did upperclass students.

Based on the preliminary results, Jennifer Ly, senior consulting manager for Student Computing, speculates that the major contributions of residence-based Facebook groups are in line with the MSU study and include:

◇ Facilitating the transition to the new residence (in particular for first-year students, answering questions and making them feel more comfortable)
◇ Building community through media-sharing (photos and videos of dorm and campus events that residents attended together)
◇ Supplementing face-to-face interactions by sharing personal information during the formation of friendships
◇ Increasing involvement, investment, and connection with the "weak-tie" network in the residence (Ly & Schiller, 2008)

The major "detractions," cited by a minority of students, were the distraction, time-wasting, or "addictiveness" of using Facebook (while continuing to use it heavily!); the potential to form preconceived notions about people from information and photos posted; and the potential to diminish face-to-face interactions (e.g., choosing to write on someone's virtual wall instead of walking down the hall) (Ly & Schiller, 2008).

A Second Life for Residence Halls

Although we are a long way from equipping residence halls with Holodecks—the virtual reality technology envisioned in the 1980s by the writers of *Star Trek: The Next Generation*—the old college residence hall is moving into today's most popular Multi-User Virtual Environment (MUVE), Linden Lab's Second Life. Hundreds of colleges have created virtual campuses in Second Life, and many conduct courses or portions of courses there, attended by the avatars (3-D virtual representations) of instructors and students. The residence halls are not far behind:

◇ Sarah Robbins, who teaches first-year writing courses at Ball State University, uses Second Life extensively to "[encourage] learning beyond designated learning spaces and times via increased levels of student engagement and community cohesion" (Robbins, 2007)—a goal that sounds remarkably like that of residential life. Indeed, *The New York Times* reported that Ball State students (surely those of Professor Robbins) "log in from their R.L. [real life] dorm rooms to decorate their avatars' virtual rooms" (Lagorio, 2007, ¶5).

◇ At MIT's Second Life campus, incoming students can visit virtual dorms to help them decide where they wish to live. The virtual residences, intended to "reflect something of the dorms' spirit and culture" (Naone, 2008, ¶1), were created by students for a contest sponsored by the Office of Educational Innovation and Technology.

A terrific cocurricular or extracurricular project would be to have students construct together an "alternate reality" version of their residence hall. Like Facebook, MUVEs offer community-building possibilities that traditional tools do not. In Second Life, the laws of physics do not apply, so residents of the Virtual Dorm can fly or teleport between "distant" locations and can bring into their dorm room or lounge essentially any educational or social resource they can find, buy, or build. They can creatively experiment with their identities, as do many Second Life residents, by altering their appearance and gender. They can extend or supplement real-space residential programming by inviting virtual guest speakers for live, interactive discussions on any topic of interest, complete with multimedia artifacts, transcripts, and archives to revisit later. The possibilities for enhancing and complementing residential community life with MUVEs like Second Life are "virtually" unlimited.

Being Proactive with Virtual Tools

The work and examples described above argue that the new interactive technologies with which most Net Gen students are familiar before they come to campus can indeed complement and enhance traditional community-building tools in the residences. Moreover, these new tools allow us to encourage student learning and development in ways that were simply not possible before. To take advantage of these tools, student affairs and residence life professionals should be proactive, not merely reactive. They should plan together—in staff training, workshops, and retreats—how to use student-owned devices, residence web sites, multimedia production, electronic discussion, social networking, and immersive environments to serve their goals.

Both professional and student staff should also anticipate problems and how to handle them. It is nearly certain that "stuff will happen" online, so we should not be surprised when someone overreacts, posts inappropriate material, makes offensive comments, or worse. "Students may do stupid things on the Facebook," Stutzman (2006) reminds us. They will do stupid things in the virtual dorm lounge just as for generations they have done stupid things in the real-life dorm lounge. Most have not been expelled for their real-space lapses, but rather given the opportunity to learn from their mistakes. Interpersonal or social slip-ups in virtual space, as in real-space, are often teachable moments. While we learn to negotiate these new terrains, residential staff should exercise caution about intervening or overreacting, possibly robbing students of the chance to construct effective learning communities together.

New Media Literacy

Finally, it is important to recognize that the Net Gen is not homogeneous nor are its members uniformly literate with technology (any more than "digital immigrants" are uniformly illiterate with technology). On the contrary, students reveal a range of skills and participation in new media. A recent study showed that skill level with presentation software, graphics, Web pages, and audio and video ranged variously by gender, area of study, and class year (Salaway, Katz, & Caruso, 2006). Notably, first-year students are less skilled than their upper-class peers; they "arrive somewhat insecure and unskilled in producing presentations, creating spreadsheets, or using specialized software" (Salaway et al., p. 16).

Moreover, the notion of literacy itself is changing, expanding to include "cognitive/critical thinking skills in a technological environment" (Educational Testing Service, 2006, p. 4) and new media authoring and production. As Jenkins notes,

> It is [not] simply a matter of teaching them how to use the technology—that's the equivalent of confusing penmanship with composition. To be literate, [students] need to develop whole sets of social skills and cultural competencies which surround the technology. (2006b, ¶47)

Those new competencies need to address computer privacy and security, safe and responsible computing practices, and copyright issues. Under seemingly unending pressure from the Recording Industry Association of America (RIAA), the Motion Picture Association of America (MPAA), and DMCA enforcement, colleges now routinely require entering students to participate in copyright and file-sharing educational programs. A more organic and holistic approach, however, would be to contextualize copyright issues for first-year students as part of academic integrity and responsible computing.

Many entering students also need guidance in the transition from high school to college uses of social networking sites and file-sharing applications. In college, the stakes are higher. Faculty, administrators, potential employers, and campus police are among those joining the "invisible audiences" (boyd, 2007) for student Facebook and MySpace profiles and other online activities. Students may not fully appreciate the persistence and searchability of the information they share online (boyd), nor the Internet's vast archiving power. Neither may students be conversant with the corporate terms of use for Facebook and MySpace, how to report abuses, or how to change default privacy settings. As for file-sharing and copyright, the RIAA and MPAA continue to focus enforcement efforts on college campuses and to threaten students with lawsuits. Students need to understand not only the potential consequences for violating copyright laws but also technical skills like how to change the default sharing behaviors of file-sharing applications.

To address "net savviness," some colleges are revamping orientation programs and rethinking "University 101" courses and workshops. At Stanford, we now include issues of copyright, privacy, and social networking in the Introduction to Computing class offered in first-year residences. Unfortunately, only about one fifth of our first-year students take the optional course. Carnegie-Mellon University offers a better, and exemplary, model for educating entering students about net savviness and new media literacy. "About Computing@Carnegie Mellon"—formerly known as the Computing Skills Workshop—is a required, peer-taught, three-unit mini-course (half-semester) for incoming first-year students "recently rewritten to integrate computer, library and information ethics skills into a holistic model of information fluency" (Hood & Carnegie Mellon Libraries, 2008). The curriculum includes CMU-specific services (e.g., e-mail, the course management system, campus calendar, networking services, central file storage, and help center); policies and guidelines for academic integrity, copyright, and network usage; university library services; Web page creation; safe computing; Excel; and other campus computing resources (Harkins & Zimbigl, 2007; Carnegie Mellon Computing Services, 2008).

Even without a model new media literacy/responsible computing requirement like CMU's, our tech-savvy but unevenly skilled Millennial students continue to need robust computing support. Entering students still need basic computing and networking help as they transition to campus systems. They also need assistance protecting their personal devices from the viruses, spyware, and security attacks that are common on college networks. With a "participation gap" replacing the "digital divide," students now need new kinds of support—help with multimedia authoring, presentation skills, social networking, responsible computing, and critical thinking about technology. The vision of distributed, community-based peer computer consultants, articulated by Merriman (1997), was never more appropriate. While many universities successfully employ centralized support models, others have stayed with or moved to residence-based, peer consultant models. The advantages of a community-based approach seem especially relevant today: one on one, face-to-face support for communities of users; leadership opportunities for students; convenient, local, responsive, timely, nearly 24/7 support; and scalable, economical tech support (Merriman). Plus now, it is our Net Gen students, not faculty or staff, who tend to be the early adopters and experts with new technologies. To help us face the challenges of 21st century literacy, we may need student technology educators in our college residences more than ever.

Notes

[1] Folksonomies—"a portmanteau of the words *folk* and *taxonomy*" (Folksonomy, 2008)—are user-created ways of organizing or categorizing information. In contrast to taxonomies (like library subject-indexing), which are created by experts, folksonomies are "bottom up," created collaboratively by readers or consumers. Users generate online folksonomies by "tagging" or categorizing information with intuitive labels.

[2] Mashups are digital collages that recombine existing work to create a new or derivative work. Music mashups may consist entirely or partly of previous musical compositions. Video mashups are edited together from multiple sources. Software application mashups combine code or data from multiple web applications to create hybrid functionality; for example, a mashup created by the Chicago Police "integrates the department's database of reported crimes with Google Maps in order to help stop crime in areas and warn citizens of areas where the crime rate is high" (Mashup, 2008, ¶17).

[3] Wikis are user-editable web sites. Like *Wikipedia*, they use a simple interface so that non-experts can easily edit and upload content to the Web. Wikis are used in higher education for courses, research, documentation, and team projects.

[4] Social bookmarking "is a method for Internet users to store, organize, search, and manage bookmarks of web pages" (Social bookmarking, 2008). With *del.icio.us*, for example, Web users can compare notes about bookmarked sites with others, and they can find new sites that other people have labeled with the same terms.

[5] User tagging or social tagging is the practice of categorizing content with intuitive labels to construct collaborative folksonomies (see above).

[6] Location tagging or "geotagging" means adding geographical information, typically longitude and latitude, to web sites or other media. Location tagging of shared digital pictures, for example, offers a way for communities to connect virtual and physical spaces in which they interact.

⁷Notable exceptions are the work of Keith Hampton and Barry Wellman on wired suburban neighborhoods (e.g., Hampton, 2007; Hampton & Wellman, 2003) and Kavanaugh et al. (2005) on the Blacksburg (VA) Electronic Village.

References

Abilene Christian University (ACU). (2008). *Envisioning the 21st-century campus.* Retrieved June 24, 2008, from ACU Connected web site: http://www.acu.edu/technology/mobilelearning/researchers/envisioning/index.html

Andersen, A., & Samagh, S. (2003). *Stanford university residence dorms: Virtual and real-space community.* Retrieved November 15, 2007, from Program in Writing and Rhetoric 3-25, Stanford University web site: http://www.stanford.edu/class/pwr3-25/group4/index.html

boyd, d. (2007, May). Social network sites: Public, private, or what?" *The Knowledge Tree,* 13. Retrieved June 28, 2008, from http://kt.flexiblelearning.net.au/tkt2007/edition-13/social-network-sites-public-private-or-what/

Branscum, D. (1997, October 27). Life at high-tech U. *Newsweek,* 78-79. Retrieved July 1, 2008, from http://www.newsweek.com/id/97264/page/1

Bransford, J. D., Brown, A. L., & Cocking, R. R. (Eds.). (2000). *How people learn: Brain, mind, experience, and school.* Washington, DC: National Research Council.

Campus Computing Project. (2007). *The 2007 national survey of information technology in U.S. higher education* [Summary]. Retrieved June 22, 2008, from http://www.campuscomputing.net/survey-summary/2007-campus-computing-survey

Carnegie Mellon Computing Services. (2008). *Computing@Carnegie Mellon.* Retrieved June 27, 2008, from Carnegie Mellon University web site: http://www.cmu.edu/c-cm/index.htm

Caruso, J. B., & Salaway, G. (2007). *Key findings: The ECAR study of undergraduate students and information technology, 2007.* Boulder, CO: EDUCAUSE Center for Applied Research. Retrieved June 22, 2008, from http://net.educause.edu/ir/library/pdf/ERS0706/EKF0706.pdf

Cheung, A. (2003). *A vast weave of threads: How instant messaging facilitates inter-dormitory network communities among undergraduates at Stanford University.* Retrieved June 25, 2008, from Program in Writing and Rhetoric 3-25, Stanford University web site: from http://www.stanford.edu/class/pwr3-25/group2/projects/cheung.html

Collura, H. (2007, August 8). Facebook pages concern parents of college freshmen. *USA Today* [Online]. Retrieved June 25, 2008, from http://www.usatoday.com/news/nation/2007-08-07-facebook-housing_N.htm

Dugdale, S., & Long, P. (2007, March 12). *Planning the informal learning landscape.* EDUCAUSE Learning Initiative Webinar. Retrieved June 18, 2008, from http://www.educause.edu/ir/library/pdf/ELIWEB073.pdf

Duke University Office of Information Technology. (2007, August 23). *Leading IT magazine honors Duke Digital Initiative.* Retrieved June 24, 2008, from the Duke University web site: http://www.oit.duke.edu/news/gen-announce/cio100award.html

Educational Testing Service. (2006). *2006 ICT literacy assessment preliminary findings.* Retrieved June 27, 2008, from http://www.ets.org/ictliteracy/prelimfindings.html

EDUCAUSE Learning Initiative (ELI). (20008). *Learning space design.* Retrieved July 11, 2008, from http://www.educause.edu/LearningSpace/5521

Ellison, N. (2007, December). *Facebook use on campus: A social capital perspective on social network sites.* Paper presented at the ECAR Symposium, Boca Raton, FL. Retrieved July 4, 2008, from http://connect.educause.edu/Library/ECAR/FacebookUseonCampusASocia/45935

Ellison, N., Steinfeld, C., & Lampe, C. (2006, June). *Spatially bounded online social networks and social capital: The role of Facebook.* Paper presented at the Annual Conference of the International Communication Association (ICA), Dresden, Germany. Retrieved July 2, 2008, from http://www.msu.edu/~nellison/Facebook_ICA_2006.pdf

Ellison, N. B., Steinfield, C., & Lampe, C. (2007). The benefits of Facebook "friends": Social capital and college students' use of online social network sites. *Journal of Computer-Mediated Communication, 12*(4), Article 1. Retrieved July 4, 2008, from http://jcmc.indiana.edu/vol12/issue4/ellison.html

Folksonomy. (2008, July 11). In *Wikipedia, the free encyclopedia.* Retrieved July 11, 2008, from http://en.wikipedia.org/wiki/Folksonomies

Fox, S., & Madden, M. (2006, January 22). *Generations online.* Retrieved November 15, 2007, from the Pew Internet and American Life Project web site: http://www.pewinternet.org/PPF/r/170/report_display.asp

Hampton, K. (2007). Neighborhoods in the network society: The e-neighbors study. *Information, Communication & Society 10*(5), 714-748. Retrieved June 25, 2008, from http://www.mysocialnetwork.net/downloads/eneighborsplace18.pdf

Hampton, K., & Wellman, B. (2003). Neighboring in Netville: How the Internet supports community and social capital in a wired suburb. *City & Community, 2*(4), 277-311.

Harkins, C., & Zimbigl, L. (2007, March 13). Teaching digital responsibility. *Research Bulletin*, 6. Boulder, CO: EDUCAUSE Center for Applied Research. Retrieved June 27, 2008, from http://connect.educause.edu/library/ERB0706

Hawkins, B. L., & Oblinger, D. G. (2007, September/October). The myth about the need for public computer labs. *EDUCAUSE Review*, 10-11

Holeton, R. (1997). *Wired frosh: A case study of electronic community building in a freshman dorm.* Retrieved June 15, 2008, from Stanford University web site: http://www.stanford.edu/~holeton/wired-frosh/index.html

Holeton, R. (2003). *dorm.net/Residential Rhetorics.* [Course web site]. Retrieved June 18, 2008, from Program in Writing and Rhetoric 3-25, Stanford University web site: http://www.stanford.edu/class/pwr3-25

Holeton, R. (in press). How much is too much new media for the Net Generation? In C. E. Ball & J. Kalmbach (Eds.), *Reading and writing new media.* Cresskill, NJ: Hampton Press.

Hood, D., & Carnegie Mellon Libraries. (2008, February 19). *Information literacy @ Carnegie Mellon.* Retrieved June 27, 2008, from Carnegie Mellon Libraries web site: http://www.library.cmu.edu/InformationLiteracy/program.html

Howe, N., & Strauss, W. (2003). *Millennials go to college: Strategies for a new generation on campus.* Washington, DC: American Association of College Registrars.

Jenkins, H. (1992). *Textual poachers: Television fans and participatory culture.* New York: Routledge.

Jenkins, H. (2006a). *Convergence culture: Where old and new media meet.* New York: NYU Press.

Jenkins, H. (2006b, November 16). *How to teach high-tech* [Chat transcript]. The Chronicle of Higher Education Live Discussions. Retrieved June 27, 2008 from http://chronicle.com/live/2006/11/jenkins/

Jones, S., & Madden, M. (2002, September 15). *The Internet goes to college: How students are living in the future with today's technology.* Retrieved November 15, 2007, from the Pew Internet and American Life Project web site: http://www.pewinternet.org/PPF/r/71/report_display.asp

Kaiser Family Foundation Program for the Study of Entertainment Media and Health. (2005). *Generation M: Media in the lives of 8–18 year-olds* (Publication No. 7250). Retrieved November 15, 2007, from http://www.kff.org/entmedia/entmedia030905pkg.cfm

Kavanaugh, A., Carroll, J. M., Rosson, M. B., Zin, T. T., & Reese, D. D. (2005). Community networks: Where offline communities meet online. *Journal of Computer-Mediated Communication, 10*(4), Article 3. Retrieved July 4, 2008, from http://jcmc.indiana.edu/vol10/issue4/kavanaugh.html

Kuh, G. D., Schuh, J. H., Whitt, E. J., & Associates. (1991). *Involving colleges: Successful approaches to fostering student learning and development outside the classroom.* San Francisco: Jossey-Bass.

Kuh, G. D., Kinzie, J., Schuh, J. H., Whitt, E. J., & Associates. (2005). *Student success in college: Creating conditions that matter.* San Francisco: Jossey-Bass.

Lagorio, C. (2007, January 7). The ultimate distance learning. *The New York Times.* Retrieved June 29, 2008, from http://www.nytimes.com/2007/01/07/education/edlife/07innovation.html?_r=1&oref=slogin

Lander University. (2008). *Student laptop requirement.* Retrieved June 24, 2008, from Lander University, Information Technology Services web site http://www.lander.edu/its/students/laptop_requirement/

Lenhart, A., & Madden, M. (2005a, July 27). *Teens and technology: Youth are leading the transition to a fully wired and mobile nation.* Retrieved November 15, 2007, from the Pew Internet and American Life Project web site: http://www.pewinternet.org/PPF/r/162/report_display.asp

Lenhart, A., & Madden, M. (2005b, November 2). *Teen content creators and consumers.* Retrieved November 15, 2007, from the Pew Internet and American Life Project web site: http://www.pewinternet.org/PPF/r/166/report_display.asp

Lessig, L. (2004). *Free culture: How big media uses technology and the law to lock down culture and control creativity.* New York: Penguin.

Life Science Early Awareness Program (LEAP). (2008). Brochure. Seaver College of Science and Engineering, Loyola Marymount University, North Hall, 1 LMU Drive, MS 8160, Los Angeles, CA 90045-2659.

Ly, J., & Schiller, J. (2008, June). *The real world: Facebook.* Paper presented at the ResNet Symposium, University of New Brunswick, Fredericton, NB, Canada. Retrieved June 28, 2008, from http://resnetsymposium.org/rspm/public/files/proposal/19/the_real_world-facebook_slides.pdf

Mashup. (2008, July 11). In *Wikipedia, the free encyclopedia.* Retrieved July 11, 2008, from http://en.wikipedia.org/wiki/Mashup_(web_application_hybrid)

Maslow, A. H. (1943). A theory of human motivation. *Psychological Review, 50,* 370-96.

Massachusetts Institute of Technology (MIT). (2008). *Collaborative workspaces & tools.* Retrieved June 28, 2008, from MIT Information Services and Technology web site: http://web.mit.edu/acis/labs/collaboration_tools.html

Merriman, J. (1997). *A community strategy for customer service: Creating distributed student support in the residential environment.* Proceedings, CAUSE Annual Conference. Retrieved June 27, 2008, from http://net.educause.edu/ir/library/html/cnc9741/cnc9741.html.

Milne, A. (2007). Entering the interaction age: Implementing a future vision for campus learning spaces today. *EDUCAUSE Review, 42*(1), 12-31.

Nachbaur, A. (2003). *College students and instant messaging: An analysis of chatting, flirting, and using away messages.* Retrieved June 25, 2008, from Stanford University, Program in Writing and Rhetoric 3-25 web site: http://www.stanford.edu/class/pwr3-25/group2/projects/nachbaur.html

Naone, E. (2008, January/February). A second dorm life: Design competition for virtual MIT dorms. *Technology Review* [online version]. Retrieved June 29, 2008, from http://www.technologyreview.com/article/19935/

Oblinger, D. (2003, July/August). Boomers, Gen-xer and Millennials: Understanding the new students. *EDUCAUSE Review,* 37-47. Retrieved June 28, 2008, from http://net.educause.edu/ir/library/pdf/ERM0342.pdf

Oblinger, D. G. (Ed.) (2006). *Learning spaces.* Boulder, CO: EDUCAUSE [e-book]. Retrieved June 24, 2008, from http://www.educause.edu/LearningSpaces/10569

Oblinger, D., & Oblinger, J. (Eds.) (2005a). *Educating the net generation* [e-book]. Boulder, CO: EDUCAUSE. Retrieved June 18, 2008, from http://www.educause.edu/books/educatingthenetgen/5989

Oblinger, D., & Oblinger, J. (2005b). Is it age or IT: First steps toward understanding the net generation. In *Educating the net generation* [e-book]. Boulder, CO: EDUCAUSE. Retrieved March 15, 2006, from http://www.educause.edu/educatingthenetgen

Oregon Libraries Network. (2008). *L-net.* Retrieved June 22, 2008, from http://www.questionpoint.org/crs/servlet/org.oclc.home.TFSRedirect?virtcategory=12250

Pascarella, E. T., & Terenzini, P. T. (2005). *How college affects students, Vol. 2: A third decade of research.* San Francisco: Jossey-Bass.

Prensky, M. (2001). Digital natives, digital immigrants. *On the Horizon, 9*(5). Retrieved July 15, 2006, from http://www.marcprensky.com/writing/Prensky%20-%20Digital%20Natives,%20Digital%20Immigrants%20-%20Part1.pdf

Robbins, S. (2007, March). *Second Life in a university writing course: Increasing engagement and community* [abstract]. Paper presented at the Purdue Teaching and Learning with Technology Conference, Lafayette, IN. Retrieved June 29, 2008, from http://www.itap.purdue.edu/tlt/conference/april4-abstracts.cfm

Salaway, G., Katz, R. N., & Caruso, J. B. (2006, December 22). *The ECAR study of undergraduate students and information technology, 2006.* Boulder: CO, EDUCAUSE Center for Applied Research. Retrieved June 27, 2008, from http://www.educause.edu/ir/library/pdf/ers0607/ERS0607w.pdf

Social bookmarking. (2008, July 11). In *Wikipedia, the free encyclopedia.* Retrieved July 11, 2008, from http://en.wikipedia.org/wiki/Social_bookmarking

Stanford Student Computing. (2008). *Results from the annual residence evaluation: 2007-2008.* Retrieved June 24, 2008 from the Stanford University web site: http://rescomp.stanford.edu/info/survey/2007-2008/undergraduate.html

Strange, C. C., & Banning, J. H. (2001). *Educating by design: Creating campus learning environments that work.* San Francisco: Jossey-Bass.

Stutzman, F. (2006). *How university administrators should approach Facebook: Ten rules.* Unit Structures [blog]. Retrieved June 18, 2008, from http://chimprawk.blogspot.com/2006/01/how-university-administrators-should.html

Tidebreak, Inc. (2008). Product information. Retrieved June 25, 2008, from http://tidebreak.com/

Tuckman, B. W. (1965). Developmental sequence in small groups. *Psychological Bulletin, 63*(6), 384-399.

Tuckman, B. W., & Jensen, M. A. C. (1977). Stages of small-group development revisited. *Group & Organization Management, 2*(4), 419-427.

UC Berkeley Office of Student Development. (2008). *Academic services in the residence halls.* Retrieved June 24, 2008, from the University of California, Berkeley web site: http://academiccenters.berkeley.edu/computing/

Weller, M. (2008). SocialLearn: Bridging the gap between Web 2.0 and higher education. Blog post in Feldstein, M. (Ed.), *e-Literate* blog (http://mfeldstein.com/). Retrieved June 24, 2008, from http://mfeldstein.com/sociallearn-bridging-the-gap-between-web-20-and-higher-education/

Western New York Library Resources Council. (2008). *Ask Us 24/7.* Retrieved June 22, 2008, from http://www.askus247.org/info/aboutaskus.asp

Young, J. R. (2008, March 17). How to combat a campus gossip web site (and why you shouldn't). *The Chronicle of Higher Education* [online edition]. Retrieved June 28, 2008, from http://chronicle.com/free/2008/03/2136n.htm

Zeller, W. J. (2008). Living-learning programs in the digital age. *The Journal of College and University Student Housing, 35*(1), 66-77.

Chapter Four

Living-Learning Programs for First-Year Students

Karen Kurotsuchi Inkelas, Matthew Soldner,
and Katalin Szelényi

Among the various programs available for first-year students in residence halls, living-learning (L/L) programs may be one of the hottest trends in the past 20 years. Designed to make a seamless college experience, L/L programs (alternately termed residential learning communities) seek to merge the academic and social spheres of students' lives (Schroeder, 1994; Shapiro & Levine, 1999). Similar to what have become known as learning communities, L/L programs generally have an academic theme (e.g., creative writing, foreign language, engineering, or honors programs) around which a group of similarly interested students coalesce and subsequently participate in theme-focused activities (e.g., taking courses, studying, attending workshops and/or lectures, or participating in cocurricular activities together). Living-learning programs, however, extend learning communities by integrating their activities into students' residence halls, providing space where students with similar interests live together (Inkelas & Associates, 2004). Thus, students' academic interests and social lives intertwine, and both are potentially enriched as a result.

The History and Development of Living-Learning Programs

Although no official registry of L/L programs at U.S. postsecondary institutions currently exists, several sources suggest that they are a popular intervention. For example, the Residential Learning Communities International Clearinghouse (n.d.) includes more than 180 programs on its web site, and a recent national study of living-learning programs included student participants in 613 different living-learning programs on 48 campuses across the United States (National Study of Living-Learning Programs, 2007). Although the living-learning program is a fairly recent phenomenon, the origins of these programs date back to the residential colleges at Oxford and Cambridge (Ryan, 1992). These English models (one dating back to 1264), focused primarily on personal morality but included formats in which faculty "fellows" instructed students in the same buildings where the students, and often the fellows, lived. This format dominated early colonial colleges but was largely discontinued as American institutions of higher education matured into modern, research-focused universities. The English model found a limited foothold again in the 20th century, most notably in some Ivy League universities (Ryan).

The modern progenitor of the living-learning program, however, is widely acknowledged to be Alexander Meiklejohn at the University of Wisconsin at Madison. Concerned with the civic development of undergraduates at Wisconsin in the early 20th century, Meiklejohn created a two-year program called the Experimental College that closely examined the history and development of democracy, while challenging students to live by the democratic ideals they studied (Shapiro & Levine, 1999). From these roots, today's L/L programs have evolved into an eclectic mixture of programming with dozens of different foci.

Types of Living-Learning Programs

Because no complete listing of L/L programs is available, it is difficult to identify all of the variations across U.S. college campuses. One study, however, offered a preliminary typology of L/L programs by theme. The 2004 National Study of Living-Learning Programs (NSLLP) conducted a survey of student outcomes in relation to participation in a L/L program and included approximately 24,000 students spread across 34 postsecondary institutions. Each L/L student in the study participated in one of nearly 250 living-learning programs, later organized by the NSLLP researchers into thematic categories. The sorting process revealed 14 different categories of living-learning programs, although some categories included more than one type of program. The categories include:

◇ *Civic/Social Leadership Programs,* which emphasize social leadership and service, and include (a) civic engagement programs, (b) leadership programs, and (c) service-learning/ social justice programs
◇ *Cultural Programs,* which focus on domestic or international interests, and include (a) international/global programs, (b) language programs, and (c) multicultural/diversity programs
◇ *Disciplinary Programs,* which are based in a single, formal academic discipline, and include (a) business, (b) education, (c) engineering and computer science, (d) health services, (e) humanities, (f) general science, and (g) social science programs
◇ *Fine and Creative Arts Programs,* which celebrate different forms of the creative arts, such as music, poetry, and photography
◇ *General Academic Programs,* which provide general academic support with no particular theme
◇ *Honors Programs,* which offer a rigorous curricular environment for invited, high-ability students
◇ *Multi-Disciplinary Programs,* which are large programs split into smaller groupings with distinct themes
◇ *Outdoor Recreation Programs,* which emphasize sports or outdoor skills
◇ *Research Programs,* which afford their participants the opportunity to work on a research project individually, in groups, or with a professor
◇ *Residential Colleges,* which offer a broad range of courses in cultural or social pursuits in the classic liberal arts tradition
◇ *Transition Programs,* which focus on the first-year transition from home to college, and include (a) new student transition programs and (b) career/major exploration programs
◇ *Upper-Division Programs,* which cater to juniors and seniors and provide cocurricular experiences that complement their academic and/or career interests

◇ *Wellness/Healthy Living Programs,* which foster healthy lifestyles through substance-free environments, fitness programs, and/or health education
◇ *Women's Programs,* which work with women students and include (a) women in leadership programs and (b) women in math, science, and engineering programs (Inkelas & Associates, 2004)

While Transition Programs focus specifically on the first-year experience, particularly on the adjustment from home to college, all of the above types of programs (with the exception of Upper-Division) work with first-year student populations. Indeed, among those programs participating in a national study of L/L programs, 89% work with first-year students (National Study of Living-Learning Programs, 2007). Thus, while programs may focus on a wide range of themes, nearly all have an obligation to address the first-year experience in some way. The empirical and professional literature offers some guidance for ways in which practitioners can structure L/L programs with the goal of facilitating successful outcomes among first-year students.

Components of Effective Living-Learning Programs: Suggestions From the Literature

Essentially, L/L programs can provide three elements to students' college experiences that are facilitative of their learning, growth, and development: (a) intimate environments for shared success, (b) increased peer interaction and collaboration, and (c) frequent and sustained opportunities for faculty interaction (Lenning & Ebbers, 1999; Love, 1999; Shapiro & Levine, 1999). As far back as 1962, Newcomb argued that the most powerful college environments for students are those with "propinquity," or those that have a relatively small number of students who intermingle regularly and with a common purpose. Living-learning programs attempt to create such environments by linking together students with similar interests in a common living environment. Thus, students share both the academic and social domains of their lives. Moreover, L/L programs often provide students additional resources to enhance their academic and social experiences, such as career advising, cultural outings, and cocurricular programs. Through this intimate environment, L/L programs attempt to create a residential climate that simultaneously welcomes and supports its students while challenging and stretching their intellectual and social development.

Second, L/L programs provide the physical setting where students with similar interests can interact with and learn from one another. This increased interaction can be facilitated through formal activities, such as study groups or workshops, or in more informal ways, such as roommate chats or impromptu meals out. Such peer interaction can serve to bolster the power of propinquity (Newcomb, 1962) and subsequently help the student feel more bonded to his or her group and, by extension, the institution itself (Hurtado & Carter, 1997). In addition, when a community of peers forms, students can learn from one another through a diversity of perspectives shared in a supportive environment (Hughes, 1994). For these and a host of other reasons, the higher education literature has consistently shown what Astin (1993) asserted: "The student's peer group is the single most potent source of influence on growth and development during the undergraduate years" (p. 398).

Finally, L/L programs can provide students access to their professors in more sustained and organic surroundings. Instead of interacting with faculty only in the classroom or during office hours, L/L program students often have the opportunity to communicate with professors during a special lecture, over a shared meal, or as part of their programs, either formally (e.g., faculty advisors) or informally (e.g., preparing a meal together). Some programs may even pair students with faculty on projects, such as research studies, internships, and/or community service activities. Time and again, the higher education literature has linked increased student learning and development to greater amounts of faculty interaction (Pascarella & Terenzini, 2005).

Surprisingly, while the concept of L/L programs and the components outlined above have been discussed in the literature and even the popular media (e.g., Bonisteel, 2006), little research has been conducted on the effectiveness of L/L programs in facilitating the lofty goals to which they aspire. Indeed, much of the research on L/L programs has been based on the results of internal assessments of individual L/L programs on a single campus (Inkelas & Weisman, 2003). While these studies, individually, were informative, they provided an incomplete portrait of the overall effectiveness of the wide-ranging types of L/L programs around the country. As a result, even less is known about the capacity of L/L programs to improve the undergraduate experience for first-year students. The National Study of Living-Learning Programs attempted to fill this void by creating a standardized instrument to measure the contributions of a broad range of L/L programs on student learning and development. In the process, the NSLLP has helped to reveal empirically the ways in which L/L programs facilitate first-year student success.

The National Study of Living Learning Programs

The National Study of Living Learning Programs (NSLLP) is a multi-year, multi-institutional study that explores the influence of L/L membership on students' attainment of important collegiate learning outcomes. First conducted in 2004 and then again in 2007, the NSLLP provides both a snapshot of students' experiences as well as a longitudinal view of their change across time. To do so, the study gathers a wide array of data, including students' pre-college academic characteristics and expectations, their experiences while in college, and their self-reported cognitive and socio-cognitive growth via a Web survey. A sample including some or all students participating in a L/L program at the given institutions was compared with a group of resident students who, while demographically similar to the first group, live in a traditional residence hall (TRH) environment. The NSLLP data allow us to make the most definitive statements to date about the myriad relationships between students' experiences in L/L programs and the outcomes they achieve.

The findings below are all drawn from the spring 2007 administration of the NSLLP. A total of 48 institutions offering 613 L/L programs participated in the study, yielding responses from 22,258 students. Of that number, 11,456 respondents (51%) were L/L participants and 10,802 (49%) were students living in a traditional residence hall environment. Here, we focus only on the experience of the 14,057 first-year students in the sample, 7,947 of whom participated in a L/L program. Demographic information about this group appears in Table 4.1. Chi-square tests allow us to determine whether demographic differences exist between the L/L and comparison group, providing important context for further analyses. Three findings are of note. First, these results indicated a disproportionately high number of Asian American and multiracial students in L/L programs, and a somewhat lower than expected number of White students. Second, L/L students were also disproportionately likely to have reported higher high school grade point averages. Finally, mothers/female guardians and fathers/male guardians of students in the comparison group were less likely to have any collegiate experience than the parents/guardians of students participating in L/L programs. With these differences in mind, we turn to exploring the outcomes first-year students reported by virtue of their residential experience.

Table 4.1
Demographic Characteristics of First-Year NSLLP Respondents ($N = 14,057$)

Characteristic	L/L %		TRH %		Sig. Diff.	
Gender						
Male	34.7		34.8			
Female	65.1		65.0			
Transgender	0.1		0.1			
Race						
African American/ Black	4.7		5.2			
Asian American or Pacific Islander	7.7		6.4		**	
American Indian or Native American	0.3		0.2			
Latino/Hispanic	3.9		3.9			
White/Caucasian	75.9		77.9		**	
Multiracial	6.5		5.3		**	
Other	0.8		0.7			
High School GPA						
A+ or A	41.9		35.2		***	
A- or B+	40.0		43.4		***	
B	13.7		16.4		***	
B- or C+	3.9		4.4			
C or C-	0.5		0.5			
D+ or lower	0.0		0.0			
Parental Education	*Mother*	*Father*	*Mother*	*Father*	*Mother*	*Father*
High school only	16.5	15.3	17.8	17.3	***	***
Some college	20.9	27.5	21.6	26.8		
Bachelors or above	62.7	57.2	60.6	55.9		

** $p < .01$. *** $p < .001$.

The Relationship Between L/L Participation and the Experiences of All First-Year Students

As noted above, anecdotal evidence and single institution studies have suggested that L/L programs of all sorts can be beneficial to the success of first-year students. Is this the case on the national level? To answer that question, we explored differences between L/L students and their TRH peers along five elements of the student experience: (a) transition to college, (b) perceptions of the residence environment, (c) peer interactions, (d) interactions with faculty, and (e) career and academic self-confidence.

Transition to college. First-year students participating in L/L programs reported smoother social and academic transitions to college than their peers living in a TRH environment. They also indicated a stronger sense of institutional belonging than the TRH students (all findings, $p \leq .001$). Although the differences between L/L and TRH first-year students were statistically significant, the magnitude of the differences (i.e., effect size) was small. Thus, participation in L/L programs provides a modest advantage in making a successful transition to college.

Perceptions of the residence environment. L/L first-year students reported that their residence environments were more academically and socially supportive than their peers who were not participating in L/L programs. They were also more likely to take advantage of residence hall resources, such as study groups or computer labs, than first-year students not in L/L programs. These differences were statistically significant at the $p \leq .001$ level, with medium-sized effects.

Interactions with peers. First-year students participating in L/L programs indicated that they had more frequent conversations than their TRH environment peers about academic, vocational, and social issues. Similarly, first-year L/L students reported more positive interactions with diverse others than did first-year students who were not in L/L programs. While all of these differences were statistically significant at the $p \leq .001$ level, effect sizes were once again modest.

Interactions with faculty. First-year students who participated in L/L programs reported more frequent contact with faculty members, be it directly related to coursework or non-course-related faculty mentorship, than did their peers who did not participate in an L/L program. Again, these differences were statistically significant at the $p \leq .001$ level, but effect sizes remained small.

Career and academic self-confidence. First-year students who participated in L/L programs reported greater confidence in their academic skills ($p \leq .01$) and in their likelihood of successfully completing college ($p \leq .001$) than their peers in TRH environments. However, L/L students were less likely than their non-L/L peers to feel that they would have a successful and balanced professional life after graduation ($p \leq .001$). All effect sizes were small.

The Experience of Distinct First-Year Student Populations

The findings above suggest that first-year students participating in L/L programs did indeed report a college experience different from their peers who were not participating in a L/L program. Importantly, however, it is not possible to say that participation in a L/L program caused these differences, only that there was a *relationship* between participation and the outcomes described. Next, we consider whether the generally beneficial character of L/L participation could also be found when we consider first-year students from different demographic backgrounds. Here, we explored several outcomes, including students' (a) transition to college and sense of belonging, (b) perceptions of their residence environment and use of hall resources, and (c) confidence in their success during college and after college graduation.

First-generation college students. Past NSLLP research has suggested that first-generation students who participate in L/L programs report a smoother academic and social transition to college than do first-generation students living in the TRH environment (Inkelas, Vogt, Daver, &

Brown Leonard, 2007). While our analysis of 2007 NSLLP data also suggested that L/L programs facilitated a smooth social transition ($p \le .001$, small effect), preliminary investigations have yet to corroborate whether L/L participation similarly facilitated academic transition. First-year L/L students in the 2007 NSLLP did report, however, a greater sense of institutional belonging than did their TRH environment peers ($p \le .05$, small effect).

Generally, first-year, first-generation students participating in L/L programs reported more positive assessments of their residential environments than did their first-generation peers not participating in a L/L program. First-year, first-generation L/L students reported that their residence halls' academic ($p \le .001$, small effect) and social climates ($p \le .001$, medium effect) were more supportive than did students in the TRH environment. L/L students were also more likely to take advantage of special resources found within the hall ($p \le .001$, medium effect).

Finally, our comparison of L/L and TRH students' confidence in their academic skills, chances of collegiate success, and prospects for a successful and balanced professional life uncovered no statistically significant differences.

First-year male and female students. Interestingly, no significant difference existed between women and men when comparing L/L students and their counterparts living in TRH settings. However, women and men within L/L programs did report uneven experiences. While no statistically significant difference emerged between men's and women's academic transition to college or their sense of belonging, first-year men reported a smoother social transition to college than did women ($p \le .001$, small effect). Men and women also seemed to perceive the L/L residence environment differently. First-year women were more likely to report that the residence hall climate was more socially and academically supportive ($p \le .001$, small effects), while first-year men were more likely to report that they were taking advantage of the resources the hall offered ($p \le .05$, small effect). Finally, first-year women in L/L programs reported higher confidence in their future collegiate success than did their male counterparts ($p \le .001$, small effect).

First-year students from non-dominant racial groups. Given our general finding that first-year L/L students tend to report higher scores on a number of important measures when compared to their peers in the TRH environment, we might hypothesize that this same pattern would hold true within individual racial groups. Our results suggest, however, that such is not the case. Only among White students did outcomes for L/L students consistently exceed those attained by their TRH peers. For Asian Pacific American (APA) and Latino first-year students, all outcomes were stronger among L/L students in comparison to TRH students, except for sense of belonging for APA students and use of residence hall resources and academic transition to college among Latinos. Finally, for African American students, the only difference between L/L and TRH students was their perception of the academic climate in the residence halls.

Finally, we explore race-related effects within L/L programs. The NSLLP analyses show that, for the majority of our factors, students from different racial/ethnic backgrounds did report differences in their outcomes. While no race-related differences existed for students' academic and social transitions to college, differences were found on every other measure. Table 4.2 summarizes all significant differences by race. Using the construct of students' sense of belonging as an example, multiracial students reported a greater sense of belonging than Asian American students, and both Latino and White students reported a greater sense of belonging than either African American and Asian American students.

Table 4.2
Significant Differences by Race Within Living-Learning Programs

Construct	Significant difference
Sense of belonging	Multiracial > Asian American Latino, White > African American, Asian American
Academically supportive residence hall climate	Latino > Multiracial, Asian American White > Asian American
Socially supportive residence hall climate	Latino, White > African American
Use of residence hall resources	African American, Asian American, Latino > White
Confidence in college success	Multiracial > Asian American White > African American, Asian American, Latino

$p \leq .05$

It is important to note, however, that not all racial/ethnic groups were included in the above analyses. The small number of students identifying as American Indian/Native American in our dataset ($n = 38$) made both analyses statistically impossible for this group. Also absent from these analyses were students who listed their race as "other," due to interpretation difficulties.

Implications for L/L Practice

Our descriptive results indicating positive relationships between L/L participation and a range of outcomes for first-year students are promising. However, it is only by further examining environmental factors that we can get a better sense of the actual aspects of L/L programs that are associated with improved first-year student experiences in residence halls. Such empirically based investigations of the relationships between L/L environments and educational outcomes are especially useful for higher education practitioners in creating and sustaining effective L/L programs. Our ensuing analyses thus address this concern by examining whether specific facets of L/L programs are associated with four key outcomes for first-year undergraduates: (a) academic transition, (b) social transition, (c) sense of belonging to the institution, and (d) confidence in college success.

Importantly, our findings for all first-year L/L program participants in the 2007 NSLLP were significantly higher on all four of these outcomes than for TRH participants. In taking these findings to the next step, we conducted four hierarchical multiple regression analyses for L/L students only, where we first statistically controlled for students' background characteristics, such as race, gender, father's and mother's education, parental income, average high school grades, and a quasi-pretest for each outcome indicating students' precollege attitudes. These statistical controls, contained in the first two blocks of our regression analyses, were crucial in allowing us to gain a better understanding of how the various L/L program environments contribute to the outcomes, over and above students' personal backgrounds. In the third block of the regression analyses, we included seven key environments commonly associated with L/L programs: (a) discussing academic and career issues with peers, (b) discussing sociocultural issues with peers, (c) course-related faculty interactions, (d) faculty mentorship, (e) use of cocurricular residence hall resources, and perception of (f) an academically supportive and (g) socially supportive residence hall climate. Table 4.3 displays the findings of our analyses, indicating the direction of statistically significant relationships at the $p < .05$, .01, and .001 levels. While Table 4.3 represents all three blocks of the regressions, the following discussion focuses only on the key L/L program environments.

Table 4.3

Predictors of Four Student Outcomes in Living-Learning Programs

	Student Outcomes			
	Academic transition	Social transition	Sense of belonging	Confidence in college success
Student backgrounds				
African American				
Asian American			---	---
Latino/Hispanic		+	++	
Other ethnicity			-	
Gender: Female		---	---	+++
Father's education				+++
Mother's education				++
Parental income	+	+		+++
Average high school grades	+		+++	+++
Pretests (attitudes prior to college attendance)				
Importance of academic success	+++			+++
Importance of knowing others in residence hall		+++		
Importance of sense of belonging			+++	
College environments				
Discussed academic and career issues with peers	+++	+++	+++	+++
Discussed sociocultural issues with peers				
Course-related faculty interaction	+++			++
Faculty mentorship				
Use of cocurricular residence hall resources	++		+	---
Residence hall climate is academically supportive	+++	+++	+++	
Residence hall climate is socially supportive	+++	+++	+++	+

Note. The regression analyses explained 13% of the variance for academic transition, 21% for social transition, 25% for sense of belonging, and 20% for confidence in college success.
$+ p < .05$. $++ p < .01$. $+++ p < .001$.
$- p < .05$. $-- p < .01$. $--- p < .001$.

Interactions with Peers and Faculty

First-year students' discussions around issues of academics and careers were a significant, positive predictor of all four of our outcome measures. Importantly, then, the more students in L/L programs engaged in such conversations with their peers, the easier their academic and social transition became, the stronger their sense of belonging to their schools, and the higher their confidence in their ability to succeed in college. By contrast, students' discussions regarding socio-cultural issues with their peers had no measurable relationships with any of the four outcomes. While these findings do not reveal the actual content of students' discussions, it is likely that the thematic foci of L/L programs bring a natural impetus for students to engage in academic and career-related conversations with each other which, in turn, facilitate students' transition, sense of belonging, and confidence in college success.

First-year students' interactions with faculty present a considerably less straightforward picture. Course-related faculty interactions, for example, appeared to facilitate L/L students' academic transition and confidence in college success, but had no relationship with social transition and sense of belonging. This is not surprising. After all, students' conversations with faculty members about their courses have much to do with their academic experiences, but less with their social life in college. Surprisingly, faculty mentorship, our other measure of faculty-student interactions, focusing on informal and career-related conversations, was not related to any of the four outcomes. However, descriptive analyses showed that very few first-year students enjoyed a mentoring relationship with a faculty member, perhaps because they had spent just slightly more than one semester on campus at the time the NSLLP survey was administered.

Residence Hall Resources and Perceptions of Climate

The degree to which first-year L/L participants used cocurricular residence hall resources, such as career workshops, community service projects, peer study groups, and peer counselors, had a significant, positive relationship with academic transition and sense of belonging. However, the relationship between this variable and students' confidence in college success was negative. While at first glance, this finding might appear to be perplexing—after all, resources in an educational setting are rarely thought of as worsening the educational experience—it is important to emphasize that our analyses are not capable of establishing the direction of the relationship between our environmental variables and the student outcomes. Indeed, it is likely that residence hall resources are not the cause of a decline in confidence. Rather, first-year students who are unsure of their ability to succeed in college may be more likely to turn to residence hall resources in search of help with academics. From this perspective, the fact that L/L programs tend to provide more resources for their students than traditional residence halls is a laudable aspect of the living-learning environment.

Our findings related to students' perceptions of the residence hall climate are especially notable. In fact, both academically and socially supportive residence hall climates hold the potential to enrich the student experience by facilitating their academic and social transition and increasing their sense of belonging. In addition, socially supportive residence hall climates were also related to students' confidence in succeeding in college. What is especially important to emphasize about these findings is that the advantages of an academically supportive L/L environment are in no way limited to academic outcomes and, likewise, social support systems appear crucial in helping students achieve not only social, but also academic outcomes. These findings present an important indication of the ways in which L/L programs can remain true to their calling to integrate the social and academic aspects of students' lives by providing a space for both living and learning.

Our findings on the national level provide a good indication of what colleges and universities can do to create new L/L programs or strengthen their existing offerings in service of the first-year experience. However, translating these results into actual practice may present challenges to practitioners. With this in mind, we conclude this chapter by offering recommendations for successful L/L practice with first-year students.

Characteristics of Effective L/L Programs for First-Year Students

One of the limitations of best practice models in the living-learning literature is that "model" programs are often chosen based on reputation instead of empirical data. The results from the NSLLP focus our attention on the components of L/L programs that are particularly important for the success of first-year students from a data-driven standpoint. When considering first-year students' transitions to college, sense of belonging and confidence in college success, we offer the following recommendations for L/L programming:

◇ Programs should encourage and find outlets for peers to interact with one another around academic and vocational subjects. Greater academically focused peer interaction was significantly associated with all outcomes—the transition to college, sense of belonging, and college confidence. Successful models of L/L programs include curricular and cocurricular features promoting academic and career discussions that, with effective planning, flow seamlessly between the classroom and the living room. One fruitful practice is the implementation of credit-bearing seminars where L/L participants and faculty explore program themes.

◇ Programs should strive to create climates in which students feel academically supported and in which the environment is socially and culturally inclusive. For example, program staff should be trained to be attentive to academic issues, including the formation of study groups, scheduling, and academic requirements. Moreover, in the NSLLP, students responded favorably to residence hall climates in which peers were supportive of one another and in which students from diverse backgrounds were celebrated. The residential locus of L/L programs can create abundant learning opportunities concerning issues related to diversity and multiculturalism. The diverse cultural practices and observances of the different students living in the program can be introduced over the course of the year. In addition, these activities can be coupled with academic content, such as a fireside chat conducted by a professor or member of the community on the history, symbolism, and meaning of the cultural practice or event.

◇ For the academic transition to college, it is important for first-year students to have more frequent interactions with professors via any means (e.g., in a class, outside of class, during office hours) and to use residence hall resources such as career workshops, peer study groups, and community service projects. L/L programs that do not already offer these cocurricular programs as options should implement them. Programs that do offer them, but find that they are not used to their full potential, should work with participants to make them more applicable to their needs.

◇ While the above programming recommendations are designed to be offered to all students, it is important to remember that students from diverse backgrounds experience college differently. The NSLLP data found that Asian Pacific American and Hispanic/Latino first-year students tended to have a less strong sense of belonging to their campuses, as did female first-year students. In relation, Hispanic/Latino and female first-year students reported a more difficult social transition to college. Therefore, L/L program staff should pay special attention to the needs of these populations when working to facilitate a positive first-year experience.

To realize the lofty expectations and demands placed upon living-learning programs, the use of empirical data to inform local practices is a strong first step in ensuring effective and quality programming. Given the critical nature of the first-year experience, this undertaking is of vital importance to higher education.

References

Astin, A.W. (1993). *What matters in college? Four critical years revisited.* San Francisco: Jossey-Bass.

Bonisteel, S. (2006, August 22). From treehouses to RV parks, students embrace dorm alternatives. *Fox News.com.* Retrieved January 9, 2007, from http://www.foxnews.com/story/0,2933,208180,00.html

Hughes, M. (1994). Helping students understand and appreciate diversity. In C. C. Schroeder, P. Mable, & Associates (Eds.), *Realizing the educational potential of residence halls* (pp. 190-217). San Francisco: Jossey-Bass.

Hurtado, S., & Carter, D. F. (1997). Effects of college transition and perceptions of the campus racial climate on Latino students' sense of belonging. *Sociology of Education, 70,* 324-345.

Inkelas, K. K., & Associates. (2004). *National Study of Living-Learning Programs: 2004 report of findings.* Retrieved September 13, 2007 from http://www.livelearnstudy.net/images/NSLLP_2004_Final_Report.pdf

Inkelas, K. K., Vogt, K. E., Daver, Z. E., & Brown Leonard, J. (2007). Living-learning programs and first-generation college students' academic and social transition to college. *Research in Higher Education, 48*(4), 403-423.

Inkelas, K. K., & Weisman, J. (2003). Different by design: An examination of outcomes associated with three types of living-learning programs. *Journal of College Student Development, 44,* 335-368.

Lenning, O. T., & Ebbers, L. H. (1999). *The powerful potential of learning communities: Improving education for the future.* ASHE-ERIC Higher Education Report, *26*(6). Washington DC: The George Washington University, Graduate School of Education & Human Development.

Love, A. G. (1999). What are learning communities? In J. H. Levine (Ed.), *Learning communities: New structures, new partnerships for learning* (Monograph, No. 26, pp. 1-9). Columbia, SC: University of South Carolina, National Resource Center for The First-Year Experience and Students in Transition.

National Study of Living-Learning Programs. (2007). Retrieved September 13, 2007, from http://www.livelearnstudy.net

Newcomb, T. M. (1962). Student peer-group influence. In J. Adelson (Ed.), *The American college* (pp. 469-488). New York: John Wiley & Sons.

Pascarella, E. T., & Terenzini, P. T. (2005). *How college affects students: A third decade of research* (Vol. II). San Francisco: Jossey-Bass.

The Residential Learning Communities International Clearinghouse. (n.d.). Retrieved September 13, 2007, from http://pcc.bgsu.edu/rlcch/index.php

Ryan, M. B. (1992). Residential colleges: A legacy of living and learning together. *Change, 24*(5), 26-35.

Schroeder, C. C. (1994). Developing learning communities. In C. C. Schroeder, P. Mable, & Associates (Eds.), *Realizing the educational potential of residence halls* (pp. 165-189). San Francisco: Jossey-Bass.

Shapiro, N. S., & Levine, J. H. (1999). *Creating learning communities: A practical guide to winning support, organizing for change, and implementing programs.* San Francisco: Jossey-Bass.

Chapter Five

Social Justice as a Strategy for Residence Hall Community Development

Mary L. Hummel

Attendees at the Campus of the Future conference in July 2006, identified the following themes as the top driving forces of change on college campuses regardless of the type of institution: (a) rising student expectations, (b) technological change, and (c) population changes (Highnite, 2006). The changes in population place increasing pressure on colleges and universities to design programs that are not only sensitive to students' diverse experiences but that also help students gain an understanding of and appreciation for diverse others. According to Hughes (1994), campus residence halls provide a potentially powerful environment for encouraging openness to diversity because of extended opportunities for students to interact with peers and for staff to implement programs that expose students to multicultural issues. Residential learning communities are an excellent vehicle to pilot programs to meet expectations of preparing students to work in a diverse fast-paced society. Yet, it will simply not be enough for individuals to be present in a community; rather, intentional education and experiences are needed to help students understand and appreciate each other's contributions to society.

A key question for higher education is how to increase students' openness to learning with regard to social justice and diversity. Gurin (1999) argued that gains in students' openness to diversity are related to the overall diversity of the student body (i.e., structural diversity); opportunities for positive interactions among diverse groups of students (i.e., informal diversity); and exposure to curricula that include knowledge about diversity (i.e., classroom diversity). Yet, diversity education is often viewed as tolerance for differences, rather than the deeper appreciation of or acceptance of the differences among individuals in a society. For this reason, this chapter adopts social justice as an educational framework, arguing that it encompasses a more comprehensive context and model for change. Social justice incorporates a definition of social oppression, a developmental model of the social identity process, and the societal relationships of systems of oppression. The education model is both a process and a goal, which includes a vision of society where the distribution of resources is equitable and all members are physically and psychologically safe and secure (Bell, 1997).

This chapter examines a conceptual framework for social justice education, beginning with definitions of terms and societal context. An overarching residence hall community education model is examined with specific program examples. Implications for the use of technology in social justice education and assessment findings are also included. The final section discusses implications and recommendations for the broader campus context.

Conceptual Framework

The theoretical foundation for this chapter is based on social justice as an educational goal. According to Bell (1997), the goal of social justice education is full and equal participation of all groups in a society that is mutually shaped to meet their needs. Social justice includes a vision of society in which the distribution of resources is equitable and all members are physically and psychologically safe and secure (Bell).

Social justice education helps students think about issues of group identity and how group identity can be used to oppress (Bell, 1997). Hardiman and Jackson (1997) suggest that social oppression exists when one social group, knowingly or unconsciously, exploits another social group for its own benefit. The Hardiman and Jackson model in general is based on how we come to understand our own multiple social identities. The process involves how we explore our own abilities, interests, and values in relation to group membership. Because we belong to various groups, we develop multiple identities (Martin & Nakayama, 2000). With these multiple identities then, we are at various times in position of oppressor and oppressed. Understanding the interaction of these roles and the impact on community development is essential for learning to take place. It is in this context of seeking to bring about societal change and understanding the forces that have contributed to the existing system, rather than the more superficial level of tolerating differences, which frames this discussion.

The focus on social justice education is recommended for first-year students for several reasons. During the first year, students are open to meeting new people, encountering new ideas, and expanding their comfort zones in ways that the transition to college supports. In addition, as many students move off campus with friends following the first year, it may be the only time in their college experience or perhaps their lives, in which they will have such a unique opportunity to participate in a learning environment with a rich, diverse group of individuals.

Several key principles should guide the development of a residential social justice model. First, it is critical to consider the institutional context and find the appropriate fit of variables within each unique setting. The next step to develop a vision statement, complete with language that has commonly shared definitions. Partnerships with academic and student affairs faculty and staff are another key ingredient. Finally, involving students in the implementation and as key leaders in the day-to-day interactions is important in integrating change in the life of the community. The case study that follows is an illustration of this approach to infuse social justice education into the first-year residence hall experience.

First-Year Residence Hall Experience Model: A Case Study

The University of Michigan has a history of leadership in social change. This commitment has been incorporated into both its University Housing Mission Statement and a longstanding document, the Living at Michigan Credo, which states in part:

Many students use their college years to explore and develop their personal identity and values. We believe this exploration can best take place in an environment that is open to and respectful of individuals across the spectrum of human differences and distinctions. It is the responsibility of every member of the Housing community, staff and students alike, to work to create and maintain such an environment. We pledge to work collectively to examine our values and conduct, and to question those values when they reflect an origin of fear, anger, or ignorance. Acts of bigotry are acts of hatred against us all, and they will not be condoned or tolerated. We must all share in the responsibility of confronting unacceptable behavior, and in providing an example of involved citizenship. (Levy, 1999)

Based on this vision statement, the charge was given to residence life professional staff to create an educational framework for a new residence life program. The first step in this framework was education of the paraprofessional and professional staff. A partnership among the psychology department, the Office of Intergroup Relations, and the Residence Education Office was created to develop and evaluate a course for residence life staff. Large meetings and small groups were jointly facilitated by faculty and staff. Each partner shared in course evaluation, assessment development, and implementation.

The goals of the course were based on the belief that resident staff at Michigan are direct links between the university and undergraduate students (particularly first-year students). The staff, thus, play a critical role in defining and articulating community standards and expectations. In particular, the residence life staff has significant potential to become a catalyst for the creation of a stimulating, supportive, and educationally purposeful multicultural community. Residence life staff participated in the class as a part of the staff selection process. Participation and successful course completion as a prerequisite for staff selection made a bold statement about the values of the organization and what it means to be a part of this effort.

The course provided new residence life staff with the foundations, both intellectual and social, to work towards these goals. The course, Social Psychology in Community Settings, was designed to help residence life staff develop self-understanding, understanding of others, and strategies for engaging and building a community in the residence hall. The class goals were to (a) develop approaches to building positive communities, (b) learn about differences and commonalities among cultural groups, (c) understand the role of privilege in intergroup relations, and (d) discuss personal and social development. The course used a combination of readings, lectures, classroom exercises, and practical experiences to help students reach these goals (Bessette & Hummel, 1999).

Each class session followed an outline of specific readings, experiential activity, discussion, and a journal reflection. Topics began with student and identity development, interpersonal and intercultural communication and conflict, and specific identity development and oppression. The small group activities were co-facilitated by housing/student affairs staff members and returning residence life student staff.

The class was evaluated in several significant ways. Each week, the facilitators asked for feedback using a short questionnaire. The overall class was assessed using the university's standardized evaluation instrument. In addition, an extensive survey was administered to residence life staff after a year of experience on the job, asking questions about the relationship of the course to their work. Anecdotal evidence suggested that the staff learned and grew personally when they were faced with a particular issue on their floor and could recognize the situation and summon the appropriate tools and language to address it.

For some students, this class was not how they had hoped to spend time during the semester; however, the class evaluations suggested that it provided students with a tremendous opportunity for learning and discussion about their own identity and that of their peers. As one student reflected, "If you take your position seriously and believe in it, then by all means you can make a difference in fighting this world of social injustice."

The focus of this class is unique. Rather than just a traditional approach to building one-to-one relationships with students, which still continues to be key, the class also asks the staff to create community within the floor and the hall based on social justice goals. In addition, it illustrates the strength of what can be developed through partnerships between academic and student affairs faculty and staff in both planning and implementation.

In fall 2004, The University of Michigan residence education staff piloted a small program to take the "staff class" to a floor of first-year residents and to attempt to facilitate similar exercises and activities with incoming students living together in one community. Students self-selected to be a part of this community and volunteered to periodically come together for discussion, self-reflection, and community-building exercises. The idea of expanding the program was to test whether the discussions and educational opportunities of the class could be expanded to first-year students in a residence hall setting. The importance of the pilot program was to demonstrate for the university an example of the educational benefit of a diverse community of learners. The students participated in experiential exercises and subsequent discussions. There were several challenges with expanding the model to include first-year students. As Snowden (2004) stated, many first-year students are not ready to embrace the complexities and uncomfortable feelings that will arise at this stage in their maturation. In addition, these students self-selected to be a part of this experimental program and even then their energy and enthusiasm were pulled in multiple directions as the semester progressed. It was hard to keep the momentum going throughout the semester as other demands on their time increased.

Three Models of Learning Communities

The previous model attempts to infuse social justice education into the fabric of an entire residence hall system, however, three other models are more prevalent on campuses across the country. These models attempt to increase access and openness to social justice education and diversity for self-selected groups of students based on stated interests.

The differences in these models in comparison to the all-encompassing social justice framework described above is their distinct focus on a particular aspect of the educational experience. Therefore, social justice or diversity education becomes part of a means to a specific end. In the first model, increasing access/achievement is the goal while, in the second, exploration and support of differences becomes the focus. Finally, in the third model, connecting students to the larger community and learning through these experiences becomes the primary methodology. Each model has laudable goals and subsequent benefits. In the following sections, the definition, outcomes, and characteristics as illustrated through specific examples will be described.

Model One: Improving Access, Achievement, and Retention of Underrepresented Students

In the late 1980s and early 1990s, there was renewed interest in improving access, academic achievement, and retention of historically underrepresented students on predominantly White campuses. These programs set as their goal increasing access to various academic fields and the engagement of students in the academic mission of the institution. In addition, programs and services were developed to attempt to reduce the achievement and retention gap. Access and retention are critical cornerstones for the education of social justice to be achieved. Without successes in these two areas, it is difficult for meaningful interactions and discussions to take place.

One exemplary program in this regard is the Undergraduate Research Program at the University of Michigan (UROP). UROP provides a hands-on learning experience for first- and second-year students through research partnerships with faculty in all academic fields and disciplines. Students develop research and academic skills through faculty mentors, research work, research seminars, skill building workshops, and peer advising.

While admission is open to all students, UROP continues to work toward improving the retention and academic achievement of underrepresented students and to support women in science and engineering. This social justice goal of access has been a cornerstone of the program since its inception. In addition, UROP fosters collaboration between undergraduate students, faculty, research scientists, and graduate students, creating a dynamic intergenerational learning community. By participating in undergraduate research, students discover new competencies, strengthen their intellectual curiosity, and clarify their academic and professional goals.

To further enhance the opportunities, a living-learning program, a subset of the larger learning community called The Michigan Research Community (MRC), was developed. In addition to making a commitment to live together in a residence hall community MRC students are required to: (a) enroll in UC 104 – Introduction to the Research University for the fall term first year only, (b) commit to and participate in a research project for the duration of their year, (c) attend and participate in monthly Wednesday evening MRC research meetings, (d) meet with their research peer advisors monthly, and (e) actively participate in MRC events and community activities. They also attend a variety of research experiences through lectures and onsite visits; participate in facilitated study groups in introductory sciences, math, languages and writing courses; attend program-sponsored outings to cultural events in the area; and take special sections of the first-year courses.

The UROP program has been engaged in longitudinal assessment of the impact of the program on student retention, academic performance, engagement, and pursuit of graduate and professional education. UROP employs a multi-method approach to assessment and evaluation, which has yielded four major conclusions:

1. UROP influenced students' academic achievement, retention, behavior, and postgraduate educational and professional activities—all intended goals for the program.
2. Findings from several of the research projects suggested a strong connection between UROP participation and proactive behavior, with UROP students discussing how they actively interact with the academic environment.
3. Findings indicated that African American students' retention and academic achievement benefited from a program designed to integrate students into one of the core goals of higher education—research and the pursuit of knowledge.
4. Findings indicated that UROP extended its effect beyond the undergraduate experience by retaining students in the educational pipeline after graduation.

In addition, assessment of the impact of the program on student learning has found that UROP students (a) were more proactive about their education and more engaged in the university's academic life, (b) learned how to process and evaluate information, (c) gained research competency in a discipline, and (d) were more likely to pursue graduate and professional school (Gregerman, n.d.).

Another prominent example of increasing access and retention in specific academic disciplines is the variety of programs designed for creating a supportive environment for students in math, sciences, and engineering. The goals of these programs are to bring together students with similar academic and career interests to create learning communities that enhance achievement. Illustrations of these programs include Women in Science and Engineering Residence Programs at the University of Michigan, Purdue University, and Iowa State University.

Model Two: Theme-Based Programs

Perhaps one of the more common models is that of a themed hall/house, which brings together students with similar interests and provides specialized programming to enable them to explore those interests. They make it possible for both students in particular majors and non-majors to live together and explore an area in an informal setting. In addition, when focused on specific cultures, theme-based programs can provide a substantial support base to students of a particular ethnic background and an opportunity for students who are not of that particular background to learn and interact in a meaningful way.

Theme programs can include academic opportunities such as lectures, receptions for noted scholars, cultural and political leaders, film series, recitals, and seminars, and language tables. Some theme houses have faculty members from specific academic departments as advisors to the community. In others, activities are designed to draw the larger campus community to participate in events.

Stanford University offers academic, language, and cross-cultural theme houses. Six houses are organized around academic majors or languages such as East Asian Studies, Central European Studies, or Spanish. The four cross-cultural houses are the Chicano/Latino Theme House, the Native American Theme House, the Asian Theme House, and the Black/African American House. While offering social and educational opportunities similar to other residence halls, the theme houses also provide opportunities to explore history, engage in culture discussions, and attend cultural events and speakers specific to the house theme. The programs emphasize and value the cultural identity of the group and enable members of ethnic groups and others to learn about and appreciate the group's history and culture.

Both UC Irvine and UC Santa Barbara also offer a wide variety of theme-based housing with specific themes dedicated to multiculturalism (e.g., Diversity Awareness and Community in a Diverse Society). UC Irvine describes the theme housing as bringing together students with similar interests and providing specialized programming to enhance those interests. Likewise, UC Santa Barbara describes theme-based housing as students' having the opportunity to enjoy specialized programming, interact with staff specializing in the theme area, and connect with related campus student organizations. Interest floors include: Rainbow House (Supportive Community for GLBT Students and Allies); Black/African American Community; Chicano/Latino Studies; Multi-Cultural Experience; and Global Living Experience (International Students and Majors).

Model Three: Social Justice in a Broader Community Setting

An emerging model embeds issues of civility and social justice throughout the community while engaging students in service. Students participate in service or community-based projects, select academic courses in connection with the experiences, and integrate this work into their lives by sharing with others in the learning community.

CIVICUS is a two-year living and learning program at the University of Maryland, centered around five tenets of civil society: (a) citizenship, (b) leadership, (c) community building in a diverse society, (d) scholarship, and (e) community service-learning. Students enroll in common courses throughout the first two years, and course activities are closely linked with each other and the campus, local, and national communities. Students are required to participate in a minimum of four community service projects per semester, in addition to the service components that accompany some courses. In this way, the coursework and experiential activities are designed to meet the goals of developing responsible citizens in a global community.

Assessment

Increasingly, data suggest that living-learning programs are effective environments in which students may develop a positive attitude toward difference (Lenning & Ebbers, 1999). The 2004 National Study on Living-Learning Programs (Brower & Inkelas, 2004), examined data from 34 universities across the United States, comparing living-learning participants and nonparticipants. The study revealed that students were more likely to embrace new perspectives and become more open to difference when they were part of a living-learning community; yet, the findings were mixed with respect to appreciation for racial/ethnic diversity. Overall, there was no significant difference between participants and nonparticipants in appreciation for diversity, which was highest for participants in upper-division and civic engagement living-learning programs. Surprisingly, multicultural program students did not have the highest means in racial/ethnic diversity appreciation. However, the programs that were small, primarily based in residence life were higher on the outcome of diversity appreciation.

There are several implications for programmatic consideration and future research based on these results. It appears that the small group concept, as exemplified in the staff class, is a setting where students can develop greater understanding of differences. In addition, the significance of the residence hall setting is also underscored by these results. Developing these opportunities in a small group and/or residence hall setting appears to be significant.

One additional finding that prompts future study is the class level of participants. There was some evidence to suggest that diversity appreciation was highest for upperclass students. Yet, many of the programs are comprised of first-year student participants who may or may not be ready developmentally to face the complexities and ambiguities involved in these experiences. This finding may impact future consideration of the class level for the programs.

Conclusions and Recommendations

The societal and educational context of the 21st century contains the driving forces of a changing college population. One way campus educators have found to meet student needs is through the development of residentially based initiatives. In these settings, opportunities to learn from peers in unique ways and to experience academic, staff, and student partnerships may be fostered.

It is important to note that these initiatives should be uniquely designed to address the educational needs and outcomes of a particular institution. Each campus has a particular mission, values, and culture. Rather than merely transplanting any individual model, it is recommended that the unique needs of a campus are taken into account and a program designed, specifically for that situation. A new and unique campus-based learning opportunity will then emerge. There are several key programmatic variables essential to the work. Leaders with vision who are skilled in managing the potential conflicts that will arise in trying to develop multicultural communities in a residence hall setting are critical for success. Training and support staff at all levels are essential. Clear articulation of learning outcomes and an assessment plan are also necessary.

An emerging area for both implementation and study is the use of technology in supporting and enhancing community dialogue. Web sites and blogs such as Facebook and MySpace have created the ability to rapidly discover vast amounts of information (accurate or inaccurate) concerning one's new roommate/floormates. A student can now make judgments about peers on the basis of that information without ever having a face-to-face conversation. This ability has serious implications for social justice education. From selecting or rejecting roommates, to harsh inaccurate judgments and superficial encounters, participation in social networking sites can inhibit and add obstacles to a developing community setting. While there have been small, often individual, attempts, there has yet to emerge a sustained, systemic approach in this area. The use of technology by students is far beyond educators' abilities to channel and focus emerging technologies to enhance the educational process.

Finally, the development of a strong and integrated residence life response, based on a conceptual framework and learning outcomes, tied to the unique academic mission of the institution will be key to the successful creation of communities in the future. The social justice goals of increasing students' openness to diversity, creating opportunities for positive interactions among diverse groups of students and exposure to curricula, which includes knowledge about diversity, are essential not only to academic communities but to the equitable distribution and security of all society's members in the future.

References

Bell, L. (1997). Theoretical foundations for social justice education. In M. Adams, L. Bell, & P. Griffin (Eds.), *Teaching for diversity and social justice* (pp. 3-15). New York, NY: Rutledge.

Bessette, J., & Hummel, M. (1999). New focus for a paraprofessional staff class: creating multicultural communities. *Talking Stick, 17 (2),* 10-11.

Brower, A., & Inkelas, K. (2004). *Report of findings on national study of living- learning programs.* Eighth Conference on Living-Learning Programs and Residential Colleges, Indiana University, Bloomington, IN.

Gregerman, S. (n.d.). *UROP conclusions.* Retrieved January 26, 2007, from http://www.lsa.umich.edu/urop

Gurin, P. (1999). *Expert report of Patricia Gurin.* In Gratz, et al.v. Bollinger, et al. and Grutter, et al. v. Bollinger, et al.

Hardiman, R., & Jackson, B. (1997). Conceptual foundations for social justice courses. In M. Adams, L. Bell, & P. Griffin (Eds.), *Teaching for diversity and social justice* (pp.16-29). New York: Rutledge.

Highnite, K. (2006, November). What's ahead? You decide. *Business Officer.* 17- 20.

Hughes, M. (1994). Helping students understand and appreciate diversity. In C. Schroeder & P. Mable (Eds.), *Realizing the educational potential of residence halls* (pp. 190-217). San Francisco: Jossey-Bass.

Lenning, O., & Ebbers, L. (1999). *The powerful potential of learning communities: Improving education for the future. (*ASHE-ERIC Higher Education Report, 26.6). Washington, D.C.: Graduate School of Education and Human Development, George Washington University.

Levy, A. (1999). *Michigan Credo. What kind of community do we want to be?* University Housing, University of Michigan, Ann Arbor, MI.

Martin, J., & Nakayama, T. (2000). *Intercultural communication in contexts* (2nd ed.). Mountain-View, CA: Mayfield Publishing Co.

Snowden, M. (2004). Learning communities as transformative pedagogy: Centering diversity in introductory sociology. *Teaching Sociology, 32,* 291-303.

Chapter Six

Residential Programs Promoting Students' Academic Success

Gene Luna

The specialized focus on the first-year experience that began 25 years ago has brought significant change to our campuses. Curricular and cocurricular reform has occurred across the country with the realization that student retention and academic success can be significantly improved by the realignment of campus resources to better support the transitional needs of new students. Prior to this heightened awareness, campuses were often structured for administrative efficiency, with centralized services and programs and little consideration for addressing convenience or matching students' schedules.

As Terenzini and Pascarella stated in 1994,

> This bureaucratization of collegiate structures is a creature of administrative convenience and budgetary expedience. It surely has not evolved from any conception of how students learn, nor is it supported by research evidence. Organizationally and operationally, we've lost sight of the forest. If undergraduate education is to be enhanced, faculty members, joined by academic and student affairs administrators, must devise ways to deliver undergraduate education that are as comprehensive and integrated as the ways students actually learn. A whole new mindset is needed to capitalize on the interrelatedness of the in- and out-of-class influences on student learning and the functional interconnectedness of academic and student affairs divisions. (p. 32)

First-year residence halls had one function, to provide housing to the first-year class and serve as a "holding tank" in between their classes and academic pursuits. The first-year experience movement encouraged campus officials to evaluate their practices and strategies, and the first-year residence hall often emerged as a centerpiece for campus restructuring efforts. These evaluations culminated with the realization that residence halls often offered the best setting for campuses to provide convenient and timely support services and programs designed to improve academic success and retention. Although each campus has approached these goals differently, the introduction of academic support services into first-year residence hall environments has become a hallmark of campuses dedicated to supporting the transitions of new students to their campuses. This chapter provides an overview of these efforts and allows readers to understand the importance of residence hall administrators in initiating and supporting academic success initiatives in the residential setting.

First-year students arrive on our campuses each fall (and spring) with a host of academic and personal challenges facing them. The transitional issues of moving from a structured home environment onto a campus where the student is now living independently for the first time are challenging on numerous fronts. Learning to manage their time, nutritional needs, sleep, health, and academics can be daunting. Any of these issues as well as others can become serious threats to a student's academic progress and persistence to their sophomore year and beyond. Thus increasingly, colleges and universities are focusing resources, programs, and services that provide a host of opportunities for students to gain support and help for their first-year transition into a learning environment that is usually quite different from their high school experience. For first-year students living on campus, understanding how the campus residence hall communities are being used to support students' academic goals with an array of learning support services and programs is an important factor.

Colleges and universities are using these support services in their recruitment materials as they market an image of a school that will care for each individual student and provide the resources to increase student success. Many schools have developed and are marketing first-year experience initiatives that purport to engage each new student in activities in and out of the classroom that will enrich their academic experience while supporting their personal needs. Because research over the years has shown that living on campus generally increases students' likelihood of persisting to their sophomore year, more colleges and universities are requiring first-year students to live on campus where they are closer to (and more likely to take advantage of) educationally enriching out-of-class opportunities. And many of these same schools have been locating a variety of both formal and informal academic support services in and around their residence halls.

Parents and students increasingly are becoming astute shoppers, visiting numerous colleges and universities and asking not only about the academic offerings and quality of the faculty, but also about the support services and opportunities for engaged learning beyond the classroom. They want to see the residence halls and hear about residentially based programs, including learning communities. They are interested in the amenities in the halls and on campus. They are asking about student success centers, tutoring programs, and other aspects of college life that can help or hinder their student's success. Concurrently, many campuses are marketing the educational advantage of living on campus. The University of Wisconsin – Madison has conducted research showing the students living in campus residence halls actually perform significantly better on average than students living off campus (3.16 GPA for on-campus students versus 2.81 for students living off campus) (Baker, 2006). Similar research conducted at the University of South Carolina found that students living on campus were 1.7 times more likely to return for their second year than those living off campus (Luna, Fidler, & Moore, 1997).

As parents and their students have become more careful consumers of higher education, the residential aspect of campus life has been changing to respond to their wants and needs. The construction of new residence halls has proceeded at record pace over the past 10 to 15 years across the country. Similarly, existing residence halls are being renovated with significant capital investment to adjust both the style and the use of the residential space. Halls that are not adaptable to the new styles and amenities expected in today's student residences are being demolished or converted to other campus uses. The halls being built and renovated are providing a host of modern amenities and spaces for a variety of programs and services that support students' academic success. No longer are student residence halls simply accommodations; today these facilities play host to vibrant living-learning communities where students and faculty engage in enriching intellectual activities as well as more traditional social activities.

Today's and tomorrow's residence halls are offering more privacy in both student bedrooms and in the bathroom facilities. Along with this increased attention to privacy, each student generally finds his or her room has outlets for their computers and televisions, wireless computing capabilities, and even larger beds than rooms built in the 1960s and before. With the rapid adoption of wireless technologies including mobile phones, many campuses are removing their landline telephone services and providing more robust computing capabilities with services ranging from legal music downloading, video, and gaming support. These communication and entertainment amenities are increasingly being integrated by educators into learning venues and support services.

Creating and Adapting Spaces for Academic Support and Programs

College and university leadership today often talks of student engagement, integrated learning, and viewing the entire campus as part of the learning environment. From the perspective of residential programs, the language of new urbanism, in which the term live-work is used to describe the idea of people living and working in the same geographic area, is being used to describe living and learning environments. How does this idea relate to space allocation for and in our residence halls?

Most campuses host many of the services, residences, and employment opportunities one finds in most municipalities. Today's campus planners are thinking like city planners in many ways. Rather than modeling the suburban sprawl of our communities and pushing residence halls to the periphery of campus, planners today are situating residence halls within the campus proper when land is available. Residence halls being demolished are not making space for expanding academic or office buildings. The place where an outdated residence hall once stood is often redeveloped for residential use or mixed-use space with student housing (Kenney, Kenney, & Dumont, 2005).

The shift in locating campus housing in central areas of campus is concurrent with a shift in the types of public space being designed into the residential facilities, whether it is through renovating an older residence hall or constructing new residences. During the residential building boom in the 1960s and 1970s, the public spaces were primarily game rooms and TV lobbies. Taking cues from the residential colleges of Oxford and Cambridge where students lived, dined, learned, studied, debated, and often worked, today's residential designs are incorporating a variety of spaces specifically planned to support student learning and academic initiatives.

In older residence halls, spaces on the ground level proximate to the front lobby are being re-designed to include spaces for a variety of academically related services and programs. Closed spaces are being opened to bring in more natural light and to make activities in those spaces visible to passers-by. For example, students are able to see a class in session, students working on a class project, a faculty advisor in his or her office, or whether or not tutors are available. By placing these spaces along the normal circulation in a building, students continually encounter activities and opportunities for learning while being reminded of their primary purpose for being in school. And by keeping or developing residences in the more central parts of campus, students are more likely to find other campus resources, such as student success centers and the library nearby.

In the more public areas of residence halls today, students encounter smart classrooms, media labs, tutoring services, academic coaches, literature, and kiosks with a variety of student success materials and tips. Their first-year seminar may be taught in their specific residence hall. A faculty member may be living in the residence hall. Faculty and academic advisors' offices may be down the hall. Public spaces will often have both wireless and hard-wired computing capabilities. All of this is in recognition that students' learn anytime, anywhere. The residence hall environment can be a vibrant place for individual and group learning while still serving as a place for social development and personal retreat from the busy life of a college student.

At Cornell University, for instance, a renovation project for Mary Donlon Hall focused on converting its original first floor from a configuration of visually enclosed rooms used sparingly as student lounges to a vibrant visually open space that encouraged and supported academic life. Removing solid walls, opening up larger spaces and using glass and colors, the space was reconfigured with a library, multimedia seminar room, music lounge, gaming room, faculty offices, as well as a student lounge for social space. Nearby, Balch Hall, a first-year residence hall, housed a dining center and related support service spaces on its first floor. After building a new dining center elsewhere, the campus reconfigured the space into the Tatkon Resource Center with spaces designed to facilitate teaching, advising, mentoring, counseling, orientation, socializing, and student support as part of their overall first-year student experience (Strong & Chiang, 2004).

Computer labs and media centers are found in many residence hall lobbies at campuses such as Georgia Southern University, University of California, Berkeley, and the University of Wisconsin – Stevens Point. These computing facilities often provide printing, scanning, and mapping capabilities. Increasingly, these computing facilities are evolving into more complete media and technology service centers with staff, special software, editing programs, video equipment, software classes, and integrated tutoring services.

In designing residential classrooms and academic space, architects and housing staff are studying what design characteristics promote optimal learning. Research indicates that lighting, temperature, and noise are the major variables affecting student learning in the built environment. The ideal space for collaborative learning will have these characteristics:

◇ Level floor
◇ Movable seating
◇ Whiteboards on three or four walls
◇ Controlled acoustics and climate
◇ Six to ten movable four-sided tables
◇ Ample lighting, including natural light
◇ Appropriate spacing between students (2 to 4 feet) and between groups (4 to 7 feet)
◇ Ample space for 30 to 50 students (Graetz, 2006)

As the "green building" movement increases on college and university campuses, more residential learning spaces gain the natural lighting and controlled climate cited above as part of the sustainable design of those spaces. At the University of South Carolina, for instance, West Quad, which was built to sustainable criteria developed by the U.S. Green Building Council, includes a learning center with faculty offices, study rooms, several classrooms with smart technology, and a community room with all furnishings being flexible and movable. Two classrooms are divided by a wall that can recede into the ceiling to allow larger gatherings and classes. As a "green" facility, West Quad has excellent natural lighting, good acoustics, controllable climate, and continuous ventilation with outdoor air. Research has shown that such learning environments promote better learning outcomes than traditional buildings (Katz, 2006).

Academic Services

As is discussed in chapter 4, many colleges and universities have developed specific residential learning communities and residential colleges in which students are grouped according to their academic discipline or interest in a particular aspect of life or learning. Often, these overarching programs will include a variety of academically focused services and programs supporting the students living in the particular learning community.

The success of learning communities, residential colleges, and other such programs in improving retention and academic performance of student participants has raised the issue of whether these programs should be more widely available. As a result, some colleges and universities have developed academic services open to all residential students, and in some cases, all students attending the institution whether they live on or off campus.

The University of Wisconsin, for instance, has worked various components of its learning communities into each residence hall and invites all residential students to take advantage of the residentially based classes, advising centers, and study groups. The University of Georgia has established satellite academic advising offices in several residence halls that are open to any student attending the university (Baker, 2006). At the University of Michigan, Community Learning Centers (CLCs) are being developed to provide a quiet, academically supportive space in the residence halls that house primarily first-year students. Currently, a student can study individually or in groups at a CLC. Tutoring is provided on a variety of academic subjects. According to the CLC director, "Our big picture goals include plans for renovated spaces to have increased computing and presentation capacities. We want to make CLC spaces flexible enough to support living-learning classes, group study, and presentations, as well as be places for consulting and tutoring" (Gnagey, 2005).

The University of South Carolina has approached this issue in a variety of ways. After developing a residential college, an honors college residential program, and other residential learning communities in the mid-1990s, the housing and residence life staff strategically transformed their approach to better align with the academic mission of the university. First, they established intentional first-year centers by designating certain residence halls that would house only first-year students. This allowed them to focus and front load resources, programs, and staffing specifically for the needs of students in their first year of college. Concurrent with this decision, a facilities audit of public spaces that could be allocated for academic programs was conducted and a plan implemented to create a series of classrooms in which University 101 (a first-year seminar) and other classes could be taught. Additional space was allocated for computer labs that could support instruction and host various software programs related to particular academic disciplines and student services.

After the classroom project was completed and the computer labs were opened, the housing staff established Academic Centers for Excellence (ACE) in the first-year halls. The ACEs were established to enable both active and passive learning opportunities for students living on campus and were also made available to any student attending the university. Collaborative partnerships with the Writing Center in the English department and the Math Lab in the mathematics department were established, and tutors from both areas began offering services in ACE in the late afternoon and early evening. In addition to these tutoring services, a variety of materials were made available on such topics as notetaking, study skills, time management, and other academically related topics. Over the 10 years since ACE was established, the services offered have evolved and expanded to include study group formation, academic planning, and academic coaching. For example, students can take the Learning and Study Strategies Inventory (LASSI) on an ACE computer and identify aspects of their approach to academic work that can be strengthened.

Graduate students in the Higher Education and Student Affairs master's and doctoral programs serve as academic coaches in ACE, offering specific office hours and coaching appointments for students. These coaching sessions can include a review of the student's LASSI results, discussion of notetaking approaches, or anything the student needs assistance in managing. The academic coaches receive specific training in first-year transition issues, curricular issues, and resources available to assist students. The coaches can work with a student to develop an academic success plan or refer the student to an appropriate office or person on campus to help with a specific issue. Students who are not performing at a level to maintain a scholarship are often required by the Office of Financial Aid to make an academic success appointment with one of the ACE coaches.

The evolution and success of the ACE initiative in university housing has led to the creation of another ACE in the main library on campus. Additionally, university housing has created a web-based ACE where students can make an appointment with an academic coach and where faculty can schedule an academic coach to give a presentation in their class about ACE services and resources on a specific academic success topic. The web-based ACE also has a wide array of resources that can be reviewed or printed by individual students or faculty who want to provide such materials in their classes. Faculty who teach University 101 classes make frequent use of these presentations and printable handouts (ACE, n.d.).

Perhaps the most significant program developed at the University of South Carolina to address the issue of how to provide academic support to every first-year student living on campus is the Student Success Initiative (SSI). Each year, 95-96% of the first-year students enrolling at USC live on campus. Thus the services and programs provided by housing staff are critically important for the university's retention goals. The SSI became the foundational, umbrella program for USC's First-Year Center communities.

The program is composed of several initiatives designed to enhance student success and retention. Components include (a) facilitating a proactive discussion with roommates using a written contract; (b) developing strong, intentional communities among students; (c) encouraging each first-year student to connect with the university through at least one recurring extracurricular involvement; (d) providing easily accessible academic support and information to first-year students; (e) devoting staff resources to developing strong relationships between students and staff; and (f) implementing an academic intervention initiative during the spring semester (Fink & Luna, 2005).

To implement the SSI, a re-engineering of the resident assistant (RA) job responsibilities and related training was required. The SSI requires that the RAs in a first-year hall meet one-on-one with each of the residents in their defined community a minimum of four times during the academic year. Obviously, this takes a considerable amount of time, thus it was important to take other responsibilities out of the RA's job description. The primary requirement that was removed was the RA's responsibility for programming in the hall or on his or her floor. Because of the intense nature of the SSI interventions, it was determined that reducing RA-to-student ratio in a first-year hall from 1:40 to 1:20 was also necessary.

In addition to restructuring the RA role, SSI facilitation guides were developed for the RAs, which provide scripts for each of the four meetings and resource and referral information. The meeting scripts are intended to guide the conversation based on the time of year of each meeting and are often adapted to the individual RA's style. The first meetings are to be completed during the first few weeks of the fall semester and focus on transitional issues faced by first-year students. The second round of meetings are conducted around mid-semester and introduce academic support services available and gauge the students' extracurricular engagement. The third set of meetings occur at the beginning of spring semester and focus on the students' academic performance during fall. The fourth meeting happens in the second half of the semester and focuses on goals for the students' second year as well as any particular issues students may be facing. In addition, to the specific focus of each meeting, the relationship building between the RA and his or her 20 first-year students is strengthened and the knowledge the RA gains about each student helps in connecting students with similar interests, establishing study groups, and building stronger communities on the floor. The program also had the unintended, but welcomed effect of increasing participation in student activities on campus since the residence halls were not having as many RA programs competing against campus-wide events. Three years after implementing the SSI program, it was credited with increasing retention rates of first-year students by 2-3%. Because of its success with first-year students, a companion SSI program for sophomores has been developed.

Most programs, such as these at the University of South Carolina and elsewhere around the country, require strong collaboration with other campus partners both in academic units as well as other service areas. Having academic advisors conducting both group and individual advising is beyond the scope and knowledge of most residence hall staff. Similarly, having tutors and supplemental instructors for difficult classes often comes from other areas outside of housing. In developing a strong residentially based set of academic services and programs, it is important to gather ideas from a variety of campus stakeholders including faculty, other student affairs staff, and even the business areas. Hosting a meeting of the stakeholders with facilitated discussions about what will enhance the academic ambience in and around the residence halls can be a catalyst for significant advancement and support for the residential learning initiatives that emerge from the conversations.

Staffing for Academic Support and Programs

The growth in academic support services and programs in student housing has spawned a different staffing model for many college and universities' residence life departments. And as mentioned earlier, the RA position has evolved and been adapted to focus more directly on students' academic success and less on traditional programming. At some campuses, the housing department may simply provide the space for academic programs and services that are conducted by staff and faculty from other offices on campus.

The growth in students' use of various technologies has led some housing departments to create live-in computer assistants. Stanford University was an early adopter of this model and gave its residential students quick technology support on the residence hall floors as well as in their computer labs. Others are evolving their computer labs into more comprehensive media labs with staff who can help students with video and music projects or class presentations with a variety of software.

Academic consultants or coaches are beginning to emerge on various campuses. These staff, both volunteer and compensated, can provide individual and group assistance for academic and other matters. Their training and knowledge about curricular issues, study skills, strategies for success, and campus resources can enable these individuals to view students and the campus holistically and provide resources, referrals, and suggestions on almost any aspect of a student's life that might be negatively impacting the student's academic performance.

Tutoring is one of the more common academic support services found in residence life programs focusing on academic success. In some cases, such as at the University of Wisconsin – Madison, the housing department will hire tutors directly to serve students living in the residence halls (Robbins & Bauman, 2005). In other cases, such as at the University of South Carolina, the tutors may be hired by another campus office (e.g., a writing lab or student success center) and then assigned to various residence halls to make their service more convenient, which makes it more likely that students will take advantage of their expertise (Baker, 2006).

A variety of professional and paraprofessional position titles have emerged on housing department staffs at colleges and universities around the country. Director of residential learning initiatives, director of residential learning communities, resident mentors, academic program coordinators, and other such positions enable a housing department to clearly articulate a focus on students' academic success. These positions, with a singular focus on student learning, can be catalysts for faculty-staff collaboration in the residential environment to optimize the use of space and program to facilitate student success.

Conclusion

Campus housing at colleges and universities has become an integrated component of the academic mission of our institutions and a nexus for student learning. Students, faculty, and staff have developed programs and services situated in the residential environment that has proven to increase student retention while enriching the collegiate environment for all.

References

Academic Centers for Excellence (ACE). (n.d.). *ACE services.* Retrieved June 13, 2008, from http://www.housing.sc.edu/ace/services.html

Baker, R. (2006). Support system. *Talking Stick, 23*(5), 43-44.

Fink, A., & Luna, G. (2005). Maximizing peer influences: The first-year living-learning experience, *Talking Stick, 22*(5), 15.

Gnagey, L. T. (2004, December). Students find quiet, help. *The University Record Online*, University of Michigan. Retrieved March 22, 2008, from http://www.ur.umich.edu/0405/Dec06_04/01.shtml

Graetz, K. N. (2006). The psychology of learning environments. In D. G. Oblinger (Ed.), Learning spaces (pp. 6.1-6.13). *Educause.* Retrieved June 13, 2008, from http://www.educause.edu/learningspaces

Katz, G. (2006). Greening America's schools: Costs and benefits. *A Capital-E Report.* Retrieved March 22, 2008, from http://www.cap-e.com/ewebeditpro/items/O59F11233.pdf

Kenney, D., Kenney, G., & Dumont, R. (2005). *Mission and place: Strengthening learning and community through campus design.* American Council on Education. Westport, CT: Praeger Publishers.

Luna, G., Fidler, P., & Moore, P. (1997). Unpublished report, University of South Carolina.

Robbins, K. S., & Baumann, J. A. (2005). The value of living learning. *Talking Stick, 23*(2), 23.

Strong, L., & Chiang, G. (2004). Finishing touches: The first-year experience at Cornell. *Talking Stick, 21*(5), 7-8.

Terenzini, P. T., & Pascarella, E. T. (1994, January/February). Living with myths: Undergraduate education in America. *Change, 26*(1), 28-32.

Chapter Seven

Faculty Involvement in Residence Halls: Bridging Faculty and Staff Cultures Through Residential Learning Communities

Calvin J. Bergman and Aaron M. Brower

In the landmark book, *How College Affects Students*, Pascarella and Terenzini (1991) completed a meta-analysis of college impact research and concluded that:

> [A] large part of the impact of college is determined by the extent and content of one's inter-actions with major agents of socialization on campus, namely, faculty members and student peers. The influence of interpersonal interactions with these groups is manifest in intellectual outcomes as well as in changes in attitudes, values, aspirations, and a number of psychosocial characteristics. The educational impact of a college's faculty is enhanced when their contacts with students extend beyond the formal classroom to informal non-classroom settings. (p. 620)

In fact, faculty involvement in residence halls has important effects on both academic and social outcomes (Inkelas, Brower, & Associates, 2004). Unfortunately, the cultural divides between students and faculty and between student affairs and academic affairs present barriers that must be overcome for informal interactions to occur. This divide manifests itself within organizational structures, relationships, and the separation between academic and student affairs.

By integrating the social and academic parts of institutions, learning communities can provide powerful, holistic experiences for students characterized by more frequent and more in-depth faculty and peer interactions. Learning communities break down the size of large universities and foster community-building and a greater sense of coherence. When housed within residential structures, the positive outcomes associated with learning communities may be amplified. We believe that residential learning communities, also known as living-learning programs, represent the cutting edge of faculty involvement in residence halls. Moreover, much can be adapted from these models to enhance faculty involvement in more traditional residence hall settings.

In this chapter, results from the National Study of Living-Learning Programs are used to illustrate the impact of faculty involvement in residence halls on student outcomes. We then use a framework of culture and overcoming cultural barriers to describe the challenges inherent in involving faculty in residence halls. A model from the University of Wisconsin (UW)-Madison demonstrates how faculty, staff, and students can work and learn together—in a collaborative framework—within residential learning communities. In addition, we describe how extending the features of residential learning communities into traditional residence halls can be an effective strategy for increasing the involvement of faculty in all residence halls.

The Impact of Faculty-Student Interactions within Residential Learning Communities

The National Study of Living-Learning Programs (NSLLP; Inkelas et al., 2004) is the first national study of living-learning programs. Prior to this study, evaluations of living-learning programs were institution-specific, and the program elements that contributed to student learning outcomes could not be generalized beyond the individual college or university. The NSLLP surveyed 24,000 students across the country, half living in 268 living-learning programs at 34 colleges and universities, and the other half living in traditional residence halls at those same institutions.

Analyses of the NSLLP focused on identifying program elements that influenced social and academic student learning outcomes. Controlling for self-selection biases and other pre-college differences, living-learning students showed positive outcomes in a variety of areas, including:

◇ Mentoring relationships with faculty members
◇ More frequent and richer out-of-class discussions with peers about academic and social issues
◇ Perception of the residence hall as an academically and socially supportive climate
◇ A smooth transition to college
◇ Use of critical thinking skills
◇ Greater commitment to issues related to civic engagement
◇ Lower levels of drinking and fewer negative consequences from drinking

Relationships with faculty and the overall amount of faculty involvement in the living-learning program were found to be key contributors to these outcomes. In fact, those programs involving five or more faculty members showed the most positive student outcomes. The most successful programs included sections of traditional academic courses taught in the residence hall for living-learning participants and offered dedicated out-of-classroom academic programs for their students that involved faculty or teaching assistants, notably service-learning and research opportunities, study groups, academic advising and career workshops, and multicultural programming (Inkelas et al., 2004).

Results from the NSLLP also suggest that programs most successful in producing these social and academic outcomes are those that involve strong collaborations between student affairs professionals and faculty. More specifically, the most successful programs:

◇ Involve residence life professionals and academic departments or individual faculty "champions" in the creation of clear program objectives
◇ Share budget responsibilities between housing and academic departments or colleges
◇ Share administrative and program oversight
◇ Share (and mix up) central and critical roles (i.e., encourage residence life staff to co-teach courses and faculty to participate in residence life staff selection and training)
◇ Offer resources and programming that capitalize on talents from both sides (e.g., service-learning, research opportunities, study groups, academic advising, career workshops, and multicultural programming) (Inkelas et al., 2004).

Residential learning community models vary widely in the extent to which faculty, staff, and students collaborate. Some schools consider theme housing with little or no faculty involvement a form of residential learning communities. Other schools have residential learning communities that are driven by faculty members or academic departments. Yet, such initiatives lack collaboration that bridges academic and student affairs as the most successful programs from the NSLLP study. Our definition of residential learning communities has a simple principle at its foundation: Faculty, staff, and students are brought together as a community to accomplish shared learning objectives. They need each other to accomplish their learning objectives (Brower & Dettinger, 1998).

However, the collaborations required by our definition of a residential learning community may be difficult to initiate and sustain because of cultural barriers. Frequently, initiatives designed to enhance faculty involvement in residence halls are launched without an adequate understanding of the cultural barriers that need to be intentionally crossed. A heightened awareness of the cultural differences is an essential step in forging productive collaborations and meaningful faculty involvement in residential settings.

Cultural Differences between Faculty, Staff, and Students

Lustig and Koester (1993) define culture as "a learned set of shared perceptions about beliefs, values and norms which affect the behaviors of a relatively large group of people" (p. 27). Among faculty, staff, and student groups, these differences can largely be described in terms of life stage and career priorities. Barriers between groups frequently take the form of competing priorities, turf issues, and more recently, preferred means of communication. Some writers have described the stereotypes held by staff of faculty, and vice versa.

Stereotypes of Faculty Culture

Faculty work is most often described by the framework of teaching, research, and service. Depending upon institution type, the priorities within this framework vary. For instance, research very often drives the day-to-day work priorities of faculty at large research-intensive universities. On the other hand, teaching is more often the emphasis for faculty at small liberal arts colleges. Unfortunately, involvement in the residence halls rarely satisfies research or teaching obligations. At institutions where faculty involvement in the residence halls is recognized as a part of faculty work, it is most often considered a contribution of service. Generally, service is not valued in the faculty tenure and promotion process as highly as research and teaching. Among non-tenured faculty, pressures to do research and teach are especially strong. Additionally, for faculty at research universities, the emphasis on research has contributed to the involvement of graduate students in undergraduate teaching, especially in lower-level course sections. Graduate students themselves prioritize progress on their own research—their raison d'être as graduate students—over their teaching and involvement in residence halls. Finally, beyond professional activity, it is important to appreciate that faculty and graduate students often have competing personal priorities. In the end, there is little institutional reward for tenured or non-tenured faculty, as well as aspiring graduate teaching assistants, to engage students in residence halls. Rather, there is strong institutionalized pressure to prioritize some combination of research and teaching.

These pressures undoubtedly feed into stereotypes of faculty as identified by Zeller (1997). For example, stereotypes about faculty are that they:

◇ Live in a publish-or-perish reward system that keeps them from having meaningful connections with students
◇ Are primarily motivated by research and external funding dollars
◇ Have strong allegiances to their discipline rather than to the institution
◇ Have little appreciation for teaching and pedagogy
◇ View learning as an isolated, nonsocial experience
◇ Place little value on extracurricular or out-of-classroom experiences
◇ Engage in interpersonal communications marked by challenge and confrontation
◇ Use academic language that relies heavily on jargon from their discipline in order to exclude others
◇ Have little concern for students' personal problems

Clearly, these generalizations paint an unflattering portrait of faculty who feel strong pressures from their institution to publish and develop national reputations in their field. Given the nature of the tenure and promotion systems at most institutions, faculty members are making good decisions to prioritize research and teaching. When designing strategies to involve faculty in residence halls, it is important to seek ways to align this involvement with their academic priorities. Such strategies may include involving faculty through their academic interests, providing new structures for faculty and students to be engaged with each other around shared academic interests, and capitalizing on faculty desire to bring others into what they love about their field.

Stereotypes of Student Affairs Culture

Zeller (1997) identifies a similar set of stereotypes for student affairs professionals. From the perspective of faculty, student affairs professionals:

◇ Work in areas that have little connection to the curriculum
◇ Ground their practice in a body of student development theory that itself contains only cursory scholarship or research
◇ View students' experiences, and most often their extracurricular experiences, as paramount, asserting that students' "real learning" takes place outside the classroom or academic department in a way that can border on being anti-intellectual
◇ Coddle students who really do not belong in college
◇ Identify with a field that is a helping profession rather than one that has learning at its core
◇ View learning as primarily a social and highly active exercise
◇ Use student affairs language that is overly inculcated with jargon from student development and counseling disciplines
◇ Avoid confrontation and instead are overly or unnecessarily supportive
◇ Make decisions using a "bottom line" financial orientation, which devalues decisions made to support the educational mission, especially within university housing
◇ View students as customers

To be certain, the stereotypes depicted here are, of course, generalizations and perhaps exaggerated to highlight the cultural differences between faculty and student affairs professionals. Again, they are clearly unflattering; yet, unless these are recognized and addressed, communication and collaboration between faculty and staff is limited. The divide between staff and faculty is reinforced by the ways in which faculty are trained to see the world through disciplinary lenses while staff tend to be trained to see the world from a student development point of view. This compartmentalization and specialization is further complicated by the power differential between faculty and staff. When the faculty and staff cultures interact, the final decision is often aligned with the faculty point of view.

A cultural competence framework can help faculty and staff think more broadly about their differences. The key to cultural competence is a recognition of one's own cultural "trappings," which leads to a recognition and valuing of the culture of others. In the context of higher education faculty and staff, the cultural stereotypes listed above are extreme. Yet, we find that they can serve as a useful starting point for discussions that lead to greater cultural awareness and competence. Ultimately, these discussions lead to the recognition that we all share the basic higher education mission—to educate students and help them become productive citizens in a global context. Therefore, a cultural competence framework forces staff and faculty to recognize that cultural differences do exist and encourages each person to examine and talk about how these differences impact communication and collaboration.

Effective management of these cultural barriers includes frameworks that sustain collaboration between faculty and staff and the creation of functional roles for faculty within residence halls that take best advantage of their interests and academic priorities. Sustained collaborative experiences between faculty and staff are the most effective way to foster greater cross-cultural awareness, competence, and appreciation. Again, bridging the divide between academic and student affairs is important to position faculty and staff to work together to foster more frequent, meaningful interactions between faculty and students. However, another cultural divide still needs to be addressed, namely, the divide between students and faculty.

Stereotypes of Student Culture & Barriers to Student-Faculty Engagement

Beyond the life stage differences between faculty and students, cultural differences between them can also be observed on campuses in terms of what is considered "home turf" (both physical and virtual) and when this turf is occupied. The home turf of faculty consists of their office, classrooms, and laboratories in which they teach and research. To some extent, students share the classroom turf; however, this is during limited and highly structured times where faculty members are clearly in charge. The home turf of students tends to be spaces on campus that are not academic in nature, including the residence halls in which they live. Our observations suggest that students avoid faculty office hours and faculty avoid entering residence halls because stepping into the others' turf creates anxiety. This is especially true when taking this step in an unstructured fashion.

Time of day also manifests itself as a barrier to faculty-student engagement. Courses are typically scheduled during business hours. Faculty members generally avoid staying on campus into the evening hours. During the day, life in residence halls is characterized by a slow start in the morning, followed by students going to and coming back from classes and then a greater buzz of activity surrounding dinner time and the evening. Faculty offices and classrooms are busy during the day and empty at night. We have found that dinner time is the important "overlap" when faculty-student activities can be planned.

As Zeller (1997) describes, faculty communication with students can often be challenging, confrontational, and filled with discipline-based jargon that can appear off-putting. Alternatively, staff communication can be overly supportive and laden with counseling-inspired and student development jargon. Neither communication style is easy for students. Meanwhile, students are often still finding their voice as they develop academic and social confidence. In addition, new technologies mean that the task of communication is constantly evolving. For example, the window of opportunity in which students, faculty, and staff can communicate has broadened. E-mail and message boards have eliminated many time and space barriers. Interestingly, our observation is that students have become more involved with more immediate and technology-driven forms of communication: instant messaging, text messaging, and social networking web sites. These forms of communication among students may serve to reinforce a separate subculture and represent an additional barrier to student-faculty engagement.

A Residential Learning Community Model: The Framework for Cross-Cultural Engagement and Institutional Change

The University of Wisconsin-Madison launched its first residential learning community, the Bradley Learning Community, in 1995. In fall 2008, a sixth residential learning community will be launched bringing total participation among residence hall students to 20% ($n = 1,348$). The residential learning communities include:

◇ Chadbourne Residential College (liberal arts) – 815 residents
◇ Bradley Learning Community (first-year experience) – 246 residents
◇ International Learning Community (including multiple language groups) – 130 residents
◇ Multicultural Learning Community – 56 residents
◇ Women In Science and Engineering – 36 residents
◇ Entrepreneurial Residential Learning Community (fall 2008) – 65 residents

The Bradley Learning Community serves as an example of the development of cultural competence through a model that sustains engagement and fosters collaboration.

Cross-Cultural Leadership Teams and Steering Committees

The model that has evolved at the UW-Madison requires collaboration among faculty, staff, and students and fosters cross-cultural engagement, competency, and appreciation. Hallmarks of the model include shared leadership and the creation of functional roles and structures that serve to bridge cultural divides. In brief, leadership for our residential learning communities is shared among faculty, staff, and students. Each learning community has: (a) a faculty director, a faculty member who receives a part-time administrative appointment to help direct the learning community; (b) a program director, a full-time residence life staff member who oversees all aspects of the program and building in which it is housed; and (c) a half-time program coordinator, a new student affairs professional or graduate student, who assists both the faculty director and program director with anything that needs to be done within the learning community. These individuals make up the core leadership team (with some exceptions) that guides the week-to-week management of the learning communities.

In addition to the learning community leadership teams, each program has a steering committee that includes faculty, residence life leadership, student staff, student leaders, academic advisors, and other important campus stakeholders. The function of the steering committee is to guide the semester-to-semester vision for the communities and to provide budgetary oversight. This structure institutionalizes cross-cultural engagement and learning. The benefit of this broader understanding has been realized in both academic and nonacademic aspects of our learning community programming.

Lessons Learned in Developing Shared Leadership

The evolution of this leadership team model has not been without challenges and cross-cultural growing pains. The creation of the Bradley Learning Community's mission of "integrative learning" typifies this. It demonstrates how each member of the initial planning team came to realize that their image of Bradley was incomplete without input from the other members of the team.

In the early 1990s, several senior residence life staff members initiated a conversation with a few faculty members to develop a residential program for first-year students. Bradley Hall had become a de facto first-year student building due to its location on the far west side of campus and its non-descript architecture. For these reasons, demand among students to live in the hall was low. In early planning meetings, it was clear that one goal would be to focus on helping students make a successful transition into college, but how that was to be done remained vague.

One initial obstacle to collaboration was the need to convert institutional motivations into personal motivations. For example, it was clear why the Division of Housing was interested in improving Bradley Hall: It was a low-priority building that needed attention, and the idea of developing programming specific to the first-year students who were assigned there seemed sensible. However, given the lack of involvement by faculty and academic affairs in the residence halls at the time, faculty, especially those in the College of Letters and Sciences, might be expected to have little desire to be involved.

Personal motivations became clear as individuals began their planning together. A key faculty member on the Bradley planning team wanted to recreate a fully integrated core curriculum in the manner of Alexander Meiklejohn's Experimental College at UW-Madison in the 1920s. The other key faculty member saw in Bradley the chance to try out theories of education based on the creation of small-group learning and social environments. Residence life staff, too, were motivated beyond the "bottom line" stereotype of needing to fill beds. One senior residence life staff member wanted the program to focus on enhancing academic enrichment activities (e.g., study groups, advising) and realized the value of having students who were new to campus become quickly connected to faculty. Another wanted to recreate the intensity of learning she experienced as an undergraduate student at a small liberal arts college.

These motivations were the foundation for collaboration, but true collaboration only emerged when individuals crossed cultures—when they recognized that they needed each other to fulfill a personal image of Bradley. Faculty recognized that they could not truly embed learning in students' daily lives without residence hall staff; residence life staff recognized that faculty would be required to teach the courses or modules and other faculty-student activities that staff had in mind (as well as lend credibility to "learning" in students' minds). Yet each member's image of Bradley was bound by his or her own culture, and these cultural views inhibited collaboration. Faculty viewed Bradley, more or less, as traditional learning that happened to take place in the residence hall. Residence life staff viewed Bradley as a more intense and engaging, but traditional, community among students. Faculty and staff continued to see each other in traditional roles. Nevertheless, lesson one in fostering collaboration was the recognition for each faculty and staff member that the others were needed in order to achieve the, albeit culturally bound, vision for Bradley.

There was no single developmental turning point in the ongoing discussions among this initial planning group; there was not a seminal moment when it dawned on everyone that the vision for Bradley was becoming a jointly developed image that pushed the boundaries of faculty and staff. Instead, over an 18-month period, a more mutually created vision for Bradley emerged from long discussions, one particularly memorable half-day retreat, and successful conflict management. Over time, the members of the planning team stopped aligning along faculty and staff lines. Instead, each began to see what was missing from his or her own vision as the discussions among them created richer elements of a program that was becoming truly different from what any of them had envisioned.

What helped enormously in the early days was a shared sense of wanting to create something special—that desire kept individuals committed to the discussions through the inevitable conflicts and dry spells. This was lesson two: reminding each other of their shared mission to create something unique.

Finally, one residence life staff member from the core faculty and staff group was naturally "cross-cultural"—she had tremendous credibility with residence life staff and faculty alike because she spoke the language of both groups. She was the translator, but even more important, she also transcended both cultures and could embody the shared culture and vision for which all members were striving. She typified "expert power" (French & Raven, 1959)—that is, based on her intelligence and good humor, both faculty and staff were comfortable with her ability to articulate program elements that combined divergent themes, and she did so in ways that were both intellectually rich and practical. Therefore, lesson three might be to find a member of your core planning team who is culturally proficient in the worlds of both faculty and staff.

In the end, the members of the Bradley planning team grew to depend on each other in much more profound ways than they had initially intended. They developed functional relationships with each other in new and rich ways that sometimes rested on the roles they played outside of Bradley, but that more often rested on the individual strengths and abilities they brought to the relationship. They had become true individuals to each other rather than simply a collection of titles and position-based roles.

Faculty Involvement: Seminars, Class Sections, and Other Structures

Because faculty members generally care about student learning, involvement in residential learning communities will often hold some appeal for them. However, many faculty members prefer to be involved in their traditional academic and professional domains. Others will recognize the value of broader learning in social, interpersonal, and community domains (i.e., domains frequently associated with student affairs). Faculty members who have been involved in the residential learning communities at the university have often learned to appreciate these broader frameworks. Beyond our faculty director roles and the opportunities for additional faculty to be involved in steering committees, there are many other structured and functional roles that faculty play within the residential learning communities. These roles are typically aligned with the roles they play on campus and their academic expertise and other interests. After getting involved in more familiar ways, faculty members often broaden their frameworks for student learning and involvement in the residential learning communities to less familiar ways.

The residential learning communities at the UW-Madison have seminars that serve as the academic anchor and shared experience among faculty, staff, and students. Faculty and academic staff are involved in these seminars in familiar lecture-discussion section formats. Analogous to the typical lecture-discussion format on campus, learning community large-group gatherings (i.e., lectures) are typically incorporated into a bi-weekly community dinner; our small-group gatherings (i.e., discussions) are typically more informal, taking place within the residence halls during the alternate weeks. Beyond these "norm-stretching" seminar formats, additional faculty and teaching assistants on campus are involved in teaching course sections to learning community cohorts, often in residence hall classrooms.

After faculty and instructors become comfortable within the residence hall environment through familiar teaching and learning activities, it is more likely to involve them in less familiar, yet meaningful ways. Providing intentional structure to bridge the cultural divides is an essential element to involving faculty and instructors in less familiar ways. Without intentional structure, students tend to gravitate to other students, and faculty members tend to gravitate to other faculty in order to reduce the anxiety that is created by the unfamiliar. For instance, the Chadbourne Residential College provides a number of activities that include intentional structure such as small-group faculty/staff-student picnic discussions during orientation week and regular faculty/staff dinners throughout the academic year. Faculty, teaching assistants, and academic staff affiliated with the community participate in these events.

The basis for the small-group picnic discussions during orientation week centers around a shared reading (typically an article about transitions or educational philosophy that is sent to all participants during the summer) and the thoughts, feelings, and experiences that students are having during their first days on campus. Thus, the discussions intentionally engage both academic and social issues. All the participating faculty/staff meet together an hour before the discussion to prepare. Most helpful are the faculty/staff who have done this before who share discussion tips and experiences; they enter into these discussions in more thoughtful ways and with a more present sense of empathy for the students. Faculty/staff are paired up with student staff and leaders and meet groups of approximately 20 students on the residence hall floors. Discussion groups spread out all over campus, going to the faculty/staff member's favorite spot for a picnic dinner. After the discussions, faculty/staff gather in a private room in the student union to debrief and celebrate the beginning of another year. Similar intentionality goes into the faculty/staff dinners. Student staff and leaders greet faculty/staff participants in the lobby and ensure that faculty/staff spread out among the students at dinner and facilitate conversation. Again, the point here is that intentional structure, often times clarifying roles, is an essential element in order to set faculty, staff, and students up to be successful in traversing cultural differences in less familiar situations.

Beware of the Inertia of the Status Quo

With familiar and less familiar ways of faculty-student engagement established in the residential learning communities, an important lesson that UW-Madison has learned is that ongoing collaboration takes continual communication and attention. For example, during the third year of the Bradley Learning Community, inertia began to settle in, straining the true collaboration that had operated previously. Parties fell back into their status quo mode of operation (more familiar cultural practices), due to time constraints and also a sense that "we already know how to do Bradley; let's just repeat what has worked in the past."

As examples of status quo inertia, during that fall semester, the faculty met to plan for the seminar course that serves as the integrative-learning foundation of the Bradley experience. This was unlike previous years when the steering committee was fully included in functional ways that involved residence life staff. During the spring semester, residence life staff proceeded with Bradley Fellow (i.e., live-in student resident assistant) selection following the standardized and internal, residence life process. While there was a passing recognition that different qualities were needed for the new Bradley Fellows, well-worked residence life practices created a staff-selection juggernaut. Reverting to the status quo, residence life staff went about its business with only cursory collaboration from faculty.

Then came an "ah-ha" experience that was formative in the development of the model of sustained collaboration. Part way though the student-staff selection process, one of the most active faculty members—one of the original champions—discussed his concerns about the lack of faculty involvement in the process. These concerns caught Bradley's program director (a residence life staff member) by surprise. He had also fallen back into the status quo paradigm. In the context of these discussions, the way in which the staff had become marginalized from the seminar planning process was also discussed. The value of having staff members involved in seminar planning had been to keep the first-year student development and transition to college issues in the foreground; whereas, the value of having faculty involved in Bradley Fellow selection had been to keep attributes of integrative learners as selection criteria in the foreground.

Through effective conflict management and the structure of our leadership team and steering committee, which institutionalizes sustained cross-cultural engagement, we overcame the influence of the status quo that pushed these cross-cultural contributions into the background. In addition, we overcame these strains due to sufficiently strong personal relationships with each other and our shared vision for the program. We also strengthened an important principle of experimentation borrowed from Meiklejohn (1932) and his Experimental College: that everything we do, each and every year, must be reinvented by the current faculty, staff, and students. This constant renewal has helped us find ways to sustain a "honeymoon effect" and create an environment that promotes ownership each year among faculty, staff, and students.

In *Learning Reconsidered 2*, Steffes and Keeling (2006) argue that "fundamentally, the effort to support collaboration is a process of cultural change" (p. 72). The process we engaged in while developing the Bradley Learning Community mirrors many of the suggested strategies they offer for effective collaboration. These include:

◇ Starting small
◇ Identifying and supporting champions, but avoiding overdependence
◇ Focusing on real problems, not theoretical opportunities
◇ Initiating the conversation
◇ Expecting and managing conflict
◇ Evaluating the outcomes

We believe our process also includes hallmarks of the successful programs highlighted by the National Survey of Living-Learning Programs (NSLLP) study. The Bradley Learning Community provided the opportunity for faculty and staff to become program champions, featured shared administrative oversight, and capitalized on the skills and resources of team members while seeking to involve them in ways that moved outside their traditional roles.

Improving Faculty-Student Interaction in Traditional Residence Halls by Expanding the Features of Residential Learning Communities

UW-Madison's residential learning community model, characterized by shared leadership and broad collaboration, has positioned the residence life program to expand many features of the residential learning communities into all of the residence halls, thereby increasing faculty involvement throughout the entire system. Residence hall class sections, a practice that was started in residential learning communities, are now integrated into all residences halls. In fall 2007, up to 35% of residents enrolled in cohorts with other students in their residence hall. Approximately 125 sections of the courses that residence hall students (and first-year students) most frequently take were offered in residence halls, including:

◇ Calculus and Analytic Geometry I & II
◇ General Chemistry
◇ Advanced General Chemistry
◇ Freshman Composition

◇ Introduction to Speech Communication
◇ Introduction to American Politics and Government
◇ Integrated Liberal Studies Courses as Residential Learning Community Seminars

To extend the impact of aligning course section enrollment with residence hall assignment, we have created 11 classrooms in our residence halls where these special class sections meet. As a measure of University Housing's commitment to this effort, top notch classroom space was included in the two new residence halls that recently opened on campus, and resources are made readily accessible to achieve high satisfaction among instructors and students in all the classrooms. In existing residence halls, common area rooms were renovated and transformed into classrooms, and furniture and AV equipment was purchased. Up to 23% ($n = 1,580$) of residents have classes in their residence hall in about 80 sections of residence hall class sections and First-Year Interest Groups (FIGs).

Due to the positive reputation of our residential learning communities and the establishment of residence hall class sections, residence life was considered a key campus stakeholder in the development of the FIG program. Unlike residence hall class sections, which are most often linked to specific residence halls, FIGs are linked to broader "residential neighborhoods" (i.e., specific residence halls located close to each other). FIGs consist of three courses (ideally taught in a coherent, integrative fashion). In fall 2007, 16 FIGs were offered, including:

◇ The United States and the Korean War
◇ Communication and Disability
◇ Race, Racial Conditioning, and the Oneness of Humankind
◇ American Studies: Bodies, Vision, Politics
◇ Engineering, Communication, and Design
◇ Health Care Systems in Contemporary America
◇ Impact of Computer Technology
◇ Childhood and the Family
◇ Making Meaning in an Evolutionary World
◇ Race, Place, and Story: Arts Against Oppression
◇ Cultural Issues for Health Care Professionals
◇ Introduction to African American Dramatic Literature
◇ Engineering, Communication, and Design
◇ Seeking Truth, Living with Doubt
◇ Urban Youth and Youth Development Policy

The alignment of class sections and FIGs with residence halls and residential neighborhoods, which essentially aligns course enrollment with residence hall assignment, serves to transplant the cultural norms and priorities of faculty and instructors into the residence hall environment. Academic program coordinators (APCs), experienced residence life student staff members assigned to each residence hall community, serve as classroom hosts and work with the faculty and instructors to facilitate out-of-class activities. These staff members are an additional example of how features of our residential learning communities have been expanded to all of the residence halls. Residential learning communities allocate a significant amount of their additional resources to expand their staff support. APCs provide support for the learning community features that have been expanded to our traditional residence halls. For instance, APCs are responsible for the classroom facilities, including classroom supplies and AV equipment (e.g., TV/VCR/DVR cabinets, LCD projectors,

DVD video cameras), and providing an orientation to instructors and faculty to the classroom and residence hall before classes begin.

Prior to the start of the semester, APCs instigate and provide resources for instructors to extend their involvement with their students and within the residence halls beyond class time. All instructors are issued $25 meal debit cards and are encouraged to use it to eat with their students. APCs discuss the potential of review sessions, study groups, office hours in the hall, and inform the instructors of $50 that is allocated for each class in support of out-of-class activities. APCs discuss the instructor's vision for the course, review course syllabi, and engage in conversations with instructors to identify areas to build upon. To be certain, we have learned within our residential learning communities, active ongoing communication is the most important task in order to build and sustain effective collaborative relationships. Throughout, we strive to leave the impression that our role is to ensure a positive classroom experience—better than other alternatives on campus—and that we "magically" remove obstacles in order to make the instructors feel as if it is easy to do things with their students in and out of class.

At research universities, like the University of Wisconsin-Madison, most of the course sections of large introductory courses are taught by graduate teaching assistants. Therefore, most of the instructors teaching our residence hall class sections and working with our APCs are TAs. Within the academic departments, we strive to promote teaching residence hall class sections as a resumé-builder and an opportunity to engage students and teach in innovative ways. TAs who have a genuine interest in the teaching enterprise often self-select to teach residence hall class sections. With our FIGs program, tenured faculty members create the FIG, identify the two other linked courses (typically sections of large introductory courses taught by TAs) and teach the core course. The vision for the FIG program is to foster integrative learning among the three courses that make up each FIG and to bridge the in- and out-of-classroom divide. Similarly, the faculty members who get involved with our FIG program typically want to engage with undergraduates and love teaching. This results in TAs and FIG faculty inclined to collaborate with APCs, which results in significant engagement among faculty, TAs, and students within the residence halls.

We have found that residence hall class sections accelerate community building. The alignment of course enrollment with residence hall assignment breaks down the size of both large lectures and large residence halls into cohorts where students are more inclined to connect social and academic integration. Instructors and faculty comment on the accelerated community building and engagement within the classroom. Students live together and get to know each other more quickly. To extend this community building, activities are planned for the cohorts, and faculty interact with students in less formal ways in the residence halls and dining rooms.

To be sure, the faculty directors and other faculty who are involved in the residential learning communities, as well as the numerous instructors and faculty who teach course sections in all the residence halls, deserve recognition. In response, the APCs have developed our Favorite Instructors program. This program is simple: At the residence hall desks, students nominate their favorite instructors. Then, the APCs send these instructors a certificate of recognition and appreciation. Though simple, faculty members greatly appreciate this recognition. Faculty members often respond with unsolicited notes expressing how meaningful being recognized by students as a favorite instructor is to them. Examples from fall 2007 include:

⋄ "I just wanted to say thanks to you and your team (and the students) for the Favorite Instructor Award!! Wow. I wasn't expecting that but I really do appreciate it."
⋄ "Please pass on my thanks for the favorite instructor awards you recently sent from both Ogg and FAST Halls. They mean a lot to me. In my opinion, thoughts like these from the

students are the most valuable kinds of recognition. It is nice to know that I might have made a difference in a few students' lives."

◇ "I try to make class worthwhile and interesting for the students, so it's really rewarding to hear that they appreciate the effort."

All these instructors and faculty—roughly 200 each year—are more formally recognized at the annual Academic Partners Recognition Reception, which University Housing organizes and sponsors at the end of each academic year. This event serves as a bookend to all the learning community and classroom activity (and out-of-class activity involving instructors and faculty) that occurs in the residence halls each year. Remarkably each year, the extent and depth of instructor and faculty involvement continues to grow as the cultural divides are slowly bridged through cross-cultural experiences and growing cultural competence and appreciation.

Conclusion

Forging and nurturing faculty and staff collaborations in residence halls takes work but is worth the effort in terms of students' academic and social gains. In fact, it is difficult to imagine how universities accomplish their missions when faculty and staff do not collaborate. In this chapter, a framework of collaboration based on crossing cultures has been presented: (a) understanding and appreciating the culture of "the other," (b) appreciating that "the other" is necessary to realize shared learning objectives, and (c) continuing to become more cross-culturally competent oneself. But first and foremost, collaborations occur only when the individuals involved genuinely need each other to get their work done. Common purpose is the first-principle to forging collaborations; when common purposes do not exist, collaborations simply cannot be forced or manufactured. No amount of cross-cultural ability or awareness can overcome a lack of common purpose.

Therefore, collaborations must have a genuine purpose—faculty and residence life staff coming together to develop a residential learning community. It is through their shared vision of that residential learning environment and program that the individuals involved recognize that they need each other and the value of crossing into each other's culture. This chapter also illustrates how the structure of residential learning community leadership teams and steering committees serves to sustain collaboration and ongoing cross-cultural awareness, competence, and appreciation. Similarly, intentional structure that aligns faculty priorities with student interactions in residence halls is essential to broaden faculty involvement from the leadership of residential learning communities to daily life in all residence halls. Most significantly, providing seminar courses in all the residential learning communities, and linking course enrollment with residence hall assignment in all the residence halls, provides a base that often leads to more informal interactions and activities between faculty and students.

Crossing cultures is risky for faculty, staff, and students; it often makes them feel as though they are visitors in their own institutions. Crossing cultures also takes courage and commitment. In the face of stepping out of one's comfort zone, it is not easy to keep one's "eyes on the prize." The intentionality and structure that we describe in this chapter to manage this risk has resulted not only in the establishment of residential learning communities at the University of Wisconsin-Madison, but it has also transformed faculty and instructor involvement throughout the residence halls and collaboration campus-wide.

References

Brower, A. M., & Dettinger, K. (1998, November/December). What is a learning community? Towards a comprehensive model. *About Campus*, 15-21.

French, J. R. P., & Raven, B. (1959). Bases of social power. In D. Cartwright (Ed.), *Studies in Social Power* (pp. 150-167). Ann Arbor: University of Michigan.

Inkelas, K. K., Brower, A. M., & Associates. (2004). *National study of living-learning programs: 2004 report of findings*. Retrieved February 28, 2007, from http://www.livelearnstudy.net/images/NSLLP_2004_Final_Report.pdf

Lustig, M. W., & Koester, J. (1993). *Intercultural competence: Intercultural communication across cultures*. New York: HarperCollins College Publishers.

Meiklejohn, A. (1932). *The experimental college*. New York: Harper.

Pascarella, E. T., & Terenzini, P. T. (1991). *How college affects students*. San Francisco: Jossey-Bass.

Steffes, J., & Keeling R. P. (2006). Creating for collaboration. *In Learning Reconsidered 2: A Practical Guide to Implementing a Campus-Wide Focus on the Student Experience*. Washington, DC: ACPA, ACUHO-I, ACUI, NACA, NACADA, NASPA, NIRSA.

Zeller, W. J. (1997). Two cultures united: residential programs of the 21st century. *The Journal of College and University Student Housing, 26*(2), 7-13.

Chapter Eight

Leadership Development and Advising First-Year Student Leaders

Norbert W. Dunkel and Mary Kay Schneider Carodine

Developing student competencies in leadership and civic engagement have become essential components of a quality undergraduate education on many campuses. Significant attention has been given to creating curricular and cocurricular opportunities designed to ensure that graduates are leaving their institutions with the skills and knowledge they will need to be effective leaders in their future professions and communities. For first-year students, their introduction to these opportunities often occurs in the residential setting and becomes a foundation for the pursuit of increasingly higher levels of civic engagement and leadership development as they move through their undergraduate careers. Ultimately, the first-year residential programs provide the initial experiences that will lead to the achievement of institutional goals and outcomes related to student leadership and civic engagement. First-year residential opportunities include floor, hall, and complex government positions, residence hall association membership, hall community services, and service-learning projects that may be linked to freshman interest groups (FIGs) or living-learning program classes.

This chapter opens with an overview of leadership theories and the skills and competencies that can be developed through involvement in residence life. A description of the range of first-year leadership and civic engagement opportunities in the residential setting follows. As an important catalyst for student development along these lines, the role of the advisor and other professional staff overseeing these opportunities is discussed. The chapter closes by addressing the importance of intentionally linking first-year opportunities to broader campus and community initiatives.

Leadership Skills, Competencies, and Outcomes

Leadership development entails creating involvement opportunities where students can increase their understanding of leadership theory, practice specific skills, and apply their knowledge in a supportive environment. In order to do this effectively, residence hall staff should be well versed in leadership development theory and use this knowledge to inform their practice.

Leadership scholars suggest that leadership can be learned and taught. Students can come to understand both the process and outcomes of leadership through their involvement. The Social Change Model of Leadership Development (Higher Education Research Institute, 1996) provides a valuable framework for involvement in residence halls. Some key assumptions of the model are:

◇ Leadership is concerned with affecting change on behalf of others and society.
◇ Leadership is collaborative.
◇ Leadership is a process rather than a position.
◇ Leadership should be values-based.
◇ All students (not just those who hold formal leadership positions) are potential leaders.
◇ Service is a powerful vehicle for developing students' leadership skills. (p. 10)

The Social Change Model is organized around the concepts of Individual Values (consciousness of self, congruency, and commitment), Group Process Values (collaboration, common purpose, and controversy with civility), and Community/Societal Values (citizenship) (Higher Education Research Institute, 1996). Individual values include awareness of beliefs and values and behavior that is consistent with those beliefs and values. Commitment refers to the psychic energy that motivates individuals to serve the collective effort. Group process values include a shared vision or purpose that is arrived at through consensus and achieved by "capitalizing on the multiple talents and perspectives of each group member" (HERI, pp. 22-23). Because differences in perspective may lead to conflict, group process values also focus on airing disagreements openly and approaching them with civility. There is also a recognition that conflict may lead to creative solutions. Community values or citizenship is the process of connecting the individual or collaborative group to the larger community or society for the purpose of affecting positive change in the community.

The premise of the model is that seven values are the critical elements of leadership development and that leadership is about positive social change, which serves as the "hub" of the model. The Social Change Model can be used to help students understand the components of their involvement as well as provide a framework for reflection and education. For first-year students, the Individual Values are critical as they help students define themselves and their values, gifts, and talents, and then help them determine how to work with others in a group. The Group Values assist students in understanding how to work with others and provide a platform to discuss group development. Finally, citizenship encourages students to see themselves as a part of the larger whole, whether that be the residence hall, the university community, or the surrounding community. It can also guide first-year students to think about what change they can make through hall governance, student events, and service projects. This leadership framework gives advisors a foundation for educational discussions and a progression of training.

The work of Kouzes and Posner (2002a; 2002b) provides another framework for helping students understand their practice of leadership and that of others. In *The Leadership Challenge*, five practices of exemplary leaders are highlighted, including (a) modeling leadership behaviors, (b) inspiring commitment to a vision for the future, (c) encouraging innovation and risk taking, (d) valuing others and empowering them to contribute to a common purpose, and (e) celebrating achievements and recognizing the contributions of team members to achieving collective goals. The Leadership Challenge can be used by residence hall staff to help students understand their strengths while also learning to value the practices of others. This theory presents leadership as a group process where everyone has something to contribute.

Finally, the Leadership Identity Development (LID) Model presents a stage-based model that "has implications for working with individuals as they develop their leadership identity and for facilitating groups as they develop empowering environments for shared leadership" (Komives, Longerbeam, Owen, Mainella, & Osteen, 2006, p. 401). Stage one, Awareness, involves "a beginning recognition that leadership [is] happening 'out there somewhere'" (Komives et al., p. 406). Students tend to see authority figures and national figures as leaders. They transition to stage two as adults recognize their potential. In stage two, Exploration/Engagement, students begin to explore their interests and develop friendships through this involvement. At this point, they develop skills and self-confidence and transition to understanding that they have leadership potential.

In stage three, Leader Identified, students believe that "leadership [is] a position, and therefore, the person in that position [is] the leader" (Komives et al., p. 407). At this stage, students who are followers look to the leader for direction and expect him/her to take action. Komives et al. found that most students in the study entered college with leader-centric views. The transition from stage three to four occurs when students

> [change] the way they [think] about themselves in relation to others. As students [spend] time in stage three, they [begin] to take on more complex leadership challenges that [promote] the recognition that they [can] not do everything themselves and that the talents and skills of group members [are] vital for organizational success. (Komives et al., p. 409)

In stage four, Leadership Differentiated, students begin to see that leadership is positional as well as exhibited by all group members, even if they do not hold a position.

Stage five, Generativity, occurs when students show "an ability to look beyond themselves and express a passion for their commitments and care for the welfare of others" (Komives et al., p. 411). Students are more concerned with the "sustainability of their groups. They [are] particularly interested in teaching and developing younger peers who needed their support, affirmation, and mentoring to develop their leadership capacity" (Komives et al., p. 411). This stage illustrates how resident assistants and older students can serve as mentors and empower first-year students. By stage six, Integration/Synthesis, students have "integrated their view of themselves as effective in working with others and [have] confidence they [can] do that in almost any context" (Komives et al., p. 412). Students see leadership as occurring in all aspects of a group, not just as a positional leader. They see themselves as teachers and learners and recognize that they are continually in a state of self-development and have much to learn from others in the group.

Helping students develop interpersonal competence, expand their self-awareness, and build self-efficacy are the three central ways that residence hall staff can facilitate leadership development as evidenced by the Leadership Identity Development Model (Komives et al., 2006). Creating intentional involvement and leadership opportunities should further first-year students' understanding of themselves and their skills and competencies. Residence halls serve as the perfect place for this learning to occur, and leadership development theory helps inform this learning.

First-Year Leadership and Civic Engagement Opportunities

The benefits of living in a residence hall during a student's first year of college are well documented (Hammond, 1998; Pascarella & Terenzini, 1991; 2005; Winston & Anchors, 1993). These benefits are derived from the nature of the intentionally structured residence hall programs, activities, and communities. Residence life staff, academic staff, and faculty—serving as program and organization advisors, administrators, and educators—research and develop these structured experiences. The environment of the residence halls is also rich with informal involvement and leadership experiences.

Residence halls offer numerous opportunities for first-year students to become involved from serving as a floor representative in hall government to participating in a housing-wide association. Involvement may range from membership or participation to a major leadership position overseeing hundreds of members of an association. Descriptions of common involvement opportunities follow.

Floor/Hall/Area Government

As Cowley (1937) notes, residence hall governments can be traced to the 1920s when Amherst College gave students the opportunity to make decisions and offer recommendations about policies and procedures (as cited in Dunkel & Porter, 1998). Today's first-year students will likely attend a floor meeting within one week of moving into their residence hall. At this meeting, they will introduce themselves to the members of the floor, learn about residence life policies, and receive information on the services and programs available to them. One or two of the students may be identified to serve as the floor representative(s). The floor representative(s) will attend hall government meetings communicating the interests and thoughts of the floor residents to the larger hall-wide community. The floor representative(s) may call meetings of the floor residents, assist paid staff to organize and facilitate floor programs, or recruit other students to participate in hall-wide programming efforts.

The hall government will, in turn, be composed of the floor representatives in addition to the hall government president, vice president, treasurer, and secretary. The hall government will generally receive funds to support hall and floor-level programming, provide equipment and services from a hall government office, and may represent the residence hall to an area government (on large campuses) or residence hall association.

The area government is composed of hall government representatives for neighboring or nearby residence halls. In many cases, students elected to serve on an area government give up their hall-specific positions. The area government will organize programming efforts, fundraising, community service events, and other activities. Given the campus, either the hall government representatives and/or area government representatives will serve in the campus-wide residence hall association.

Involvement in a hall or area government provides students tremendous benefits through the acquisition of skills. These organizations are established to be inclusive, process-oriented, and empowering. Within this type of organization, students will gain skills in listening, building coalitions, learning at individual and team levels, promoting self-leadership, collaboration, giving and receiving feedback, and learning (Komives, Lucas, & McMahon, 1998).

Residence Hall Associations (RHAs)

The Midwest Dormitory Conference, founded in 1954 by Iowa State University, the University of Colorado, the University of Missouri, and the University of Northern Iowa (Dunkel & Schuh, 1998), led to the establishment of the National Association for College and University Residence Halls, Inc. (NACURH). NACURH now represents more than 450 affiliated institutions and their residence hall associations.

Institutionally, the students involved in a residence hall association (RHA) represent the campus residence halls to the housing and campus communities. The RHA is often responsible for "programming, policy formulation, and addressing quality-of-life issues for the residence hall program" (Verry, 1993, p. 47). The RHA generally has individual committees such as budget, programming, movies, fund raising, sustainability, community service, and other initiatives in which students become involved. While some first-year students may choose to become involved in the RHA as an elected hall or area government representative, others may volunteer to serve on one of its many committees.

National Residence Hall Honorary (NRHH)

Following their first term or their first year living in the residence halls, students may apply for election to the National Residence Hall Honorary (NRHH). The NRHH was created by

NACURH, Inc. in 1964 "to provide recognition to residence hall students and leaders" (History of NRHH, n.d.). NRHH activities vary by campus but often include induction ceremonies, annual recognition banquets, leadership retreats, conferences, social events, hall or campuswide programs, and fundraisers.

Leadership Houses

Residence life units have created leadership development living-learning communities for first-year students. These students live in a "leadership house" on a residence hall floor where a sophomore, junior, or senior serves as a mentor to younger residents. The first-year students participating in this type of program receive the benefits of mentorship such as developing an awareness of campus, increased knowledge of resources, community development, and long-term friendships. As first-year students, they have an opportunity to develop their interpersonal and decision-making skills with the possibility of being identified as a mentor the following year.

Departmental Committees

Housing operations develop numerous committees to provide direction, advocacy, feedback, information, and reports to guide decision making and planning. Housing units that maintain a philosophy of student involvement allow students to sit on these various committees. The students may be appointed through the residence hall association, area/hall/floor governance structure, through recommendations from housing staff, or through application processes. The types of committees typically existing in university housing include budget, projects, awards and recognition, staff selection, strategic planning, sustainability, programming, community service, and rules and regulations.

Academic Initiatives

Students living in residence halls are increasingly able to select living in a residential learning community. These learning communities integrate the academic community with the residential environment. Their main purpose is to expand the learning experience for college students beyond the classroom. These communities can be structured using a variety of approaches that are all intended to complete the students' college experiences by providing them with a supportive learning environment, community development programs, educational programs, and stronger relationships with faculty and staff. Within these communities, students have the opportunity to be a part of a seamless living-learning environment surrounding a specific theme or topic. Students in residential learning communities are assigned to the same residence halls; mentored by upper-class peers who also reside in the same location; and are immersed in programs, activities, and may take university courses taught on-site related to the theme of the community. Learning communities may include an honors residential college, international house, career exploration program, first-year student program, academically related program (e.g., fine arts, engineering, language), wellness, or global learning. Students living in these communities often take classes together taught on site in "smart" classrooms; relate to faculty who live, have offices, or teach on site; receive academic advising and tutoring on site; or have modified facilities to support their learning community. These modifications may include a studio or gallery to support a fine arts program; a large food preparation area to support an international house; space for tutors and advisors to support an honors college; or offices to support faculty and staff assigned to the program.

Informal Involvement and Leadership Opportunities

In addition to the leadership experiences already outlined, students may also take on leadership responsibilities such as serving as the intramurals chairperson for the floor, organizing a community service project, presenting a program on an area of expertise, or simply planning outings for fellow residents. Resident assistants should be encouraged to create informal involvement and leadership opportunities in addition to the more formal leadership opportunities that exist in residence life.

Following early involvement in residence hall organizations and activities, many students choose to remain involved in the residence halls while others may choose to augment their residence hall activities with campus and/or community activities or move entirely to involvement outside the residence halls. The groundwork of leadership knowledge, skills, and experience that is built within the residence halls prepares students to take active roles on campus and in the broader community.

The Role of the Advisor and Other Professional Staff

Since the inception of residential governing bodies at Amherst in 1928, the role and purpose of advisors to residence hall associations and area and hall government has continued to evolve (Coleman & Dunkel, 2004). Working with resident students and student leaders involves understanding their organizations, motives, and leadership development. It also requires skills and knowledge beyond general supervisory skills. Advisors play numerous roles working with students and hall governance organizations, such as: (a) mentor (assisting students to understand the one-on-one learning relationship), (b) supervisor (assisting students to understand the concepts of teambuilding, performance, communication, recognition, self-assessment, and evaluation), (c) teacher (assisting students in their success and the success of their communities), (d) leader (assisting students in their leadership development), and (e) follower (assisting students to understand the nature of the leader/follower role) (Dunkel & Schuh, 1998).

Advisors also teach lessons such as group development, meeting management, Robert's Rules of Order, and conflict management. An advisor assumes new roles and responsibilities in working with volunteer student organizations as compared to working with paid staff members or student leaders. The advisor should understand which of these responsibilities is most important and the role he or she should play within the organization. An advisor must also educate students about their roles and the leadership development involved.

Dunkel and Porter (1998) conducted a national study of RHA advisors and found that 92% of RHA advisors were full-time, professional housing staff and 8% were graduate or undergraduate housing staff. Further, they identified the top five most important responsibilities:

1. Meeting regularly with the RHA executive board to clarify questions or provide insight on issues
2. Serving as resource person by providing information to the executive officers as necessary
3. Interpreting institutional policies by providing background information, clarification, or identifying any interpretive mistakes to institutional policy or rules
4. Attending meetings and activities to show support for student efforts and to establish a two-way relationship with officers and members
5. Motivating and encouraging members by recognizing the differences in motives for each individual and the larger organization

These responsibilities should be discussed by the RHA executive officers and advisors immediately following the election of new officers in order to establish expectations. While many first-year students may not serve in RHA executive board positions, it is important for the advisor to assist the executive board in the education of all student members regarding the duties of these roles. The open understanding of each role and its responsibilities is valuable to student members who are considering increased involvement or running for a leadership position. An advisor's role becomes increasingly important as a residence hall organization moves from providing basic programs and services to areas of community service and service-learning as these areas involve additional theoretical and conceptual understanding.

To help prepare advisors for their complex roles, Dunkel and Porter developed the Basic Adviser Recognition and Training (ART) program in 1997. This program identified five core advisor competencies and participants were also required to take a course in each area including advisors as an information resource, student/group development theories and models, recruitment and retention, working with executive boards, and meetings and activities. Participants were also required to take three of the following elective courses: (a) legal issues, (b) how diversity affects RHAs, (c) conferencing, (d) motivation, (e) working with the national communications coordinator, (f) advising NRHH chapters, or (g) bid writing and presenting for awards or conference site hosting. Finally, in order to receive the Basic ART certification, advisors must have advised a residential student organization for at least two years, attended a NACURH-affiliated conference, and attended a NACURH business meeting.

The Basic ART certification program was further enhanced by adding a Master ART program developed by Kevin Linkous and Chad Clark in 2002 (McMahon & Pierce, 2006). This certification program required advisors to complete five additional master core components: (a) providing long-distance advising to state, regional, and national boards; (b) understanding conference advising from bid to completion; (c) teaching ART concepts in staff training; (d) establishing supportive departmental relationships for RHAs; and (e) incorporating ART fundamentals into other advising opportunities. Additionally, the advisors must have completed three years of advising experience post-ART certification, published an article for a regional or national publication, and presented at least two ART programs at regional or national conferences.

Residence life staff should make a commitment to furthering their advisory knowledge and skills to best educate students as leaders in the service of others. The advisor may further encourage student members to seek broader involvement in the campus and community. Some of the principles and opportunities follow.

Building Linkages to Broader Campus and Community Initiatives

Student involvement and engagement in residence halls serves many purposes including individual development, leadership development, and increasing an understanding of one's responsibility to the community. One goal of leadership development is increased civic engagement, which the Pew Charitable Trusts define as:

Individual and collective actions designed to identify and address issues of public concern. Civic engagement can take many forms, from individual voluntarism to organizational involvement to electoral participation. It can include efforts to directly address an issue, work with others in a community to solve a problem or interact with the institutions of representative democracy. Civic engagement encompasses a range of specific activities such as working in a soup kitchen, serving on a neighborhood association, writing a letter to an elected official or voting. (Carpini, n.d.)

Yet, research indicates a decline in civic engagement among entering students. Even though students are participating in individual and group community service projects, they are less likely to participate in local and national governance (e.g., voting). Ehrlich (2000) suggests that "the decline in political participation by young people" highlights the importance of promoting civic responsibility in college. In fact, he argues

> Institutions of higher education should help students to recognize themselves as members of a larger social fabric, to consider social problems to be at least partly their own, to see the civic dimensions of issues, to make and justify informed civic judgments, and to take action when appropriate. (Ehrlich, 2000)

Residence halls can serve as an environment to expose students to community issues while providing training and opportunities for involvement. Community service and service-learning assist in addressing one's responsibility to a broader community while promoting civic engagement. Service is a process and a relationship in which a student works with a community or an individual to identify needs, develop a mutual purpose, and work to affect socially responsible change while empowering others. Residence life staff should ensure meaningful service, intentional reflection, and evaluation.

Residence life advisors can use the Principles of Good Practice for Combining Service and Learning (Honnet & Poulsen, 1989) to create leadership and service opportunities that assist students in their development and increase their social and civic engagement. These principles suggest that an effective service program:

1.   Engages people in responsible and challenging actions for the common good
2.   Provides structured opportunities for people to reflect critically on their service experience
3.   Articulates clear service and learning goals for everyone involved
4.   Allows those with needs to define those needs
5.   Clarifies the responsibilities of each person and organization involved
6.   Matches service providers and service needs through a process that recognizes changing circumstances
7.   Expects genuine, active, and sustained organizational commitment
8.   Includes training, supervision, monitoring, support, recognition, and evaluation to meeting service and learning goals
9.   Ensures that the time commitment for service and learning is flexible, appropriate, and in the best interest of all involved
10. Is committed to program participation by and with diverse populations. (pp. 1-4)

The principles also articulate for students the things to consider in order to best serve all parties, while strengthening their connection to the community.

Community service and service-learning within the residence halls may occur anywhere along a continuum of food and clothing drives to philanthropies to partnerships with local schools and living-learning communities. Involvement opportunities should be created that promote the development of first-year students' leadership and civic engagement, taking into consideration the range of their initial personal development.

Ideally, service can serve as a launching pad for residential students to learn about leadership, community issues, and connect with upperclass students. Good models exist on many campuses and can serve as resources for residence life professionals as they are creating service experiences for their students. However, each program is unique and should be defined by the intended outcomes, the population to be served and their gifts and needs, and the structure that maximizes learning for all parties. At the University of Michigan (2007), they have a K-grams program whose mission is "to establish a strong community of learning for a wide range of college and elementary students, staff, and families by developing positive relationship and experiences that extend beyond the classroom." One component of K-grams is the Pen Pals program that pairs more than 1,000 college students living in traditional residence halls with elementary students for monthly letter exchanges. Participating in K-grams helps college students interact with the broader community, get involved, have fun, and develop a sense of community. Other campuses have residence halls that participate in programs like Special Olympics, Take Back the Night, or mentoring and tutoring at local elementary schools. The opportunities for residence hall students to participate in community service while learning about leadership and civic engagement are endless.

The lessons learned frequently translate back into increased understanding of diversity, sense of community, and responsibility for others. Civic responsibility, along with service, can assist students in their development as public citizens when they are active learners, reflect on their experiences, integrate their values, and act on their responsibilities. Additionally, service can assist students in synthesizing their private and public selves, which is essential for active citizenship. Residence halls serve as the perfect forum to develop civic engagement through leadership development, involvement opportunities, and community service. The role of residence life staff as educators and advisors in this process is tantamount.

Conclusion

The involvement opportunities for students living in a campus residence hall are numerous and varied. The benefits realized from early out-of-class residence hall involvement can open up greater opportunities for civic engagement and leadership. Residence hall staff and student leaders play an integral role in educating students about the types of involvement available to them as well as encouraging early involvement in their residential experience. The students' leadership development, civic and community engagement, and knowledge and skills gained from their involvement will continue well beyond graduation as they become engaged citizens.

References

Carpini, M. D. (n.d.). The Pew Charitable Trusts. Retrieved October 3, 2006, from www.apa.org/ed/slce/civicengagement.html

Coleman, J. K., & Dunkel, N. W. (2004). *50 years of residence hall leadership: NACURH, Inc.* Gainesville, FL: The National Association of College and University Residence Halls.

Dunkel, N. W., & Porter, J. D. (1998). A comparison of residence hall advisor responsibilities. *The Journal of College and University Student Housing, 27*(2), 15-19.

Dunkel, N. W., & Schuh, J. H. (1998). *Advising student groups and organizations.* San Francisco: Jossey-Bass.

Ehrlich, T. (2000). Civic engagement. In *Measuring up 2000: The state-by-state report card for higher education.* Retrieved October 13, 2006, from http://measuringup.highereducation.org/2000/articles/ThomasEhrlich.cfm

Hammond, R. B. (1998). Effects of a first-year experience program on student academics, involvement, and satisfaction (Doctoral Dissertation, Boston College, 1994) *Dissertation Abstracts International, 55*, p. 1483.

Higher Education Research Institute (HERI). (1996). *A social change model of leadership development.* Los Angeles: The Regents of The University of California.

History of NRHH. (n.d.). Retrieved February 14, 2007, from http://www.nrhh.org/history.php?menu=About

Honnet, E. P., & Poulsen, S. J. (Eds.). (1989). Principles of good practice in combining service and learning. *Wingspread Special Report.* Racine, WI: The Johnson Foundation.

Komives, S. R., Longerbeam, S. D., Owen, J. E., Mainella, F. C., & Osteen, L. (2006). A leadership identity development model: Applications for a grounded theory. *Journal of College Student Development, 47*(4), 401-418.

Komives, S. R., Lucas, N., & McMahon, T. R. (1998). *Exploring leadership.* San Francisco: Jossey-Bass.

Kouzes, J. M., & Posner, B. Z. (2002a). *The leadership challenge.* (3rd ed.) San Francisco: Jossey-Bass.

Kouzes, J. M., & Posner, B. Z. (2002b). *The leadership challenge.* Retrieved April 22, 2007, from http://www.leadershipchallenge.com/WileyCDA/Section/id-131055.html

McMahon, J., & Pierce, S. J. (2006). Training advisers. In N. W. Dunkel & C. L. Spencer (Eds.), *Advice for advisers: Empowering your residence hall association* (3rd ed.) (pp. 22-41). Columbus, OH: ACUHO-I.

Pascarella, E. T., & Terenzini, P. T. (1991). *How college affects students.* San Francisco: Jossey-Bass.

Pascarella, E. T., & Terenzini, P. T. (2005). *How college affects students: A third decade of research.* San Francisco: Jossey-Bass.

University of Michigan. (2007). *What is K-grams?* Retrieved September 22, 2007, from http://www.umich.edu/~smile/

Verry, B. (1993). The organizational structures of RHAs. In N. W. Dunkel & C. L. Spencer (Eds.), *Advice for advisers: The development of an effective residence hall association* (pp. 45-53). Columbus, OH: The Association of College & University Housing Officers – International.

Winston, R. B., Jr., & Anchors, S. (1993). Student development in the residential environment. In R. B. Winston, Jr., S. Anchors, & Associates, *Student housing and residential life* (pp. 25-64). San Francisco: Jossey-Bass.

Chapter Nine

Current Staffing Patterns Supporting First-Year Students

Joel Johnson and James Parker

A catalyst for the changes in staffing and residential cocurricular education over the last several years is the evolving, collaborative environment within the divisions of student and academic affairs at many institutions. Prompted by reports such as the *Student Learning Imperative* (ACPA, 1994), *Powerful Partnerships* (AAHE, ACPA, & NASPA, 1998), and most recently *Learning Reconsidered* (Keeling, 2004), these collaborations have generated new educational outcomes designed to improve the undergraduate experience and have had a significant impact on the staffing and organizational structures of higher education, especially in residence life units.

No longer is the primary role of staff to manage behavior, or to focus on health and wellness and social connections. Schroeder (1996) wondered what role residence life should play within an institution newly focused on student learning and on creating seamless learning environments. Similar questions have driven campus administrators and residential life staff to examine how to balance the traditional first-year student staff roles of community building, crisis management, and social integration, with the newer responsibilities supporting learning outcomes within living-learning programs. Thus, this chapter examines the transition from older staffing models to ones poised to address these new demands. Secondly, we explore how new staffing models impact budgeting, recruitment, selection, training, and assessment. The chapter also examines the collaborative creation and joint supervision of many positions between student and academic affairs. We conclude with a review of best practices, specifically examining how campuses are using staff members programmatically to positively impact the student experience in the first year. Included is an overview of a variety of intentional initiatives that use peer mentors, faculty, academic support staff, and technology staff to enhance the residential cocurricular experience.

Historical Overview of Residential Staffing

Although the roots of living-learning models can be traced as far back as the Athenian academies, the earliest American campuses developed collegiate and residential programs that emulated the English Oxford-Cambridge models. This model is grounded in the philosophy that the university is responsible for developing the whole individual including their moral character, as well as their intellectual development (Brubacher & Rudy, 1968). Within this model, the role of faculty was an important component of the student experience as faculty engaged students in every aspect of their lives—not just teaching them but also living within the residential community.

American higher education in the years after the Civil War and during the early part of the 20th century, however, began the first major shift that impacted the residential experience. During this time the land grant movement, the rise of the American research university, and the influence of the German higher education system shaped the direction and purpose of American higher education. Such changes resulted in a move away from faculty oversight of student life and in the elimination of student residences on campus. Campuses that retained student residences filled the faculty oversight void by hiring nonacademic staff to manage the residence halls. Housemothers were commonly employed and "provided a control factor, a parental factor, and a social graces factor." As such, "these women were key staff members in the institution's implementation of in loco parentis" (Frederiksen, 1993, p. 175). Between the end of World War II and the mid-1970s, the demand for on-campus housing and a changing student body, led to housing shortages and the end of in loco parentis. This same period saw the professionalization of the housing field and development of paraprofessional positions.

With the increase in the number of students on college campuses after World War II, most institutions focused on creating residential units designed to house large numbers of students rather than focusing on creating living environments that took educational or personal development into account, such as residential colleges. Creating larger living facilities meant developing a new management approach to these residential environments. In order to be cost effective and to best meet the overall needs of the students and the university, most universities hired large-scale paraprofessional staffs to help manage the residential experience. Most of these positions were "... referred to as 'counselors' or 'advisors' and would eventually come to be known by the title 'resident assistant'" (Miltenberger, 1996, p. 68). Most campuses began to hire graduate students or professional staff who provided supervision to the paraprofessional staff. These resident director positions provided a cost-effective approach to managing residence hall services, which included advising student government, adjudicating violations of the conduct code, responding to emergencies, and supervising resident assistants or resident counselors. Responsibilities of paraprofessional staff typically included programming, developing community, responding to emergencies, documenting behavior violations, and responding to first-year adjustment issues such as mediating roommate conflicts.

Beginning in the mid-1980s, higher education leaders engaged in an ongoing conversation about the quality of undergraduate education, particularly the experience of first-year students. These national conversations, along with increased calls for accountability and the development of new initiatives (e.g., living-learning programs and learning communities), several reports emerging from these conversations have highlighted the role of student affairs, and in particular the role of residential life, in improving the undergraduate experience and student learning. For example, Powerful Partnerships noted that "Much learning takes place informally and incidentally, beyond explicit teaching or the classroom in casual contacts with faculty and staff, peers, campus life, active social and community involvements, and unplanned but fertile and complex situations" (AAHE et al., 1998). With a growing understanding of the types of environments likely to encourage and support student learning, residential life began to take leadership or become a key partner in creating new learning environments. Residence life units were also actively involved in reevaluating and improving current practice. Such efforts changed the staffing landscape of residential life programs dramatically. No longer was the resident director and resident assistant model the primary—or ideal—staffing pattern for meeting institutional and student needs.

Current Trends Driving Staffing Models

While the majority of residential campuses today maintain the traditional resident director-resident assistant model of staffing, the focus on student learning in student affairs work has required many residential life programs to redesign current or create new staffing patterns. These new positions vary in their scope and responsibility from academic, technological, and multicultural to other specialized emphases (e.g., environmental education). While national trends impact staffing patterns, a host of campus characteristics such as size, institutional mission, student body demographics, and campus funding also shape the development of staffing and program advancements. Below, we provide a brief list of current national trends driving the development or restructuring of staff positions to support the first-year residential student.

Student Learning Focus

Perhaps no trend has made a bigger impact on first-year staffing across the country than the student learning movement. Programs focused on student learning such as learning communities, special interest housing, theme houses, or residential colleges are rapidly increasing. Many of these programs began as collaborative efforts between student and academic affairs, with residential life as a partner; others started as grassroots efforts created solely by residential life staff. The assessment of living-learning programs illustrates the success of these programs in contributing to the enhancement of the first-year student experience. For example, students who lived in academically thematic learning communities were proven to have higher levels of achievement, more interactions with faculty and peers, and informal academically oriented interactions more often than students not living in a learning community (Blimling, 1993 as cited in Li, McCoy, Shelley, & Whalen, 2005; Terenzini, Pascarella, & Blimling, 1996 as cited in Li et al.). Further, it has been noted that students in residential learning communities have a significantly higher level of involvement and interaction than do students living in traditional residence facilities (Pike, Schroeder, & Berry, 1997 as cited in Li et al.). The success and impact of such initiatives have pressed many institutions and housing administrators to re-consider their current staffing patterns in order to help create these intentional and intellectually rewarding environments.

Student Expectations and Needs

A unique challenge for residential life programs is responding to today's students and their parents' expectations. While the core needs of students have not changed much in terms of wanting to fit in and do well academically, the expectation of how students achieve this (and how campuses will support them in doing so) is very different today. Student and parental expectations for residential amenities, such as recreational spaces, on-demand services, and larger, private living spaces often outweigh the desire or expectation for a residential environment that provides an intellectually enriching experience (Miller, Bender, Schuh, & Associates, 2005). The competing challenges of trying to create staffing positions to support a seamless campus learning environment versus trying to meet the expectations of students and their parents for a residential community by providing the best amenities often forces residential life programs to make choices that would keep them financially competitive rather than creating an environment that enriches the academic experience.

Psychological and Personal Needs

Another trend that impacts staffing patterns is the increased frequency of mental illness among current students. In studying mental health demands on staff, Archer and Cooper (1998) found that:

> Compared with students in the past, today's students arrive on campus with more problems as a result of dysfunctional family situations, with more worries and anxieties about the future and about the serious problems facing them in modern society, with an increased awareness of their own personal demons, and with a great willingness to seek psychological and psychiatric help. (as cited in Crissman Ishler, 2005, p. 23)

The complexity of these situations and the time they demand place additional burdens on professional and student staff traditional resident director and resident assistant roles. Moreover, balancing the increasing mental health and crisis demands and additional responsibilities for new academic and student success initiatives has created a dilemma for housing administrations in regard to staffing infrastructures.

Technological Impacts on Staffing

Student experiences with technology are increasing their expectations about the service and support available in campus residences and the speed with which services will be delivered. Technology also has implications for student learning and engagement that did not exist in previous years. This situation is complicated, according to Junco (2005), by the fact that "many professionals who work with first-year students are unaware of the many ways those students are using technology that may enhance or detract from their academic and psychosocial development" (p. 223). Thus, residence life departments find themselves trying to balance administrative technology needs with student needs while trying to keep up with technological advances. As IT needs grow, many departments have either added duties to existing positions or created new positions to address IT issues. In addition, some have turned student technology over to paraprofessional staff to help with cost savings, but also as a recognition that students are often the best resources of the campus IT infrastructure.

Current Trends in First-Year Residence Hall Staffing

The result of student affairs, in particular residence life, trying to integrate students' curricular and cocurricular experiences and improve the first-year experience has been the development of new specialized positions, both professional and paraprofessional, and the restructuring of current positions within existing housing programs to create a more seamless and intentional learning environment. These positions are described in detail below.

Assistant Directors of Academic Initiatives

One of the new positions created within campus communities to meet the challenge of managing the large numbers of living-learning programs on campuses are mid- to senior-level management positions, whose main or collaborative responsibility is overseeing a department's living-learning efforts. These positions are typically charged both with the daily coordination and logistics of such programs, combined with the development and maintenance of relationships with faculty and administrators involved with the academic components of these programs. At Minnesota State University, Mankato, the assistant director for academic initiatives is responsible for the design and implementation of the First-Year and Sophomore Learning Communities. The goal of the program is to foster first-year student and faculty interaction and provide more integrated learning experiences for first-year students resulting in increased student satisfaction and retention. The position trains and supervises student paraprofessional and graduate staff involved in the program and provides leadership in the development and marketing of each learning community.

Qualifications for such positions often require a master's degree, and many prefer or require a doctorate due to the level of interaction with faculty and academic administrators. These positions call for previous full-time experience in developing and managing living-learning programs, and in-depth experiences working with and understanding faculty and academic administration. Often, these positions are responsible for and must be skilled in assessment and communicating assessment data to a diverse campus community in order to build support for programs, get budgetary collaboration with academics, and educate faculty on the importance of faculty-student interaction. Examples of such positions can be found at Iowa State University, Syracuse University, and the University of Florida.

Living-Learning Program Directors

These positions are often live-in staff members whose buildings host the first-year program, a student affairs affiliated program coordinator, or a faculty member. Depending on the staff member, there are a host of issues to balance in terms of the skill sets needed to manage the program and the demands of other responsibilities.

Because their backgrounds may vary, the directors of living-learning programs may face a significant learning curve as they enter these positions. Faculty directors often face issues related to student life and the cocurriculum for the first time in their careers and may struggle with the scope and magnitude of these responsibilities. Student affairs directors may face academic-support issues for the first time, which take them beyond the realm of their professional training and background. These struggles can frequently detract from the new director's effectiveness and keep him or her from reaching their full potential.

These positions are being filled from a wide-spectrum of professional backgrounds depending on the type of program and the particular needs of the campus. Each of these professionals brings unique strengths to the position, with none being fully prepared to manage all the living-learning program components. Whoever serves as director of these programs has to manage the balance between the curriculum of the program while creating an effective out-of-classroom experience for participants. These positions often need staff who are able to

◇ Balance the need for understanding academic and student affairs cultures
◇ Understand teaching and learning theory, student development theory, as well as program development
◇ Collaborate effectively
◇ Be an advocate for students while articulating institutional and academic goals effectively

Discipline-focused living-learning programs require staff to have a clear understanding of advising, program requirements, and the discipline's primary subject matter. The ability to create a program that enhances the classroom experience while providing the frontloaded services and resources for students to be successful in their community are also key to the director's success.

These positions may be titled in different ways depending on the program and the institution. Examples include:

◇ Coordinator of student development at Cal Poly San Luis Obispo
◇ Program coordinator for the Weston Exploration Program at the University of Illinois-Urbana-Champaign
◇ Faculty director of the Civicus Living-Learning Program at the University of Maryland-College Park

Exceptions to this model exist where there is a highly integrated and collaborative approach to these academic initiatives. Campus programs such as Ball State University's Freshman Connections have developed a team approach to managing their living-learning programs that includes faculty, residence life, students, and academic advisors. Not only does this ensure that everyone plays a role in the program, it also allows for the sharing of roles and collaboration needed to make it a success.

Learning Specialists

To meet these new staffing patterns, Zeller (1999) proposes the creation of a learning specialist who would "bring together expertise in the best of the academic affairs and student affairs fields, with a special focus on learning theory and its applications on a college or university campus" (p. 32). This specialist would need knowledge of student development and learning theories, have the ability to work within and understand the nature and unique facets of differing academic fields and to develop educationally purposeful and effective learning environments, and possess the administrative leadership skills necessary to manage the aspects of an expansive campus program (Zeller). If academic living-learning initiatives continue their exponential growth on campuses more and more departments will find themselves needing to evaluate, develop, and hire staff to fulfill this newly emerging position.

Faculty-in-Residence Positions

With decades of research showing the powerful impact of faculty-student interaction, it is not surprising that so many academic living-learning programs have interaction with faculty outside of the classroom as a main outcome for their programs. Since the 1960s, there has been a resurgence of the residential college or faculty-in-residence model. These programs include models that are degree-granting like Michigan State's James Madison College. Other residential colleges are interdisciplinary or communally based such as Rice or Yale University's long-running programs.

While residential colleges have historically been sponsored by academic affairs and administered by faculty, a large number of institutions have created programs where faculty live in and support individual living-learning programs or provide interdisciplinary academic support. These programs are often defined by a shared sponsorship where specific responsibilities are typically divided between student affairs professionals and faculty or academic personnel who live in the community. Recently, Kuh, Kinzie, Schuh, and Whitt (2005) found that institutions with effective educational practices have a "high degree of respect and collaboration... so faculty, academic administrators, and student affairs staff work together effectively. Cocurricular programs are designed to complement not compete with or undercut, student achievement" (pp. 164-165). This ethos of approaching the student's learning and cocurricular experience from a holistic, university-wide perspective is becoming a more common and effective way to respond to managing a curricular and cocurricular program successfully. Examples of successful residential college or faculty-in-residence programs are those at Cornell University, Truman State University, and San Diego State University.

Peer Positions in First-Year Living-Learning Programs

The staffing changes occurring from the development of first-year focused living-learning programs have not only affected professional staffing but have also impacted and created a whole new paraprofessional staffing pattern to support first-year students and these programs. While a great number of living-learning programs are still staffed by the traditional resident assistant role, some campuses have begun to develop specific paraprofessional positions designed to help facilitate and manage living-learning programs, using upperclass students to create a supportive environment for first-year students. Staff in these positions "are, selected, trained, and supervised to assist in peer personal and academic development while attending to environmental aspects of the living area" (Benjamin, 2007, p. 32). In particular, these staff provide a low-cost approach to managing living-learning programs by offering social and educational programming, tutoring, and discipline or major-specific mentoring. In programs that are connected to or lead by a specific college or major, upperclass students are used to helping provide an early peer network for transition to the major's culture, expectations, and common experiences. These new paraprofessional roles have titles such as learning community coordinator or upperclass mentor.

"Peer mentor job responsibilities may include such assignments as facilitating study groups, coordinating social and community building activities, and completing administrative paperwork, but as a paraprofessional staff, their primary responsibility is focused on students' development" (Benjamin, 2007, p. 32). They are usually selected based on their academic major and previous leadership experience. The skill set for these students is usually very different from that of the traditional resident assistant. Some of the skills these students need to exhibit or acquire include

◇ More in-depth understanding of the academic experience
◇ Excellence in their academic performance
◇ Excellent academic skills in terms of time management and study skills
◇ Good communication or presentation skills to help co-teach a first-year seminar or other course related to a living-learning program
◇ A strong sense of diplomacy to interact with faculty, administrators, and students

Examples of these positions can be found at Iowa State University, which features learning community peer mentors for both residential and non-residential first-year learning communities programs; The University of Missouri-Columbia; and Minnesota State University, Mankato.

Positions designed to promote first-year retention and student support. The last 20 years have seen a major shift in residential life's staffing to focus on supporting the first-year student's academic success and promoting retention. Residence life's focus is no longer exclusively about providing an auxiliary service and managing student behavior and social programming. Rather, residential life programs have begun to create positions or opportunities to collaborate with campus offices to provide academic support opportunities in the residence halls.

While many residential life programs have included responsibilities for tutoring and academic support, in the resident assistant's job description, campuses are beginning to create specific peer positions designed to help in the academic transition of first-year students. These positions provide a cost-effective approach to providing services like peer tutoring, writing support, in-hall library services, and first-year curricular initiatives such as a peer instructor in first-year courses.

The peer mentor role has historically been filled by the resident assistant within the traditional campus housing model, but with years of studies showing the powerful impact of peers, new, more specialized roles have emerged to support the first-year student. The responsibilities or skill sets related to these academic support positions require a deeper proficiency around teaching, presentation, small group management, study skills, and the ability to convey and help first-year students understand the academic expectations of their campus. Some examples of residential life positions that have been created to support academic success and promote retention are The University of Michigan's academic peer advisor, The University of Kansas' Academic Resource Center assistant; The University of Maryland-College Park's Math Success Program staff; and Minnesota State University, Mankato's learning community coordinators. On other campuses, peer tutors serve the entire first-year population but are closely aligned to residential life. Programs of this type include California State University, Monterrey Bay's Academic Skills Achievement Program; Chapman University's Center for Academic Success; and St. Lawrence University's Academic Achievement Office.

A major collaboration to support first-year retention on campuses is between first-year experience offices and residential life. Often, because so many first-year students live on campus, these two departments are found working together to bring support services and programs to the first-year student. Examples of such student staffing positions that support first-year programs include orientation peer assistants, admissions tour guides, peer tutors, community advisors, learning community or academic success coordinators, with many working directly on residence hall floors.

Positions designed to support technology. Over the last two decades, the growth of technology has impacted every facet of the college campus. Today's students are savvy and knowledgeable users of technology and have elevated expectations and needs for technology services. This is not just a consumer mentality; today's students are fundamentally different from previous generations. Prensky (2001) notes that

> Today's students—K through college—represent the first generations to grow up with this new technology. They have spent their entire lives surrounded by and using computers, videogames, digital music players, video cams, cell phones, and all the other toys and tools of the digital age. Today's average college grads have spent less than 5,000 hours of their lives reading, but over 10,000 hours playing video games (not to mention 20,000 hours watching TV). Computer games, email, the Internet, cell phones and instant messaging are integral parts of their lives. (p. 3)

The demand for technological amenities has created a new staffing structure to support student expectations. Most residential life programs have created information technology (IT) units to provide support for Ethernet and other technology services to students.

The challenge of having professional IT staff who work during the day responding to residential life staff needs and the needs of students who are using their computers late into the evening has prompted the creation of a cost-effective and convenient paraprofessional position. These staff members commonly live with and are available to students during evening hours. When the first-year halls open, student IT staff help students get connected to the university Internet infrastructure and respond to questions. Similar positions on campuses also have responsibility for providing programs ranging from using the Web for research to ethical decision making related to illegal downloading. Because today's students have grown up with and understand the latest and most current technology, residential life programs often find that peers are the most logical and effective option in educating and serving the first-year student. Examples of residential technology positions can be found at The University of Michigan, Eastern Michigan University, Longwood University, and Bowling Green State University.

As technology continues to progress at an ever-changing pace and the nature of student learning changes, residential life will be continually challenged to provide the amenities and staff to meet the technology needs of tomorrow's first-year student.

Positions designed to support adjustment needs. There are a number of examples of different peer mentor roles developed to assist and support first-year student adjustment issues. They include health aides and diversity peer mentors. Each of these new positions fall under a much more holistic label of peer mentor.

Student health is an ever-challenging matter for campuses, with many first-year students never having responsibility for their own health care. Increased alcohol use, lack of sleep, poor eating habits, and a host of stresses lead to potential health problems for first-year students. Campuses are always looking for ways to support the health education needs of students. Whether through the campus health center or in information from their RAs, institutions provide resources for healthy living as well as services to respond to students' health needs. An example of an approach by one university to help with these efforts is the peer health aide position at the University of Nebraska-Lincoln. Developed in response to an Asian flu epidemic in 1957, approximately 100 students are trained to provide assistance with minor illnesses and injuries each year. Health aides also provide health-related information and "assist with campus projects such as the Campus Blood Drive, Great American Smoke Out, health fairs, and screenings" (University of Nebraska-Lincoln, 2007).

The health aides live on residence hall floors and partner with the traditional residential assistant position in providing a unique service to students. Qualifications and training for this position offer students with experiences in health fields or majoring within community health or pre-med a service opportunity linked to their major or prior experiences. As campuses discuss the impacts of health and wellness and its relation to student success and retention, roles such as this are positive options to explore.

Another position that is finding a common place on campuses is the role of the underrepresented student or multicultural peer mentor. As institutions continually re-evaluate services designed to assist underrepresented students and their successful matriculation and retention, the role of peer mentorship and the programmatic impact such positions can make are becoming realized. Using the traditional qualifications and training of peer mentors, combined with specialized diversity training, these new roles can offer effective program delivery to diverse students on today's college campuses.

These peer mentors help underrepresented students make the academic and social transition to college. They also provide one-on-one support, help advise groups such as the residential black caucuses, plan programs, work with resident assistants in ensuring that the floor environment is inclusive, and help the residential life staff stay aware of issues in the halls related to multi-ethnic concerns. The peer mentor position may be designed to address the specific needs of African American, Native American, Asian and Pacific Islanders, and Hispanic/Latino students, women, or LGBT students. Positions such as these provide valuable support to underrepresented first-year students in their transition to the campus environment and will become increasingly important as more first-generation and underrepresented students enroll in college.

Recruitment and Training Considerations for New Staffing Models

With the development of new staffing positions comes the challenge associated with recruiting and training individuals for these new roles. As departments diversify their staffing models and some begin to hire staff without degrees in higher education or particular skill sets necessary for working with living-learning, first-year, or academic support programs, training will become a more critical factor in establishing a skilled staff.

Positions that focus on academic support should have advanced training in understanding university academic requirements and academic culture, successful study strategies, good communication and presentation skills, and good mentoring/advising skills. An excellent resource to train students who will serve in a peer mentor capacity is, Ender and Newton's (2000) *Students Helping Students: A Guide for Peer Educators on College Campuses*, which covers topics such as intercultural competence, communication skills, helping skills, leading groups effectively, strategies for academic success, and ethics.

One last training issue to consider when working with paraprofessionals is to look for opportunities for teambuilding between traditional resident assistants and other peer mentors. Because their roles intersect so often it is important that there is a positive working relationship between these staff positions.

Professional staff have an entirely different set of skills that are needed to be successful in their work with first-year student success. Training considerations for new or revamped professionals include:

◇ New professional staff who have a great deal of interaction with faculty and academic affairs administrators need training on understanding academic or faculty culture, diplomacy, compromise, and understanding institutional and departmental goals when dealing with units outside of the department. Involving academic units in training efforts for these staff members can be particularly effective.

◇ A critical challenge for residential life programs is the great diversity of staff in terms of education, training, and departmental responsibilities. As a result, training will need to be more comprehensive. Further, training will need both group and individual components to ensure that all aspects of training are covered effectively.

◇ As departments hire staff for new roles focused on living-learning programs or other academic collaborations, they may want to consider opening their search to individuals who have academic backgrounds and experience outside student affairs. Departments might find excellent candidates who lack a degree in higher education, but have the skills, knowledge, experiences, and academic connections for positions designed to enhance students' cocurricular learning experience. However, as departments move in this direction, they need to recognize the training needs of these staff members. Departments may have to add training topics, such as student development theory, program development, and higher education culture that have been taken for granted by a history of hiring staff with experience and degrees in student affairs.

As residential life programs develop and implement programs and services to support the first-year experience new staffing patterns will play a crucial component. Departments will have to put as much time and energy in recruiting and training as they do in developing these positions.

Recommendations

The following are recommendations for consideration by housing administrators in developing staffing patterns to meet the needs of first-year students.

◇ *Do not forget the history of the field.* Positions such as resident assistants and hall directors continue to be relevant in managing crises, a campus community's standards of behavior, and the social networking needs of first-year students.

◇ *Residence hall staff must be aware of the educational role they play with regard to the academic mission of the institution.* Clear learning outcomes must be established for residential life programs, combined with adequate assessment to illustrate achieved results in meeting the needs of first-year students.

◇ *Avoid the continual addition of new responsibilities to existing positions.* As the demands of new initiatives like living-learning programs grow in size and complexity, new tasks may be added to existing positions. Too often, the end result is overloaded staff, morale concerns, burn out, and shrinking candidate pools for both professional and paraprofessional positions. Program directors/staff will need to find creative and collaborative ways to redefine existing roles and create new ones to meet changing program needs.

◇ *Strategic planning based on sound internal program reviews and assessment data cannot be overemphasized.* It is important that each department and institution make a point to reflect on its role in supporting the first-year student. In their book, *Improving Staffing Practices in Student Affairs*, Winston and Creamer (1997) found that "organizations must have a clear sense of purpose and understand how each position contributes to the accomplishment of that purpose and of other assigned responsibilities if they are to make the right decisions about new personnel" (p.143). The end result will be positions that are appealing for candidates but also strive to meet the institutional goals of supporting the first-year student.

◇ *Recognize the importance of assessment.* Building institutional support for new or revamped staff roles and marketing residential life's impact on the first-year student experience is critical in a fiscally challenging climate. Assessment will be required to illustrate achievement in first-year student success as administrators, students, and society increasingly demand to see that outcomes are being met. It will be critical for departments to either hire specific staff responsible for or provide effective training in assessment to current staff so that departments and programs can maintain or develop new levels of staffing.

◇ *Develop a strategic recruitment and training program that supports the needs of new staffing structures.* The variety of new staff positions along with the traditional resident director and resident assistant roles will challenge departments to diversify their approaches to recruiting and training the staff for these new roles.

    ◇ When recruiting for positions that work with an academically focused program, it is important to think about recruiting in nontraditional venues, such as academic conferences, discipline-focused journals, career fairs related to certain fields of studies, and any other venue that might attract individuals who might have degrees or interest in the academic field of study of the first-year program.

    ◇ In terms of paraprofessional staff recruitment, collaborate with schools or departments that sponsor disciplined-focused housing to hire students who major in the programs focus area.

    ◇ Recruit paraprofessional staff through student organizations that are discipline-focused such as the business club, the biology club, or an ecology club.

Conclusion

Staffing first-year residential life programs is indeed a challenging but rewarding opportunity for student affairs practitioners. The residential life experience is one of the most powerful resources to help address the needs of today's first-year students. While there are exemplary programs and staffing across the country, it is essential that the specific institution's traditions, culture, and goals are a foundation for creating any new program or staffing model. The next decade in higher education and first-year housing programs appears to be as challenging and transformational as the last three decades. One of the greatest tools in helping to meet those challenges is a sound and effective staffing infrastructure.

References

American Association for Higher Education (AAHE), American College Personnel Association (ACPA), & National Association of Student Personnel Administrators (NASPA). (1998). *Powerful partnerships: A shared responsibility for learning.* Washington, DC: Authors.

American College Personnel Association (ACPA). (1994). *The student learning imperative.* Washington, DC: Author.

Benjamin, M. (2007). Role construction of residential learning community peer mentors. *Journal of College and University Student Housing, 34,* 31-42.

Brubacher, J. S., & Rudy, W. (1968). *Higher education in transition: An American history: 1636-1956.* New York: HarperCollins.

Crissman Ishler, J. (2005). Today's first-year students. In M. L. Upcraft, J. N. Gardner, & B. O. Barefoot (Eds.), *Challenging and supporting the first year student, a handbook for improving the first year of college* (pp. 15-26). San Francisco: Jossey-Bass.

Ender, S. C., & Newton, F. B. (2000). *Students helping students: A guide for peer educators on college campuses.* San Francisco: Jossey-Bass.

Frederiksen, C. F. (1993). A brief history of collegiate housing. In R. B. Winston, Jr., & S. Anchors. (Eds.), *Student housing and residential life* (pp. 167-183). San Francisco: Jossey-Bass.

Junco, R. (2005). Technology and today's first-year students. In M. L. Upcraft, J. N. Gardner, & B. O. Barefoot (Eds.), *Challenging and supporting the first-year student: A handbook for improving the first year of college* (pp. 221-238). San Francisco: Jossey-Bass.

Keeling, R. (Ed.). (2004). *Learning reconsidered: A campus-wide focus on the student experience.* Washington, DC: National Association of Student Personnel Administrators & the American College Personnel Association.

Kuh, G. D., Kinzie, J., Schuh, J. H., & Whitt, E. J. (2005). *Student success in college.* San Francisco: Jossey-Bass.

Li, Y., McCoy, E., Shelley, M. C., & Whalen, D. F. (2005). Contributors to student satisfaction with special program (fresh start) residence halls. *Journal of College Student Development, 46*(2), 176-192.

Miller, T. E., Bender, B. E., Schuh J. H., & Associates. (2005). *Promoting reasonable expectations.* San Francisco: Jossey-Bass.

Miltenberger, L. J. (1996). Paraprofessional staff and the first year experience. In W. J. Zeller, D. S. Fidler, & B. O. Barefoot (Eds.), *Residence life programs and the first-year experience* (pp. 67-74) (Monograph, No. 5, 2nd ed.). Columbia, SC: University of South Carolina, National Resource Center for The Freshman Year Experience and Students in Transition.

Prensky, M. (2001). Digital natives, digital immigrants. *On the Horizon, 9*(5), 1-6.

Schroeder, C. C. (1996). Focus on student learning: an imperative for student affairs. *Journal of College Student Development, 37*(2), 115-117.

University of Nebraska-Lincoln. (2007). *Health aide program.* Retrieved April 19, 2007, from http://www.unl.edu/health/students/education/healthaide/

Winston, R. B., & Creamer, D. G. (1997). *Improving staffing practices in student affairs.* San Francisco: Jossey-Bass.

Zeller, W. J. (1999). The learning specialist. *About Campus, 4*(4), 31-32.

Chapter Ten

Residence Hall Architectural Design and the First-Year Experience

Bradford L. Angelini

Architecturally, the residence hall is becoming one of the most complex buildings on campus. Students arrive on campus having very high expectations for their living environments. Campus administrators are looking to the residence hall to supplement students' changing academic needs. And top ranked universities are using new and better-equipped residence halls as recruiting tools to attract the best students. Advances in computer and communication technology have changed the way students access and share information, which requires new types of spaces on campus. Campus dining halls are also changing, as they become the centerpiece of living-learning neighborhoods and the community-gathering place for students in adjacent residence halls.

As institutions come to recognize the important role student housing plays in recruitment, retention, and successful transitions of their students, amenities and spaces for "front-loaded" academic support services (i.e., academic advising, tutoring, group study, classrooms, and faculty offices) are being included in facilities designed for new students. These spaces facilitate new student academic success and the academic mission of the university by providing an informal, student-friendly environment, designed to support new approaches to teaching and learning. The purpose of this chapter is to identify the housing needs of the incoming first-year students, describe some of the challenges that housing administrators face, and offer some examples of how colleges and universities are working to create an environment for the successful transition from high school to college.

Housing Millennial Students

In *Millennials Rising*, Howe and Strauss (2000) note that 70% of high school graduates born between 1982 and 2002 will plan to continue their education in some form after high school. As a group, Millennials are defined by seven traits: (a) a sense of their own specialness, (b) a sheltered upbringing, (c) confidence, (d) team-orientation, (e) values that are more conventional than their parents, (f) a heightened sense of pressure, and (g) a desire for achievement. These youths are also confident and optimistic, team- and rule-oriented, and very hardworking (Howe & Strauss, 2003). These students are changing the programmatic and physical makeup of college residences by requiring more community space designed for team and active learning, multiple use flexibility, and increased privacy in residence rooms.

These new college students also mirror the population of the United States in that they are increasingly non-White and non-middle class. The decade since 1993 saw college enrollments grow by 15% to 16.6 million from 14.4 million, with minority students now making up nearly 30% of the total undergraduate population (SCUP, 2007). Minority students may also be less prepared for the rigors of college-level academics due to their lack of exposure to a college preparatory curriculum. As such, today's students are arriving on campus with different learning needs and are requiring different types of learning spaces. These alternate learning spaces will look different than the traditional classrooms and will include areas for small-group discussions, places where podcast lectures can be viewed, and spaces where students can study and research in teams. Spaces to support the academic demands of today's diverse students are being included in the planning and design of new residence halls.

Considerations Driving Residence Hall Design

Learning Outcomes

An important consideration in planning new construction or renovation projects is defining the learning and developmental outcomes that a residence hall should support. The architect can then suggest the amount of space, room proportions, and organization needed to facilitate the social and educational goals of the residence hall or residential community. For example, if the outcome is to increase student-faculty interaction, the design solution will provide spaces within the residential community either in the residence hall or in an adjacent area where faculty and students will feel comfortable meeting. This can be a study lounge, a coffee shop, or space on the ground floor of the residence hall separate from living areas and with easy exterior access. Increasing faculty and student interaction also has implications for site planning and building location on campus. For example, the hall should be easily accessible to the academic core of campus so that a faculty member does not have to travel far from his or her office or lab. Housing located away from the center of campus, even with appropriate public spaces and transportation, will be less likely to encourage student-faculty interaction.

Technology

If there is one word that sums up today's generation, it is "connected." Students maintain constant contact with friends and family through cell phones, instant messaging, and social networking sites. Yet, college housing administrators are concerned about the loss of community and the loss of a sense of place with all of this "screen" technology (Kenny, Dumont, & Kenny, 2005). As students rely more on technology to communicate, socialize, research, and attend class, administrators are strategizing ways to increase the student-to-student and student-to-faculty contact that researchers such as Astin (1993) suggests is necessary for academic success. While not entirely unfounded, such concerns may reflect a failure to understand the power of technology to keep this generation of students connected. Moreover, students are not necessarily sacrificing face time to stay connected electronically. A casual observation of food courts and coffee shops on campus show that students are gathering and interacting—often around the computer screen. As such, college campuses need to provide the types of spaces where students can work together with the aid of the computer and monitors large enough for multiple viewers. These spaces can be available in residence halls or in a community center that is part of a living-learning neighborhood.

For example, the ability to view a lecture on a video screen the size of your palm or on a large screen television has changed the way information is delivered to students from the impersonal lecture hall of 250 or more students to a personal setting or place and time, to be determined by the student. A study group can gather around a video screen in a residence hall study area and watch the lecture. The students can pause the lecture to discuss points among themselves or e-mail questions to the professor. This small community learning experience encourages teamwork, dialogue, and provides a forum for even the shyest of students to communicate with the professor.

Support Spaces Within the Residence Hall

The shift toward a greater academic role by the departments of residence life has created a greater emphasis on and required more public space in residence halls. A significant portion of the ground floor of new and renovated residence halls is now dominated by classrooms, computer rooms, faculty offices, student organization meeting spaces, seminar rooms, and multi-purpose gathering spaces. The ground floor of these residence halls can be used by the campus community for classes, services such as counseling and tutoring, and dining facilities. The upper, more private residence floors are also expanding their community spaces with a mix of small- and medium-sized meeting spaces and hallways that are irregular with open spaces and exterior views, for impromptu student gatherings.

A good example of this is the new Honors Hall at the University of South Carolina, where the ground floor includes study lounges and multi-purpose rooms, a game room, a dining center, administrative offices, the residence director's apartment, and a residential wing (Figure 10.1). The corridor shift on upper floors creates distinct living areas for 12 to 14 students (Figure 10.2). Student lounges are open to the corridors to shorten them and bring natural light into typically dark hallways. The upper residence floors have 12 lounges varying in size and shape to accommodate community needs.

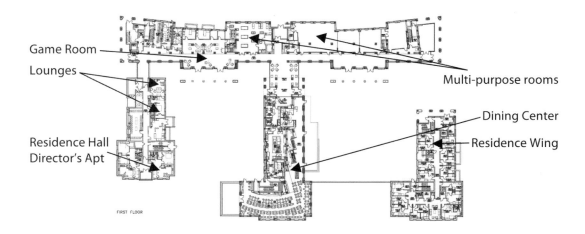

Figure 10.1. Honors Hall, University of South Carolina. By Garvin Design Group in Columbia, South Carolina.

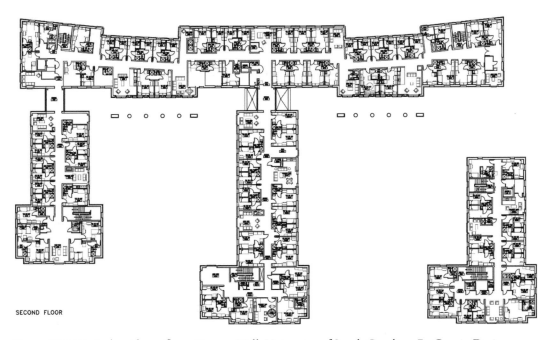

SECOND FLOOR

Figure 10.2. Typical residence floor, Honors Hall, University of South Carolina. By Garvin Design Group in Columbia, South Carolina

Another important concept that affects the types of learning spaces required is the shift to student- or learning-centered pedagogies, which changes the size, number, arrangement, and mix of classroom types needed on campus (Kenny et al., 2005). For example, academic units increasingly need classrooms for small-group activities and interactive seminars. Residence halls designed for living-learning programs can provide alternative classroom space in a student-friendly environment. Further, residence life departments can support the academic mission of the university by forming partnerships with academic departments and providing spaces for initiatives that use innovative pedagogies (e.g., learning communities).

At the University of Michigan in Ann Arbor, each residence hall had a satellite library that was connected to the main campus library. The libraries are now being converted into learning resource centers (Figure 10.3). The resource centers offer a variety of seating and technology options to enhance team learning. Individual and group seating in soft chairs with tablets or in straight-backed chairs around rectangular or round tables provide network connections for laptop computers. The area also features small, private rooms and low privacy walls to facilitate group work. This room provides the space, technology, and flexibility to support a variety of learning activities.

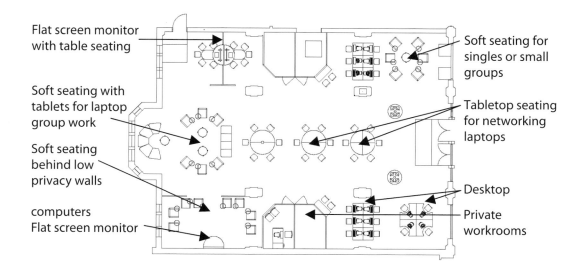

Flat screen monitor with table seating

Soft seating with tablets for laptop group work

Soft seating behind low privacy walls

computers
Flat screen monitor

Soft seating for singles or small groups

Tabletop seating for networking laptops

Desktop

Private workrooms

Figure 10.3. Learning Resource Center at the University of Michigan's West Quad housing complex.

Room Configurations

The current housing types available for students vary widely as do the philosophies about the degree to which the housing experience should support educational objectives. At one end of the continuum, is college housing that is outsourced to independent construction and management companies and that operates like a commercial apartment complex. At the opposite end, are halls that embrace the academic mission of the university by providing staff, intentional programming, and spaces designed to facilitate interaction among students, faculty, staff, and administrators (Pica, Jones, & Caplinger, 2006). Regardless of who is responsible for the construction and management of student housing, two common, but seemingly conflicting goals, for residence life are to build community and offer residents privacy. The room types for first-year students help institutions achieve both these goals in varying degrees.

Traditional double. The traditional double, like the ones recently constructed at the University of Oregon (Figure 10.4), is a simple box repeated in a line on both sides of a double-loaded corridor. This room type is the most efficient and cost-effective way to house students. There is no plumbing in the room, and the furniture, including the closets, is movable and can be configured in a number of ways. The beds can also be bunked. Because students are forced to use the public spaces and shared bathrooms, this type of hall is arguably the best layout for creating community among first-year students. During a focus group conducted by Angelini & Associates Architects at Idaho State University, a group of sophomore students who live in a new apartment style hall said they were glad they lived in a traditional hall with a central shared bathroom during their first year because they would never have met so many people in their current living situation.

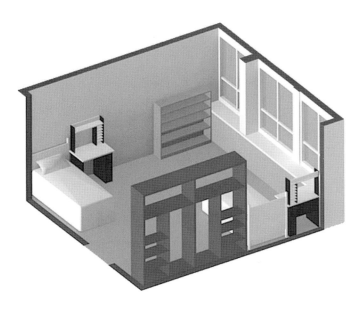

Figure 10.4. A traditional double room (13' x 16') completed in 2006 at the University of Oregon. Designed by Zimmer Gunsul Frasca Architects, Oregon.

Suite style. The adjoining suite-style room, like the ones recently constructed at Arizona State University, is made up of two double sleeping rooms, an entry/closet/vanity area, and a shower and toilet room shared by four students (Figure 10.5). Like a hotel room, the sleeping area is buffered from the corridor by the closet entry area, making it feel more private and reducing sound transmission. The furniture can be lofted to maximize floor space. The toilet and shower room is accessed by separate doors from the closet/vanity area, but this type of door-locking arrangement can be problematic for privacy and access. A better solution is to have separate shower and toilet rooms, each with privacy doors.

The adjoining suite style is currently a very popular option for first-year residence halls, and some institutions are converting older halls to a similar configuration. Because the layout fits neatly in a rectangle, it can be used efficiently in buildings designed with double-loaded corridors. The shared room is not oversized so students will be inclined to use the building's public spaces, which will encourage community building.

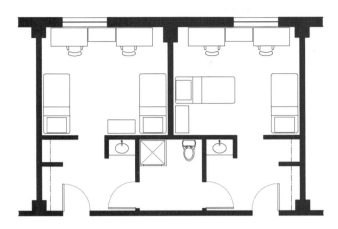

Figure 10.5. Adjoining suite-style construction (room dimensions 12' x 14'; closet/vanity dimensions 8' x 10') completed in 2006 at Arizona State University. Designed by Machido and Silvetti, Boston, MA.

Single semi-suites. A single semi-suite is a cluster of four single rooms sharing a semi-private bathroom off a private corridor (Figure 10.6). Each room includes a closet with shelves, a three-drawer chest, desk with study carrel and mobile pedestal with two file drawers, a wall-mounted corkboard, and a full-length mirror. The shared bathroom and hall help create smaller communities within larger residence halls. As such, this design transitions well from a first-year only hall to one that can accommodate sophomores and juniors who want to remain on campus. For the amount of privacy provided this is a very efficient plan that could be used in a double-loaded corridor or a cluster layout.

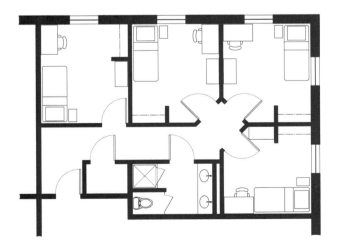

Figure 10.6. Grouping of four single rooms (12' x 10'6") in a suite designed for the University of Missouri, College Avenue Housing. Designed by International Architects Atelier, Majid Amirahmadi Architect of Record.

Apartments. Many campuses are adding apartment-style residence halls to their housing options. Figures 10.7 and 10.8 illustrate two- and four-bedroom apartments designed to be in a double-loaded corridor or a cluster arrangement in a residence hall. The apartments feature kitchens with full-size refrigerators, a cook top, double sink, and eating area. Stackable washer and dryer units are also included. This hybrid apartment building offers students the privacy of apartment living with the convenience and safety of living in a residence hall on campus. The entrance to the building is centrally located on the ground floor near learning community amenities including a front desk, administrative and faculty offices, class and meeting rooms, lounges, and recreational spaces.

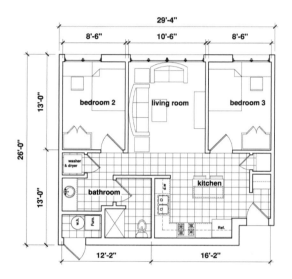

Figure 10.7. Two-bedroom apartment designed for Northern Arizona University as part of a housing master plan. Angelini & Associates Architects, Ann Arbor, MI.

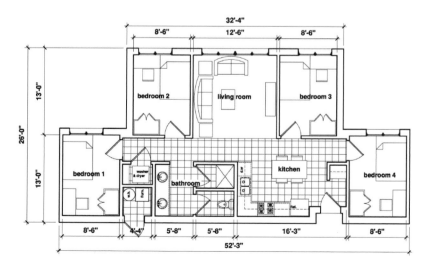

Figure 10.8. Four-bedroom apartment designed for Northern Arizona University as part of a housing master plan. Angelini & Associates Architects, Ann Arbor, MI.

Colleges and universities are feeling pressure to build apartment-style housing based on the demands by incoming students for more space and privacy; however, this is not an ideal model for first-year students where student-to-student interaction and the building of social communities are goals. A 2005 ACUHO-I/EBI Residence Assessment confirms this, finding that the number one factor for overall student satisfaction with the residence hall experience is the ability to interact with others in the hall (Pica et al., 2006). The overwhelming majority of chief housing officers responding to a similar survey believed that traditional housing with multiple occupants in one room is the most conducive to interaction and engagement, while a large majority (76%) considered the single-occupancy apartment undesirable for interaction and engagement. However, these same chief housing officers felt that a single in the super suite was the best (82%) housing option for recruitment purposes while a traditional, shared room was seen as a liability (Pica et al.).

On each campus, the decision to build a particular hall and room type is based on the goals and objectives of the institution's administration. When planning first-year housing, the primary goal should be to create an environment that supports community through student-to-student interaction and public spaces that promote group and team learning. Smaller student rooms with semi-private spaces on each residential floor and public spaces on the ground floor is the best way to provide a balance between privacy and community.

Furnishing and Configuring the Room for Flexibility

A key to satisfaction among residents is the ability to personalize their rooms. Major residence hall furniture suppliers are developing innovative ways to accomplish multiple room layouts and maximize storage using modular, interchangeable furniture parts to create personalized spaces. Something as simple as the loft bed with the desk tucked in below maximizes space and provides students with a sense of privacy. Additionally, some models allow the desk area to be personalized and decorated with changeable panels for hanging posters or artwork, shelving, task lighting, and even a flat-screen television or computer monitor.

Taking the idea of personalizing the room one step further requires not only flexible furniture but also moveable walls. For example, Angelini & Associates Architects developed a proposal for rooms with pivoting walls as part of a new construction project at the University of Arkansas. The idea is to have one wall that can slide and pivot within a modular space of fixed walls. The overall construction module is approximately 30' x 24' and includes a bath area, sink area, and small living area outside of the bedrooms. The module can sleep two, three, or four students depending on the configuration.

The Residential Neighborhood

Part of the decision-making process for students who are looking at schools today is the type of amenities offered outside the classroom. In 2000, 64% of the $9.4 billion spent on facilities construction at colleges and universities was on non-academic facilities including improving recreational facilities and building larger and more luxurious housing and dining. While "luxurious housing" options, quite often apartment-style halls, aid recruitment and build enrollment, these halls do not necessarily build the community that leads to student satisfaction (Kenny et al., 2005).

Providing "luxury" housing also comes with a high price tag. In 1998, the median residence hall room had 300 square feet and cost $37,662 per student to build. According to a construction and renovation survey conducted in the fall of 2003 by ACUHO-I, the median residence hall had 338 square feet per student configured in super suits at a cost of $50,025 per student. Apartments offered 343 square feet of living space at a cost of $52,629 per student (interpolated from data provided by Balogh, Grimm, & Hardy, 2006). The price for this type of housing is not only monetary: it also affects lifestyle. The more luxurious and amenity-packed the room, the less likely that a student will have the need to share space. With food, TV, cable, Internet access, and podcast lectures available in the room, there is little reason to use campus common spaces. This is not unlike what has happened in our American suburbs as the front porch was replaced by the backyard deck and the public park was replaced by the backyard pool, driveway basketball court, and basement exercise room. The residential neighborhood has been divided into a collection of private domains.

Thus, the question for residence life professionals is whether the public spaces in residence halls can be designed to be so inviting that students will want to leave their rooms? On way to accomplish this is to think of campus housing in terms of neighborhoods as proposed by a group of campus housing professionals during the 2006 21st Century Project Summit. A block is made up of approximately 30 students. A residence advisor lives on the block, knows each student by name, and acts as an advisor and confidant. Relationships among the block residents are face-to-face and on a first-name basis. Yet, there is a limited amount of community space on the block, and its adjacency to private spaces makes quiet study the most likely and acceptable activity. An occasional block party may be planned, and residents may engage in group activities, (e.g., intramural sports) and may have the same major and share classes (Millennia Consulting, LLC, 2006).

At the neighborhood level, the interaction is similar to a traditional residential neighborhood that shares public spaces and amenities. The neighborhood is made up of approximately 150 students and also includes administrators and faculty. The common public spaces may include public lobbies, dining facilities, a café, small retail shops, and postal facilities. Classrooms, computer labs, meeting spaces, and offices may also be in the neighborhood. Like the Union Drive Neighborhood at Iowa State University (described below), the neighborhood level is the primary locus for social activities. Name and face recognition among residents of the neighborhood is high, and interactions are frequent. Local identity and loyalty is strong (Millennia Consulting, LLC, 2006).

Residence Life and Campus Master Planning

The foregoing considerations should all be part of a campus master plan for housing. Developing a master plan provides a decision-making framework for determining how and where first-year students will be housed on campus. It also provides housing administrators with the necessary information to make informed decisions on topics including facility conditions, space requirements, financial health, and program needs (Kenny et al., 2005). Thus, a master plan is a tool to evaluate how well the existing housing facilities and programs are serving students. A master plan also serves as a benchmark for future analysis, beginning with an evaluation of the present condition through program, facility, and financial reviews. The master planners then analyze that information to recommend future decision making, using tools such as vision confirmation, a gap analysis, program development, financial modeling, and site and building planning. Examining the current physical condition of the existing halls and comparing these to facilities at peer institutions provide important information for recommendations on the renovation, demolition, and construction of new residence hall facilities. In this way, the master plan becomes an important tool in helping residence life departments meet their goals and objectives. By making cost projections and proposing project phases, the plan ensures that the goals are achievable given the self-supporting nature of residence hall budgets.

The master plan also encourages housing professionals and campus administrators to take a macroview of residence life rather than focusing on individual buildings. A single residence hall can no longer provide all the amenities, programming, and services that are expected by today's students. The trend in housing master planning is to consider adjacent residence halls, dining and athletic facilities, and classroom buildings as a neighborhood or living-learning community. A first-year neighborhood, or community of learners, will provide the programming, amenities, and services that new students require to make a successful transition and establish a foundation that will support a successful college career. The examples that follow demonstrate how this neighborhood concept is evolving on a number of campuses.

Iowa State University

A housing master plan produced for Iowa State University determined that Hesler Hall, an older hall with little architectural character and a long list of maintenance problems, should be demolished and replaced by three new halls. Friley Hall, a nearby first-year hall housing 1,200 students, and an intramural athletics building would—along with the three new buildings—form the core of a first-year residential academic community designed to help to ease the transition from a supportive home community to a campus where students know few, if any, people. A central dining hall/community center would also be constructed and would be the first building completed as part of the Union Drive Neighborhood (Figure 10.9).

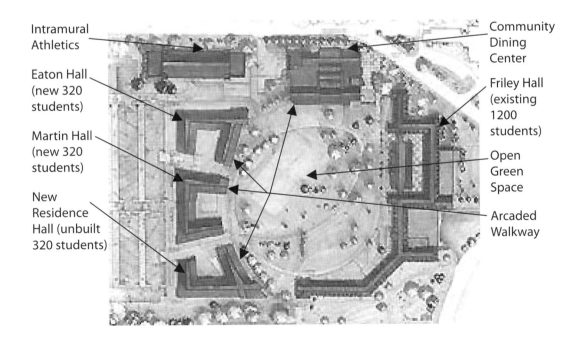

Figure 10.9. Union Drive Neighborhood, Iowa State University. Site planning by Sasaki Associates, Boston, MA.

The Union Drive Neighborhood provides services in one location, which aid first-year students in their academic success. In addition to three new suite-style residence halls, spaces and programs are provided for academic advising, tutoring, study skills workshops, counseling, and academic classes. The new 58,000 square-foot community center provides multiple dining options including themed food stations with made-to-order dishes, a bakery, and a nonalcoholic sports bar. The community center also has a convenience store, game and exercise rooms, and a post office (Figures 10.10 and 10.11). The new residence halls and the community center have a covered arcade at their base to unify the buildings and are arranged around a large open space that is surrounded by the community of buildings.

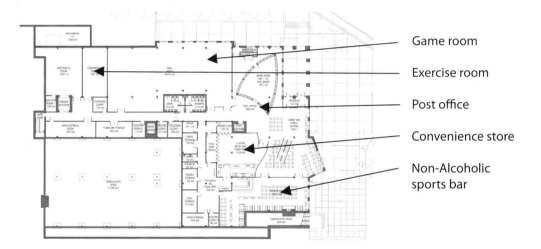

Game room

Exercise room

Post office

Convenience store

Non-Alcoholic sports bar

Figure 10.10. Lower level of dining/community center, Iowa State University. Designed by Angelini & Associates Architects, Ann Arbor, Michigan and Baldwin White Architects, Architects of Record, Des Moines, IA.

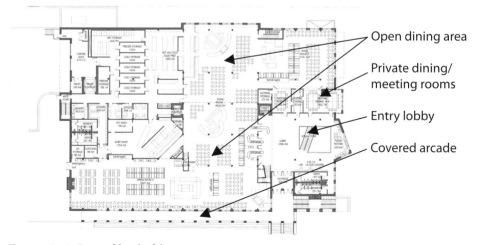

Open dining area

Private dining/ meeting rooms

Entry lobby

Covered arcade

Figure 10.11. Ground level of dining/community center, Iowa State University. Designed by Angelini & Associates Architects, Ann Arbor, Michigan and Baldwin White Architects, Architects of Record, Des Moines, IA.

Arizona State University

The Hassayampa Academic Village at Arizona State University is a 565,000 square-foot, 1,928-bed residential community being built in two phases. The buildings anchor the southeast corner of campus and are adjacent to the Law School, the Student Recreation Complex, the Physical Education Building, and outdoor intramural sports fields. A cluster of five buildings completes a community of 980 students. Both four-story (housing 156 - 172 students) and seven-story (housing 246 - 308 students) buildings are part of the complex. The floor plans are "C"-shaped, double-loaded corridors. The student rooms are four-bed semi-suites or two rooms with a shared bathroom (see Figure 10.5, for example). Double suites, accessible rooms, and residence advisor rooms are also available and are distributed throughout the building. The room furniture is loftable allowing the students more options for personalizing the room arrangement.

The public spaces in the halls are designed to support the three first-year living-learning communities: (a) the Mary Lou Fulton College of Education, (b) the College of Liberal Arts and Sciences CLAS Learning Communities, and (c) the Living Well Residential Community. The Living Well Residential Community is well suited to this location due to the adjacency of the Student Recreation Complex, the Physical Education Building, and the outdoor intramural sports fields. The spaces provided for these communities include offices for on-site advising and preregistration, meeting spaces for community involvement with youth programs, and classrooms for education faculty seminars and workshops. Spaces are also provided for on-site tutoring and peer mentoring, life skills workshops, ice cream socials, movie nights, and weekend pizza and barbecues as well as dinners with the dean. The activities take place in four-person study rooms, two-story community lounges, classrooms, tutoring facilities, coaching rooms, and conference rooms. The two-story community lounges feature kitchenettes, a television-viewing area, and wireless Internet. Because the lounges are open to two floors, the possibilities for community development are greatly expanded. The community also shares a dining facility, a central mail center, a UPS store, and a convenience store.

Fort Lewis College

Fort Lewis College in Durango, Colorado has a very interesting cluster of residence halls, the Bader Snyder Complex, built in the 1950s. Their unique design offers ideas that can be implemented in new residence hall construction. The complex is made up of six two-story buildings each housing 40 students for a total of 240 residents. The halls are freestanding and form an informal courtyard with a picnic shelter at the center. The basic floor plan is a "U" shape of rooms surrounding an interior rectangular community lounge with a centralized skylight. The residence hall is entered through a lobby at the narrow end of the community lounge. There are eight, five-person suites, four on each floor (Figure 10.12). A residence advisor's room is located on the second floor of each building, and a residence director apartment is in one of the six buildings. Two of the halls have basements with a game room, computer lab, laundry, and storage.

While the design has some flaws based on today's standards, its strengths lie in the centralized two-story community space, the double/single room options, and the small-scale community identity. The community lounge is ideally sized for 40 students to hang out, have a class or meeting, invite guest speakers, and to live and learn in a community. This is an efficient solution where both circulation and community space work as one. Students also experience the open skylight space each time they come and go from their rooms.

The five-person suite also provides opportunities for flexibility. The single room can be available for second-year students who are interested in staying in the halls and participating in the living-learning community environment. The ability to mix first- and second-year students in the living-learning community provides an opportunity for programming that is not possible with a first-year only class.

The learning communities housed in the complex include Outdoor Experience, Life House, and Hungry Mind Learners. The cost for additional stairs, elevators, and exterior materials required for this construction are balanced by the buildings' smaller size and savings for structural requirements and mechanical systems.

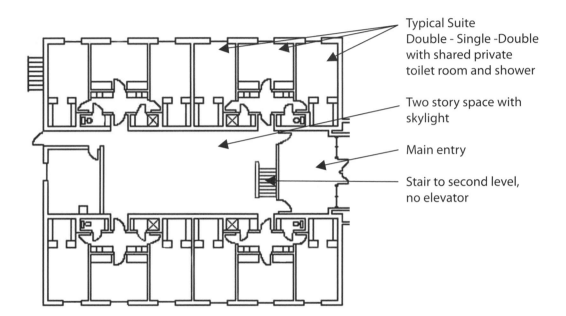

Figure 10.12. Ground floor of a residence hall in the Bader Snyder Complex, Fort Lewis College in Colorado.

Conclusion

Having positive and frequent interactions with one's peer group is the number one indicator of student satisfaction with the living environment (Pica et al., 2006). Successful residence hall design will facilitate student interactions and promote a strong sense of community. A living environment for first-year students also needs to provide academic and personal support, including programming for academic success, opportunities to meet new people and to make friends, and space to develop emotionally and become more independent. An important opportunity that living on campus allows is the ability to meet students who have different interests, backgrounds, and majors. It is important to provide spaces in and adjacent to residence halls where these interactions can occur both formally and informally, especially when students are in a living-learning community with a single academic focus. The new emphasis on the residence hall as a community of learners is transforming the physical space of housing from a place removed from the classroom to a place that is the center of academic life and student success.

References

Astin, A.W. (1993). *What matters in college?* San Francisco: Jossey-Bass.

Balogh, C., Grimm, J., & Hardy, K. (2006). ACUHO-I construction and renovation data. In N. Dunkel & J. Baumann (Eds.), *College housing: 2005 special report. 21st century project reading compendium* (pp. 31-38). Columbus, OH: ACUHO-I Press.

Howe, N., & Strauss, W. (2000). *Millennials rising.* Washington, DC: The American Association of Collegiate Registrars and Admissions Officers (AACRAO).

Howe, N., & Strauss, W. (2003). *Millennials go to college.* New York: Vintage Books.

Kenny, D., Dumont, R., & Kenny, G. (2005). *Mission and place.* Westport, CT: Praeger.

Millennia Consulting, LLC. (2006). Beginning a better dialogue: An executive summary of the 21st Century Project Summit. In N. Dunkel & J. Baumann (Eds.), *College housing: 2005 special report. 21st century project reading compendium* (pp. 18-32). Columbus, OH: ACUHO-I Press.

Pica, J., Jones, D., & Caplinger, C. (2006). Freshman housing: Current practice, planned construction, CHO perspectives on the future. In N. Dunkel & J. Baumann (Eds.), *College housing: 2005 special report. 21st century project reading compendium* (pp. 51-58). Columbus, OH: ACUHO-I Press.

The Society for College and University Planning (SCUP). (2007). *Trends in higher education July 2005.* [Virtual Seminar Handout] Ann Arbor, MI: Author.

Chapter Eleven

Safety and Security: An Important Element of First-Year Residence Education

James C. Grimm
Revised 2008 by Jim Day with research assistance from Leslie Atchley

In a 1994 feature article of the ACUHO-I *Talking Stick*, Pleskoff noted that as we prepare for the educational needs of the next generation, we must include personal safety needs at the top of the list. If possible, we must help people prepare for the potential for crime with the same vigor we prepare students for an academic major. In short, we must call our campuses to action. Pleskoff succinctly established the relationship between education and students' personal safety and identified a course of action for campus administrators. Pleskoff's call for action is no less important today. The tragic shootings on campuses (i.e., at Virginia Tech in April 2007 and at Northern Illinois University in February 2008) are just the most recent reminders of the need for campus safety plans and education programs. Concerns regarding the potential for incidents of terrorism on college campuses or in the surrounding areas have also contributed to a sense of urgency in attending to campus safety.

Colleges and universities seek to include students in communities of scholars where learning is prized and civil exploration of intellectual differences serves as a means to greater understanding. Strange and Banning (2001) note that

> Although safety and inclusion are distinct concepts, they are related in the sense that both reflect campus conditions thought to be important requisites for development and learning to occur, and contributing to one will undoubtedly enhance the other. It can be said that failure to address one can easily jeopardize the other. (p. 113)

Thus, a feeling of personal safety is a necessary precondition in order for such learning communities to exist and thrive.

Where can the task at hand be better addressed than in the residence halls? The residential setting has been a venue of choice for many social-awareness education programs including those focused on the use and abuse of alcohol and other drugs, sexuality and sexual health, diversity and human relations, and other social issues. The research noted throughout this monograph indicates that the best place to begin is with first-year students in the residence halls.

Secondary questions include: What must we do? How may we implement it? And how far shall we go with our security programs? Willis, Hines, and Johnson (1994) offer a framework from which to begin program development and/or revision:

Findings from [our research] as well as from the research literature agree that students want to be responsible for themselves, but at the same time, desire some degree of protection. In general, students and parents perceive present security measures as adequate, but also desire tightened security, especially as it pertains to visitors in residence halls. Students do not mind security procedures that do not inconvenience them or infringe upon their feeling of personal freedom. (p. 11)

Yet, a heightened level of concern following the terrorist attacks in New York, Washington, DC, and Pennsylvania on September 11, 2001 and the subsequent emphasis on homeland security along with violence on and near campuses have added to concerns about personal safety for college students. Students and their families may now be more willing to accept inconveniences associated with security measures that would heretofore been considered onerous and unreasonable. It behooves the staff to draw upon knowledge about the security risks on a given campus, the resources available, and the perceived needs of students and their families in developing security protocols and programs that inform and sensitize without producing an antagonistic environment that detracts from the overall residential and educational experience.

This chapter provides an overview of what campuses can and should do to provide safe living and learning environments for students. Given that the effectiveness of security systems is limited by students' compliance with those systems, the chapter also addresses strategies for educating students about their responsibilities in creating a safe campus. The suggestions outlined here for establishing educational programs for first-year resident students are categorized by four time frames. The first time frame occurs prior to the student's arrival at the institution; the second is during check-in; the third is the initial two- to four-week period when the resident student is forming new habits; and the fourth comprises continuing programs throughout the year. These four periods of program development are presented as an approach to a comprehensive first-year program of safety and security education and awareness.

Residence Hall Safety and Security

Residence life staff must consider three primary areas when planning for residence hall security: (a) policies and procedures, (b) staffing, and (c) security infrastructure.

Policies and Procedures

◇ Rules and regulations should be established to ensure the safety and security of residents and their belongings. As a corollary, staff should have procedures for communicating and enforcing these rules and regulations.

◇ Key policies for staff and residents should include written records of key issuance, policies and procedures for key issuance and security, procedures for lock changes in the event of a key loss, and periodic audits of records against actual key possession

◇ Fire evacuation plans for residents and staff should be easily understood, well communicated, and practiced in the form of fire drills each term.

◇ Evacuation and emergency notification plans and procedures must account for the needs of persons with disabilities. These plans and procedures should be developed in cooperation with campus or local police and emergency response agencies and should be well communicated to affected residents and staff.

◇ Solicitation policies should spell out any approved and/or prohibited forms of commercial, religious, and political solicitation in the residential facilities, along with procedures for gaining approval.

◇ Natural disaster plans should outline staff and resident roles in the event of severe weather, earthquake, or other likely natural disaster.

◇ Policies for dealing with stray and wild animals found in or around the residential facilities should be established and communicated to staff and residents.

◇ Visitation policies for residential facilities should address access and sign-in procedures for non-resident visitors; visitors of the opposite sex, if applicable; and overnight guests who are not assigned residents of a given living unit.

◇ On-call procedures should establish staff coverage in the event of an emergency. These procedures should be communicated to residents, campus police, and student affairs offices.

◇ In the wake of shooting incidents on campuses and with the availability of effective technological solutions, many campuses have adopted emergency notification systems that can quickly send e-mail, text messages, and voice mail messages to all students, faculty, and staff.

◇ Medical emergency response protocols should detail how to respond if a resident needs medical assistance, taking campus police, ambulance, and other emergency response teams into consideration.

◇ Mental health crisis response protocols should outline the assistance offered to students experiencing an emotional or psychological crisis. Special response protocols should be developed for attempted suicide or other situations where students are deemed a threat to themselves or others. These protocols often include cooperation with campus police and/or campus mental health resources.

◇ Personal crisis response procedures should also be established to support residents dealing with a personal matter other than a medical emergency or psychological/mental health emergency.

◇ Procedures in the event of a death of a resident or other person in the residence hall should outline who is responsible for notifying campus and local authorities, working with nearby and other affected residents, and responding to the media.

◇ Bomb threat procedures should be developed in conjunction with campus or local law enforcement authorities and communicated to any staff member who might possibly receive such threats.

◇ Emergency maintenance plans should outline procedures for identifying and reporting facilities problems that pose a current/potential safety hazard to occupants or that may result in damage to the facility if not repaired quickly.

◇ When applicable, emergency procedures for persons caught in elevators, which include notification of trained evacuation personnel by residential staff, should be established.

◇ Strategies for responding to mass demonstrations should be coordinated with institutional policies and procedures and communicated to staff.

◇ Procedures allowing staff to enter rooms for maintenance, cleaning, emergencies, and routine health/safety inspections should be established. Such policies should be in keeping with applicable laws and the housing contract between the institution and the residents.

Staffing

In terms of staffing, a number of considerations must be weighed to ensure the safety and security of residents. For example,

◇ How many full-time live-in staff should the campus employ? What is the desired level of experience and professional training for these staff members?

◇ Should security patrol programs in and around the residence halls be established?

◇ Should the main desk in the residence hall be staffed 24 hours a day?

◇ Who will be responsible for residence hall security? Campus police or uniformed security guards? Are campus police officers fully trained and licensed?

◇ What role do custodians and maintenance personnel play in creating a safe environment? Is an escort required for access to certain areas? How are these staff members identified to and identifiable by students?

◇ Will the residence halls, in conjunction, with other campus offices or on its own, provide escort services or safe ride programs for students?

Security Infrastructure

The security infrastructure encompasses the design of facilities, including hardware and software to control access to residential facilities and to alert residents, staff, and emergency personnel in the event of fire, criminal activity, or other emergent safety issue in the residence hall. Such infrastructure also includes signage that communicates safety and security policies and that alerts residents to potential dangers. In designing security infrastructure, consideration should be given to:

◇ Locating telephones outside buildings entrances, which may be used to contact residents or in the event of an emergency

◇ Installing blue light emergency phones, which are capable of autodialing campus police or a security office, along walkways, in parking lots/decks, and near transportation hubs and gathering places

◇ Instituting parking lot and building lighting programs, which provide adequate lighting for night-time users and which are reviewed and updated at least annually

◇ Installing viewers in student living unit doors so residents can observe and identify people outside the door without opening the door

◇ Installing security screens on ground floor windows and those that are otherwise easily accessible to intruders

◇ Installing multiple security locks on sliding glass doors in individual living units, where applicable

◇ Trimming trees and shrubbery regularly to minimize potential hiding places for intruders and to maintain adequate lighting

◇ Installing automatic door closers on individual living unit doors in accordance with fire safety codes

◇ Maintaining fire safety equipment, including fire-alarm systems and checking equipment routinely in accordance with state and local codes

◇ Installing electronic door access systems on entrances, where feasible

◇ Installing closed circuit television (CCTV) systems at exterior doors, in elevators, and specific areas of concern, whether those systems are constantly monitored or used only for investigative purposes

◇ Installing door alarms on exterior doors when there is an expectation or desire for limited access through those doors

◇ Using up-to-date communications technology such as streaming announcement boards located in high traffic areas, targeted e-mail announcements, and emergency notification announcements over campus television and radio channels to inform residents of threatening weather, environmental hazards, or other dangerous conditions on campus or in the surrounding community

◇ Installing appropriate signage such as building entry decals identifying intended users, prohibited access if applicable, and related procedures; escort required signs; trespass warning information in compliance with campus/local requirements so that trespassers may be arrested (as allowed); and notices identifying areas where there is no regular security oversight or where unsafe conditions may exist

Safety and security plans and policies should be assessed on a regular basis. The checklist included in the appendix to this chapter is adapted from the ACUHO-I Residence Hall and Apartment Safety and Security Environmental Assessment Checklist (Pleskoff & Grimm, 1993). It is intended for use by students, staff, faculty, or a safety committee as a security audit guide. The assessment form is outlined as a checklist and could be used as a rating scale, or as a review list for the committee to begin an audit program. In addition to serving as an assessment tool, the checklist can be used as part of educational initiatives designed to involve people in discussions of safety and security in the residential environment.

In addition to ensuring that infrastructure, staffing, and appropriate policies and procedures are in place, residence life staff must educate residents about their responsibility in creating and maintaining a safe living environment. The rest of the chapter addresses strategies for educating students during four critical time periods within the first college year.

Safety Education Prior to Residence Hall Check-in

Safety and security education should begin prior to the student's arrival on campus. In fact, this education can begin with the first publication or electronic communication the student receives related to housing and residence life programs. Frequently, what campuses communicate prior to enrollment is information related to the Campus Security Act of 1990. The legislation, amended in 1992, 1998, and 2000, was renamed the Jeanne Clery Disclosure of Campus Security Policy and Campus Crime Statistics Act (Clery Act) in 1998. The Clery Act is a federal law requiring colleges and universities to disclose certain timely and annual information about campus crime and security policies. All public and private postsecondary institutions participating in federal student aid programs are subject to the law and are required to publish a report by October 1st each year that contains the three most recent years of campus crime statistics and certain policy statements including those related to sexual assault and basic victim's rights, the authority of campus police, and the procedure for reporting campus crimes by students. In addition to filing the report with the U.S. Department of Education, campuses must also publish it. Publication may take place via the Internet with printed copies made available upon request. The law also stipulates specific notification requirements for current and prospective students and employees.

Initially, some institutions did not respond to the Clery Act, and others failed to publish anything close to what the federal government requires in statistics, policies, or procedures. Some colleges and universities have complied within minimal standards of the Clery Act, providing publications that meet only the basic requirements of disclosure. Over time, many institutions have turned this government mandate into a very positive approach to publicizing campus crime solutions. By using the required notification as an educational and public relations tool, a school can go beyond the obligatory disclosure to enhance and publicize a proactive program to fight campus crime. This is the approach that this chapter encourages. Attractive brochures, reports, and well-designed web sites written in a positive, proactive vein can serve as an introduction to campus awareness programs for first-year students and their families. Though the law requires only that the printed report be made available upon request, proactive institutions have sent program materials including printed reports and/or web site links as part of the information material for admitted students. These materials can also be included as part of the housing information that students receive along with their application or residence hall contract. If this information is not available, housing departments can take the initiative to develop a brochure that brings attention to security issues within the residence halls.

Part of the pre-arrival awareness program can be accomplished at new student orientation sessions. Many campuses have a first-year student orientation program during the summer months when students and parents are invited to the campus for a day or two. Though mainly academic, these programs can also cover student services, housing, food service, and financial aid. If the department of housing and residence life has an opportunity to visit or speak with a group of students and parents on housing assignments and payment schedules, there should be ample time to discuss safety and security expectations. The new student orientation program is an opportunity to provide information to students and parents about residence hall access control policies, personal safety precautions and resources, emergency communications systems, and procedures related to large scale events (e.g., natural disasters, terrorism, violence on campus). Safety and security educational content should be delivered in a coordinated and integrated fashion by orientation program presenters, which may include housing and residence life staff members as well as representatives from student life, campus police, student health, student counseling, parking services, and other offices.

When dealing with first-year college students, housing staff members sometimes forget that parents may not have attended college. If parents did attend college, the rules, regulations, policies, and expectations are quite different today than they were a generation ago, especially in the area of campus safety and security. Parents may have an incomplete understanding of what has changed on campuses since they were enrolled.

The term "helicopter parents" has been coined to identify parents of millennial students who seem to want involvement in every aspect of their college-going children's lives, assuming a hovering position and using every available means of immediate electronic communication to stay in touch with their children and campus resources. While not every parent deserves the appellation "helicopter," the hovering posture of some parents is emblematic of deep concern and willingness to become engaged. Residence life and student life staff can leverage this interest to fruitful ends by encouraging parents at orientation to help educate their students about the importance of taking an active role in protecting oneself and minimizing exposure to safety and security risks on campus and in the surrounding community. Young adults often exhibit behavior indicating a misguided belief that they are immortal, invincible, and fully protected from harm. Parents can assist colleges and universities in leading students to a more realistic view of their vulnerabilities and responsibility for their own safety.

Orientation activities are also a good time to inform parents about ways that they can stay informed about safety and security on campus. Some campuses have a specific person, office, e-mail address, or telephone number for parents to contact with concerns. Web sites and automated communications systems may also be available for parents who wish to stay current with campus security events.

Computer use policies are generally a topic for explanation at new student orientation sessions and are a good time to broach the subject of Internet security. Young people use social networking sites widely, and first-year college students will likely have great familiarity with them; however, the expanded freedoms of college life are accompanied by new electronic communications activities and opportunities, some of them risky, illegal, or dangerous. Orientation sessions are an excellent opportunity to make students and parents aware of the dangers of scams, cyber stalking, inappropriate postings to social networking sites, identity theft, academic dishonesty, illegal file sharing, spoofing, and other issues connected to Internet use.

Safety Education at Check-In and During the First Days on Campus

Students arriving on campus to check in to the residence hall are often accompanied by one parent or an entire entourage of friends and family. The students are typically unconcerned about safety and security at this point. They are more concerned about their roommate, whether all of their belongings will fit into their room, who will be living on the floor, if they will be accepted by the people in the hall or apartment, what classes will be like, if the food will be edible, and a thousand other things. As one might expect, this is a situation in which the resident assistant (RA) becomes a key player in orienting students. The RA can and should emphasize the importance of basic safety and security regulations and procedures to each resident during the check-in period.

The RA has many messages to communicate to students, and each student has a list of things to accomplish in the few days prior the beginning of classes. The RA training program can develop a list of items to be covered, at check-in and within the first two or three days, by both the RA and the new student. Timing the delivery of safety and security information is very important. Not all of it can be covered at one time, and not all of it can be done through posters, bulletin boards, group meetings, or personal conversations. A variety of approaches are required. Often, subtle reminders are more effective than a 20-minute lecture.

Residence life staff can take advantage of wait time during check-in and other opening activities by looping a video on campus security issues on monitors in the lobby. The video could focus on raising awareness of security and safety risks; recommended steps to protect personal property; availability of campus resources such as emergency call boxes, police and security staff patrols, 911 service, escort services, and shuttle service; and availability of crime prevention and self-defense education programs. Alternatively, a series of public service announcements focused on safety and security can be shown on a campus TV channel or residence hall movie channel. The university police department or campus security agency may set up a table in a centrally located area to provide brochures, samples of locks for bicycles, personal inventory cards to record model and serial numbers of valuable items, and other types of security information. This table does not have to be staffed throughout check-in but should be checked occasionally to restock material.

It is common to unlock all doors during periods of high move-in traffic. If part of the residence hall security program is limiting building access to specific entrance areas, then it is essential to provide adequate information to residents about normal procedures and to restore standard access control as quickly as possible. If electronic access control using card readers, proximity devices, or biometric readers is standard for entrance areas, encourage students and their parents to become familiar with the system early on. The use of such systems must be explained upon initial check-in, and it may also be wise to provide a brochure with details about the access control system and related procedures. Residents should also be informed if CCTV systems are in use and whether the system can be relied on to signal for help if needed.

One of the first things an RA should do as part of the introduction to students on the floor is to check on facilities. The RA can ask, "How are things? Is everything working? Does your key work? Have you tried opening your mailbox?" Simple conversational items help with the introduction of the student and parent and establish the RA as the person to inform if these things are not functional. It also encourages the student and parent to try the key to make sure it works and puts emphasis on the idea that, yes, you should be using your door key and locking your mailbox. Many times these small, seemingly insignificant suggestions make a bigger impression than a booklet that lists all the rules, regulations, and procedures.

Throughout discussion of safety, references have been made to the integral part the RA plays in education. The RA does play an important role; however, there are other individuals within the residence halls that augment this role. For example, judicial sanctions involving the collection and dissemination of information about common threats to personal safety or security of property can be educational for both the individual being disciplined and for a target peer group. Other sanctions might require a student to organize and promote a series of activities focused on self-defense or avoiding Internet fraud and safety problems. Security patrols, whether they consist of sworn campus police officers, campus or contractor supplied security guards, permanent housing department staff, or part-time student security employees become additional eyes and ears for campus security.

Several institutions have created theater groups that provide short, one-act plays in the halls relating to current social problems and security issues such as sexual assault, intoxication, tailgating at sporting events, and drug use. Emphasis here is on the long-standing role of peer education in creating effective residential programs.

Bulletin boards welcoming students to campus are vitally important and can provide very effective reminders about locking doors and checking mailboxes. They also may announce some security event or raise awareness about security concerns. This kind of information, however, should not be an overwhelming part of the bulletin board as its primary purpose is to welcome the students and let them know about floor and hall activities. As is often outlined in RA training manuals, this initial time period and its effect on the entire operation of that residence hall floor is critical.

Safety Education During the First Two to Four Weeks

The third critical programming period is significant in that it represents a period of time when students begin to develop habits and routines. Classes have begun, class work assignments are made, and time tables are set for academic, cocurricular, and social activities. It is also a time when students are beginning to make adjustments to roommates and establishing themselves on their floor and hall. Most importantly, students seem open to new information during this period of adjustment to a new environment. With all of these events and activities going on, student safety and security awareness can be heightened if tied to the activities and processes with which the student is involved. The objective is for the residence hall staff to be aware of where the student is in this adjustment period and to provide assistance for the student to make appropriate decisions. As mentioned earlier, timing and subtlety can be key elements in the staff's attempt to raise awareness. Many campuses have designed flyers placed in mailboxes or on student room doors, newsletters affixed to the inside of bathroom or toilet stall doors, and posters that can be used as subtle and effective ways of reminding students that their security is a priority for the university and should be a concern for students as well.

Security and safety programs can also revolve around specific activities going on at the college or university. In the fall term, the institution may have athletic events such as football games. Student interest in the games and the activities associated with them can open the door to programming by staff to encourage healthy and safe ways to enjoy on-campus sporting events. When there are games away from campus, students will often attend, and the staff can be proactive by planning safety and security programs that connect to students' interest in the trip. The programs could help students avoid inconvenience (and possible safety concerns) by encouraging preplanning, providing directions to the event and information about the event location. Tips on safely using public transportation along with being aware of unsafe areas in the community are important information. Other activities that students may plan are camping trips, nature hikes, visits to museums, and sporting events. The staff can promote security measures that need to be considered in a variety of venues. Including safety and security concerns in programs or as part of activities/events as a method of raising awareness is a positive and proactive approach. Though the students may be continuously involved in these kinds of activities throughout the year, the first time they are involved can have a lasting effect on the decisions that are made when participating in future events. A wise staff person takes a proactive approach to program planning for campus events and includes personal security as an element of the plan.

This period of time is also an opportunity for the university police or campus security agency to begin making available programs in the area of crime prevention and personal safety. One very successful program is "Operation ID," where the police department encourages students to have their appliances and personal electronic devices (e.g. laptops, IPods, cell phones) engraved with a unique identifier. These identifiers are then kept on file with the police department and, in case of theft, will assist the police in recovery of the items. In addition to being an excellent service, the event itself establishes a rapport between university police and resident students. Many times campus police are seen as "traffic cops," those who hand out tickets or arrest students for underage drinking, creating a negative image of campus security. If the student can see the campus security or police officer in a positive light (e.g., as someone who is providing a service such as Operation ID or as a resource for personal safety issues), a more trusting relationship can be established. Safety and security programs can be unobtrusive, and subtle but consistent reminders can be very effective. It is crucial to remember, though, that safety and security programs will not affect everyone in the same way, nor will any one type of program delivery effectively reach all students. A varied approach to programming, therefore, is essential.

Another source of information that can be provided during this time period is a safety bulletin board. Each hall should have a safety-security bulletin board in the main lobby. This board should contain listings of resources, services, and programs available through all safety and security agencies whether they are in the city, county, or on campus. A safety bulletin board for the residence halls can provide both general and specific information. It can list crimes that have taken place within that residence hall and on campus, which will alert students to the type of crimes being committed and the steps that can be taken to avoid that crime happening in their own lives.

Residence life and campus security staff members have been successful at implementing focused, comprehensive, and integrated safety and security awareness and education programs during a short period of time. These programs generally occur within the first month of the academic year and include information, presentations, and activities mentioned above and others that may be relevant to the situation at a particular institution. A safety week program can include information and presentations to respond to the needs of female students, who have been found to experience a chilly climate in terms of campus safety (Kelly & Torres, 2006). Complementary programming can be offered at the same time to educate male students about their roles and responsibilities in creating safe living and learning environments on campus.

Safety Education as a Continuous Annual Program

In *Student Housing and Residential Life*, Schuh and Triponey (1993) note,

> It would be difficult to find many people on the contemporary college campus who would not agree that developing a comprehensive program to meet the needs of residential students is essential to creating an environment in which students can learn and grow. (p. 423)

Although this statement pertains primarily to developing a planned involvement program for resident students, it can also be applied to most problem-solving situations, including an ongoing safety and security program. Examples of educational programs that can be offered throughout the year include the following:

◇ As mentioned earlier, Operation ID and similar partnerships with campus law enforcement not only encourage personal responsibility for safety but also diminish the adversarial nature of the police officer-student relationship.

◇ Sexual assault awareness programs should target both men and women, outline potential risks and discuss the responsibilities that both men and women have in preventing sexual assault.

◇ Resident life staff can sponsor personal safety programs incorporating campus-specific information and guidelines. For example, one program might include providing whistles to be used as an alarm device during a threatening situation.

◇ Alcohol education programs should provide information on campus and local policies, such as likely sanctions for violations; discuss the connection between alcohol use and sexual assault, unwanted sexual activity, and sexually transmitted diseases; and highlight responsible drinking behaviors and treatment resources.

◇ A safety week conducted early in fall term might incorporate many of the above educational initiatives, offering a multi-pronged approach to raising awareness, promoting safe behaviors, and identifying resources.

◇ More passive educational programs might include posters and door hangers promoting safe behaviors, pointing out risks, reporting recent or ongoing safety and security-related incidents. Campus crime statistics can be published in the campus newspaper or via the Internet to maintain an accurate level of knowledge about risk and criminal activity in the environment.

Developing a comprehensive safety education plan for the academic year should include a variety of programs. The sequence can be developed around the student needs at a particular time, such as an emphasis relating to security of personal belongings during a vacation period. To be able to provide information to the student when he or she needs it is not an easy task, yet timing is of major importance.

As programs, brochures, and other resources are developed to raise student awareness, sometimes there is more concern about cost effectiveness than about information effectiveness. However, ongoing assessment efforts can help allay concerns about program costs while demonstrating the program's impact on crime rates, security violations, and other relevant measures. Assessing the effectiveness of activities in each of the four time frames should be undertaken regularly, as should a summary assessment of residence hall safety and security education programs. It will be necessary to adapt to new conditions and include emerging technology and resources in order to maintain and improve the desired level of security and safety awareness.

The key elements of a first-year resident security program are timeliness, expectations, reinforcement, consistency, repetition, and the staff's ability to know and read their students. Willis et al. (1994) note,

> Security in residence halls is only as good as those who are most affected by it...Student attitudes appear to be the key to the success or failure of any security system. The heart of campus safety continues to be the balance of students' perceptions of freedom with perceptions of security and control. (p. 12)

Just as the RAs need to establish a solid first impression, the institution along with housing and residence life must establish safety and security measures immediately as a high priority for first-year residents. If the staff, faculty, and even the president provide the impression that security is important, then the first-year resident will also feel it is important. It is a difficult challenge, but one that can be met with committed involvement of all parties concerned.

References

Kelly, B. T., & Torres, A. (2006). Campus safety: Perceptions and experiences of women students. *Journal of College Student Development, 47*(1), 20-36.

Pleskoff, B. (1994, December). Preparing for campus crime assessment is a crucial first step toward prevention. *Talking Stick, 8-9.*

Pleskoff, B., & Grimm, J. (1993). *Residence hall & apartment safety & security environmental assessment checklist.* Columbus, OH: ACUHO-I.

Schuh, J., & Triponey, V. (1993). Fundamentals of program design. In R. Winston & S. Anchors (Eds.), *Student housing and residential life* (pp. 423-442). San Francisco: Jossey-Bass.

Strange, C. C., & Banning, J. H. (2001). *Educating by design.* San Francisco: Jossey-Bass.

Willis, S., Hines, E., & Johnson, W. (1994). Residence hall security as perceived by students and parents at two public universities. *The Journal of College and University Student Housing, 24*(2), 8-13.

Appendix

Campus Housing Safety and Security General Checklist

This safety/security checklist is of a general nature and pertains primarily to facilities and programs. It is perhaps best employed as a preliminary step to thorough environmental assessment.

Rate each item on a 1 to 5 scale, with 1 as low and 5 as high.

_____ Written safety and security policies and procedures

_____ Housing safety and security committee

_____ Written long-range plan (five years)

_____ Plans are included in annual housing budget

_____ Annual security audit conducted

_____ Housing master key policy

_____ Housing key inventory with records of keys issued, periodic staff key audit

_____ Lost key/card policy and procedure with records

_____ Lock core changed with each key lost

_____ Nonresident access policy and procedures

_____ Safety/security publications for residents

_____ Communication process for informing residents of crimes

_____ Procedure for students to report a crime

_____ Well-lighted hall entrances and exits

_____ High risk areas posted and lighted

_____ Shrubbery trimmed in potential risk areas

_____ Adequate "blue light" emergency phones on campus

_____ Phone at hall entrance doors

_____ Bike racks convenient and lighted

_____ Security screens on ground floor windows

_____ Level of security at all entry doors

_____ Level of security at all exit doors

_____ Electronic entry door access system

_____ CCTV at entry doors

_____ CCTV at exit doors

_____ CCTV in elevators

_____ CCTV at other high risk areas

_____ Propped/open door sensor/alarm

_____ Level of security of interior doors (metal door frames, solid doors, one-inch deadbolt locks, door viewers)

_____ Level of desk services for security

_____ Level of nonresident access control

_____ Safety/security bulletin board in each hall

_____ Fire alarm system per applicable code

_____ Fire drills conducted and recorded

_____ Fire sprinklers installed and inspected per code

_____ Panic alarm in resident bedrooms

_____ Adequate security plan implemented during breaks

_____ Nighttime escort service available

_____ Regular nighttime security patrols around/in halls

_____ Published procedures for reporting security problems, concerns

Chapter Twelve

Residential Programs for Other New Students: Serving Graduate and Transfer Students

William J. Zeller

Residence life departments committed to supporting the transition and success of new students should explore the expansion of their program and service offerings to include all new student populations—specifically new transfer and graduate students. Because many of these students choose to live on campus at the beginning of their careers, the residence life department has a unique opportunity to serve as a primary connecting point for them to the rest of the university.

Yet, these "other" new students have not traditionally been provided with the same focused attention as first-year undergraduates. Campus staff and faculty have often assumed that these students have the requisite skills and maturity levels needed to immediately succeed in a new campus environment, especially if they are perceived as already having achieved success in higher education. As a result, many campuses have traditionally foregone the development of similar campus-wide initiatives for new transfer and graduate students who are arriving on their campuses each fall. Moreover, transfer students entering as juniors and new graduate students are often more closely affiliated with their academic departments than with the campus at large. For graduate students in particular, their orientation to the campus and connection to campus resources have often been the responsibility of their academic department rather the campus itself. However, these students are often in need of general support services and programs that will facilitate their successful transition to the campus and help them connect to the broader campus community.

Moreover, departmental efforts are often sporadic and inconsistent, leaving many of these new students without the information and tools they need to successfully transition into, and connect with, the broader campus community. A recent national survey on graduate student attrition, for example, found that a lack of integration into the department or the university was the most frequent response given for why student were leaving their institutions prior to graduation (Golde & Dore, 2001). In their need for affiliation, new graduate students are very similar to their first-year undergraduate counterparts. At the same time, new transfers and graduate students have unique needs in making the transition from their previous institution to the culture of a new campus.

Research shows that the adjustment process for transfer students is also likely to be complex—including academic, social, and psychological aspects resulting from the environmental differences between two- and four-year institutions (Laanan, 2006). Townsend and Wilson (2006) found that on many campuses, institutional leaders have concentrated institutional efforts on retaining first-year students through such activities as residential learning communities, freshman interest groups and first-year seminars. Far fewer efforts have been exerted to ensure the retention and success of community college transfer students. (p. 440)

It can therefore be assumed that higher retention of graduate and transfer students might be achieved if their academic and social integration to the campus was strengthened through the same kinds of intentional efforts historically focused on new first-year undergraduates.

This chapter provides an overview of recent trends in graduate and transfer student education that support the development of specialized programs for these new student populations and explores the steps residence life professionals can take to design residential programs that are uniquely suited to address the needs of their campus and its students.

Residential Initiatives for New Graduate Students

Campuses with residential communities specifically designated for graduate students have an important opportunity to provide transitional and educational support programs for them and their families. By doing so, institutions may achieve higher graduate student retention rates, lower incidents of mental health issues, and strengthen educational success and professional development initiatives.

At many research universities, attrition rates of doctoral graduate students are 50% within the first three years of study (Lovitts, 2001). Graduate students are also experiencing significant mental health issues (Hyun, Quinn, Madon, & Lustig, 2006).

In addition, Golde and Dore (2001) indicate that a significant mismatch exists between the purpose of doctoral education, the aspirations of students, and the realities of their careers both within and outside academia. They contend that doctoral students continue to pursue careers as faculty members, and graduate programs persist in providing narrow career training, despite the paucity of academic jobs available. Ninety percent of all research university doctoral students who begin graduate programs do not land tenure-track positions in research universities (Golde & Dore). Realizing this, many graduate students seek opportunities to explore alternate career options, which are not being provided within their academic departments.

In response to these issues, many leaders in higher education (Carnegie Foundation for the Advancement of Teaching, n.d.; Golde & Dore, 2001; Woodrow Wilson National Fellowship Foundation, 2001) are calling for a broadening of the curricular and cocurricular components of graduate education. Collectively, these reports are giving significant attention to:

◇ Designing new and enhanced retention initiatives
◇ Developing interdisciplinary research and curricula
◇ Creating stronger connections to the campus, peers, and faculty
◇ Expanding career development to include non-academic career preparation
◇ Promoting greater diversity within graduate education
◇ Creating physical spaces for community
◇ Encouraging social events

A discussion of specific strategies and considerations for responding to the challenges outlined in these national efforts follows.

Principles of Good Practice

Pontius and Harper (2006) have developed seven student affairs principles for good practice in graduate student engagement. These include: (a) continually striving to eradicate marginalization among underrepresented populations; (b) providing a meaningful orientation to the institution; (c) investing resources in communication with graduate and professional students; (d) facilitating opportunities for community building and multicultural interactions; (e) partnering with academic schools and departments to create engagement plans for students; (f) enhancing career and professional development; and (g) systematically assessing satisfaction, needs, and outcomes. In many ways, these principles can provide a new construct for graduate student residential life programs and staffing responsibilities.

Graduate Student Development

Student development theory has been used as a foundation for understanding and working with undergraduate students for decades. Understanding the developmental stages of traditional-aged undergraduates has helped student affairs practitioners and academic faculty educate their students more successfully. Nonnamaker (2004) has introduced a three-stage model for graduate Ph.D. student development that can serve as an important tool for understanding the commonly encountered challenges facing graduate students as they progress through their graduate careers. The three stages include:

◇ *The Entry Stage (from first year through qualifying exams).* The three main goals of this stage include maintaining motivation, managing academic demands, and developing a clear sense of purpose and direction.
◇ *The Engagement Stage (Years 2-5).* This stage has two main goals, including self-preservation and academic achievement.
◇ *The Exit Stage.* The two main goals of this stage include disengagement from the role of student and reintegration into a new career.

These stages offer unique insights into the graduate student experience, and can serve as a foundation for the development of residential programs and services for graduate students.

Forming Campus Partnerships

In order to create a residential program for new graduate students that supports institutional objectives, residential life staff should initiate discussions with academic and student affairs colleagues across campus to assess institutional curricular and cocurricular goals for graduate students. From these conversations, collaborative partnerships can be explored, which will hopefully result in a quality residential program. As Guentzel & Nesheim (2006) note, "Sharing responsibility for the experiences and learning of graduate and professional students will decrease the fragmentation of the student experience, as well as the isolation, and should enhance the student experience, improve social integration, and lower attrition rates" (p. 103).

At the center of these cross-campus collaborations should be discussions about the foundational elements of residential graduate programs. While the goals and needs of a particular campus will determine to what extent these elements will be incorporated in such programs, on all campuses residential life staff can take the lead in bringing these issues to the surface.

Foundational Elements of Graduate Residential Programs

Recruitment. Conversations with graduate student recruitment staff on campus can create opportunities for making the institution more attractive to prospective students. Specifically, conversations can explore how the graduate residential program can help make the campus more attractive to highly recruited graduate students and enhance the competitiveness of the campus. Other topics might include guaranteed housing, the types of housing options best suited for graduate students and their families, how best to communicate the benefits and services of living on campus, and the provision of tours to visiting students being recruited to the campus.

Career development. At research universities, in particular, graduate students often find it difficult to explore alternative career options within their academic departments. There is generally a lack of support and resources for such exploration, and many report that they are often ostracized from their departments if they show any interest in a career outside of the research-faculty track. These attitudes prevail despite the inability of many Ph.D. graduates to successfully land tenure-track research faculty positions after graduation (Golde & Dore, 2001). The residential community can become a "safe haven" for graduate students wanting to explore alternative career options in industry, entrepreneurship, consulting, and teaching. By partnering with campus career planning professionals and academic department representatives, residential communities can offer career workshops and programs that will help graduate students explore alternative and nontraditional career options. The residential community may also encourage the development of clubs or organizations for graduate students interested in specific alternative career paths.

Retention. The residential community can serve as a "front line" resource for identifying and supporting at-risk graduate students. Conversations with campus colleagues should explore opportunities for defining how the graduate residential program can support the retention of graduate students and how residential life staff can work with campus colleagues to refer at-risk graduate students to appropriate campus resources.

Orientation. The residential program can be a focal point for orienting new graduate students to the campus and the surrounding community. Specialized residential programs can help students connect to their new communities and their resources and quickly acclimate them to their new surroundings. These initiatives can be developed in collaboration with academic department orientation programs so they can complement and not compete with each other.

Diversity. Supporting underrepresented student needs and interests should be a component of a residential first-year graduate program. In addition, the residential communities should be a locale for enhancing all graduate students' understanding and sensitivity to diversity issues.

International graduate students. Many campuses have large numbers of international graduate students whose needs for specialized support services are high. New international students and their families must adjust quickly to the U.S. culture, which may vary considerably by region, and to the campus and their academic department. The residential life program can serve as a significant resource for these students and can assist in their transition to the campus and surrounding community. Conversations with graduate and international staff can contribute to the development of a successful residential graduate program for these students.

Mental health and wellness. Supporting graduate student health and wellness can be an important contribution of a residential FYE program model for graduate students. Studies of graduate student mental health and stress issues indicate that a significant need exists for campuses to identify and support graduate students who are experiencing emotional difficulties. A recent survey at the University of California, Berkeley indicates that 95% of respondents felt overwhelmed in the last 12 months, and 45% had experienced an emotional or stress-related problem that significantly affected their well being and/or academic performance. Nearly 10% had seriously considered suicide in the past 12 months. Despite these reported problems, fewer than 2% indicated they would first contact a campus mental health provider or member of the faculty to discuss an emotional or stress-related problem (Hyun et al., 2006), meaning that residence life staff may need to step in to help students connect with appropriate resources.

Interdisciplinary connections. Many institutions have established goals to facilitate the development of interdisciplinary research and educational connections between graduate students and between graduate students and faculty. Graduate residential communities already provide opportunities for students to meet and socialize with one another across disciplines. With more intentionality, residential life programs could be structured to provide graduate students with an opportunity to have more beneficial interdisciplinary interactions with peers and faculty. From these interactions, incentives from the campus could be provided to promote interdisciplinary collaboration in research, teaching, or other academic work.

Convenient provision of support services. Because graduate students may not be using departmental or campus resources, the residential community may be the best area to provide proactive intervention services for students in need. Specialized services such as career planning, counseling, and international student services could be offered as satellite services within the residential community. In addition, residential programs can help graduate students find recreational and social outlets in order to help them achieve a healthy and balanced lifestyle. Strong collaborations with campus mental health professionals and campus recreation staff can facilitate the development of programs and services uniquely designed to fit the needs of graduate student populations.

Graduate student use of residential technologies. Graduate students' use of residential technologies is often quite different than their undergraduate counterparts. In particular, their research and teaching responsibilities often require them to have technological services similar to those of the faculty, requiring access to research and teaching systems away from their academic departments. Residential technology administrators must collaborate with campus and departmental technology representatives to ensure that the residential technology services are as seamless as possible to graduate students and support their teaching and research responsibilities.

Community service-learning. Many graduate students continue to participate in community service and service-learning activities while they are in graduate school. In addition, colleges and universities are increasingly interested in having graduate students extend their research and teaching expertise into local communities. These programs can be supported by graduate housing residential staff in a number of ways. Graduate residential programs can serve as a center for coordinating some of these activities. In addition, staff can assist other campus partners in the coordination, communication, and other support services needed for these programs. These activities will ultimately be strengthened by close collaboration with academic and other student affairs professionals on campus.

The Graduate Student First Year Initiative at UC Irvine

The Department of Student Housing at the University of California, Irvine (UCI) has embarked on a progressive effort to enhance and support the academic and cocurricular experiences of our graduate students. As an institution, UCI has established a strategic goal to become a national model for curricular and cocurricular graduate education by providing an "on-campus experience for graduate students [that] will be among the best in the nation, with exceptional opportunities for research, housing, and co-curricular activities" (University of California, Irvine, 2004).

In support of this goal, the Department of Student Housing has developed a unique outcomes-based residential program that supports both the transition of new graduate students to the campus and their academic success. With the majority of new graduate students living on campus,

The Graduate First Year Initiative (GFYI) is designed specifically to address the transitional and developmental needs of graduate students by coordinating and front-loading university resources and services to graduate students within their residential communities (http://www.housing.uci.edu/gfyi/). As such, GFYI has three main areas of focus: (a) the expansion of housing to graduate students, (b) a guaranteed on-campus housing for all first-year Ph.D. and MFA students, and (c) programmatic efforts to support these students.

Housing expansion and graduate guarantee. In fall 2006, UCI implemented a long-standing goal of guaranteeing on-campus housing for all new first-year Ph.D. and MFA students. In order to achieve this goal, 1,400 new graduate student bed spaces have been added to the on-campus housing inventory. Approximately 80% of the incoming Ph.D. and M.F.A. students will choose to live on campus, thus making the student housing communities the connecting point between the university and the new graduate student cohort.

Program design. The GFYI was designed to fulfill identified needs drawn from a series of assessment activities including surveys, focus groups, and university and national research findings. From these assessments, a graduate student learning outcomes document was developed to provide a structured framework for the programs and services offered and to guide program assessment. The three main components of the graduate student learning outcomes are:

◇ Increase use of nonacademic and academic campus and community resources
◇ Provide academic and personal development support and enhancement
◇ Help provide social connections, both in the residential community and academically across the campus

In addition, the demographics of the graduate student population have created opportunities for incorporating specialized programs and services to address the needs of specific target populations. These populations include students with partners (41%), families with children (16%), and international students (32%). The service and program offerings introduced in the initial year include:

◇ An orientation to campus and community resources for students, spouses, and families, including walking tours offered in several languages
◇ A series of workshops designed to help international students with their adjustment to the campus and the U.S. culture
◇ A series of programs on financial planning and stress reduction related to finances
◇ A campus-wide welcome event and reception, complete with entertainment
◇ A mentoring program featuring emeritus faculty on panels, dinners, and social events to address issues related to faculty careers, interdisciplinary research, and graduate student and professional development

Future plans. UCI continues to prioritize the successful transition of new graduate students and strives to create a campus environment that provides the resources and tools that will allow them to lead successful careers at our institution and beyond. To that end, the GFYI will expand its service and program offerings in the future to support students' developmental and career goals. Collaboration with a variety of academic and academic support agencies will be essential to successfully fulfill the articulated outcomes and goals of the campus. In addition, a comprehensive assessment model is being developed. Other possible options include:

◇ A web portal and electronic portfolio initiative that will provide graduate students with a personalized structure for accessing campus resources and compiling their academic and cocurricular activities

◇ The development of a residential living-learning program for graduate students modeled after the Council of Graduate Schools' "Preparing Future Faculty Initiative"

◇ The creation of "Professional Interest Groups" to enhance the graduate career preparation along with cocurricular clubs and organizations

◇ The development and creation of a campus-wide graduate student resource center

Residential Programs for Transfer Students

New transfer students can also benefit from a specially designed residential program. Transfer students have adjustment and transition needs that are both similar to, and different from, their native peers. For example, they have similar priorities for making a successful transition to their new campus. In their qualitative study of transfer students at a large research university, Townsend and Wilson (2004) found that transfer students need many of the same specialized programs and services as new first-year students, if for a shorter period of time. Other challenges faced by transfer students are related to the differences between the sending institution (frequently a two-year college) and the receiving institution.

Attending classes taught in large lecture halls by faculty whose priorities are research-focused is very different from the small, teaching-centered classroom of the community college. New transfer students may also have difficulty forming social relationships with peers who have previously established social networks. In fact, Townsend and Wilson speculate that those campuses that have very successful first-year experience programs create such strong campus social networks that they may inhibit transfer students from forming peer relationships. The residential setting may in fact be the ideal location for providing the smaller academic and social connections to the campus that are so beneficial at the very beginning of the transfer student's career. If successful, students can quickly assimilate into the larger campus community once they have made this initial adjustment.

Transfer students are, however, different from first-year students, and some may not be as receptive to these types of services as are new first-time, first-year students. They have typically found academic success at another higher education institution, and their previous success and maturity may diminish their receptiveness to the supports being offered to their first-year peers.

Transfer Student Housing Assignments

Many campuses struggle with decisions regarding the assignment of new transfer students to their residential communities. There is no best model for housing transfer students, and each campus needs to make decisions that best fit the unique philosophies and programs of their campus. There are three fundamental choices that campuses need to consider: (a) housing transfer students with first-year undergraduates, (b) providing specialized housing options for transfer students, or (c) housing transfer students with upper-level peers.

Housing transfer students with new first-year students has both positive and negative implications. On campuses with established residential FYE programs, providing services and programs to transfer students can be achieved without the duplication of resources and expenses. However, transfer students often have an aversion to being identified with new undergraduates, and housing these two groups together can often send the wrong institutional message regarding the status of transfers on campus.

There are also potential benefits to housing transfer students with new first-year students. Being part of a community of peers can provide the most supportive environment for new transfers. In addition, specially crafted program offerings can address the unique transitional and adjustment needs of new transfer students and will more likely attract them to participate. Yet, housing transfers together may inhibit their ability to connect with their nontransfer peers. In addition, it often creates a need to duplicate services and programs that are already being offered to first-year students.

Assigning transfer students to upper-level student housing communities can be beneficial in allowing new transfers to connect with peers who are established on campus and within the same class levels. These peers can serve as mentors and resources for new transfer students. When the communities are designed appropriately, they may be the best option for new transfer students. However, special attention still needs to be given to their unique needs, especially at the beginning of their first term, and specialized programs and services still need to be offered within these communities. Clustering transfer students together within upper-level housing communities is another option for campuses to consider.

A Residential Program for Transfer Students

Although the components of a successful residential transfer program should in many ways mirror residential FYE programs, particular emphasis must be given to the unique needs of transfer students and the accelerated timeline that they have for transitioning into the campus and matriculating to graduation. Townsend and Wilson (2006) suggest that transfer students need a bit of handholding and encourage campuses to implement transition resources to support academic and social integration to the campus during the first few weeks of the new term. Thus, the components of a successful residential program for transfer students should include:

◇ Connection to campus recruitment activities
◇ Connection to transfer student orientation
◇ Provision of transitional support activities
◇ Introduction to academic support services
◇ Introduction to campus involvement opportunities
◇ Opportunities for building connections with peers, faculty, and the campus

These components are discussed in greater detail below.

Recruitment activities. Participation in the recruitment of new transfer students to the campus should be a component of a residential transfer student program. Quality residential life opportunities for new transfer students should be viewed as a recruitment advantage for the campus, and successfully communicating and marketing these opportunities are important recruitment strategies. Specialized campus marketing materials for new transfer students should communicate the importance of living on campus for new transfers.

In addition, the residential program should be articulated as a campus initiative, not just a residential life initiative. Tours of transfer student housing facilities during on-campus transfer student tours should be included. Campus and departmental web sites and marketing materials should be consistent in their communications about the residential transfer program and should be given a high profile on these web sites.

Orientation. Townsend and Wilson (2006) state that large universities may need to reexamine and rethink their approach to orienting new transfer students. Some transfer students may need a comprehensive ongoing introduction to the curricular and cocurricular resources, something many campuses do not currently provide. The residential community can be an ideal setting for sponsoring all or part of this program. The orientation of new transfer students who have chosen to live on campus should be a stated outcome of a residential transfer program.

Transitional support services. Transfer students have immediate needs for support to facilitate their seamless academic and social transition to the campus community. Residential programs can provide great assistance by immediately helping transfer students learn to navigate the campus, learn where essential resources are, and conveniently find assistance when needed. New transfers are often living away from home for the first time and supporting their adjustment to independence is important. These types of services will be of great assistance, particularly during the first stage of their career. It would be worthwhile to consider adding staff and/or volunteers to serve as a resource for transfers over the first few weeks—allowing them to become independent as quickly as possible. Transfer students from previous years could be excellent resources for this critical need.

Academic support services. Residential communities can be the ideal location for the "front-loaded" provision of academic support services specifically designed for new transfer students. Academic advising, tutoring, technology support services, career planning services, counseling services, and study group assistance can generate higher levels of interest and participation when they are located within transfer student residential communities. Specially crafted services and programs that are conveniently located where students live can overcome the reluctance many transfer students feel toward the use of services that appear to be targeted specifically toward first-year students. Residential life professionals can work to create satellite spaces and offices within transfer residential communities suitable for use by campus academic support offices.

Campus involvement opportunities. Townsend and Wilson (2006) remind us that "institutions should not assume that transfer students are uninterested in co-curricular activities" (p. 452). Thus, a residential transfer student program should be designed to help new transfers quickly find opportunities for involvement on campus. Residential staff and community members can intentionally seek out transfer students for involvement. In addition, campus and residential student government positions and committee assignments can formally appoint transfer students to designated positions. Not only will they have a voice in community issues, but they will also have the opportunity to engage in community activities.

Connections with peers, faculty, and the campus. Perhaps more than any other new-student population, transfer students have a great need to quickly establish connections with peers, faculty, and the campus community as they transition into their new surroundings. Their peers include other transfer students and returning upper-level students. Other transfer students (both new and returning) can serve as an important support network and mentoring resource for new transfer students. Residential communities and their programs can be structured to provide opportunities for transfer students to build these connections. Orientation activities, early social events, and other programs can be intentionally structured to help new transfer students connect with this peer resource.

Returning upper-level students, particularly those serving in leadership positions within the residential community, can also be cultivated to help new transfer students transition successfully into the upper-level student culture of the campus. Without intentionally creating these opportunities, new transfer students may have difficulty building connections with their returning student peers.

Residential programs can also provide transfer students with opportunities to build connections with faculty—both within and outside of their departments. Particularly on large campuses, creating opportunities for having out-of-class connections with faculty is a way to introduce transfer students to an important component of the upper-level student experience. Faculty and staff who were transfer students as undergraduates are a resource that residential programs can use for these types of programs.

Conclusion

Developing first-year residential programs for other new student populations can significantly support institutional goals for recruitment, retention, and student learning. The transitional support needs of graduate and transfer students are equally as important as the needs of first-year students. Residential life professionals must collaborate with campus professionals responsible for working with these new student populations in order to design facilities and services to meet their transition needs.

References

Carnegie Foundation for the Advancement of Teaching. (n.d.). *The Carnegie initiative on the doctorate*. Retrieved July 2, 2008, from http://www.carnegiefoundation.org/programs/sub.asp?key=29

Golde, C. M., & Dore, T. M. (2001). *At cross purposes: What the experiences of doctoral students reveal about doctoral education*. Philadelphia, PA: The Pew Charitable Trusts. Retrieved February 11, 2008, from http:// www.phd-survey.org

Guentzel M. J., & Nesheim, B. E. (2006). Throwing pebbles at Stonehenge: Advocating for graduate and professional students. In M. J. Guentzel & B. Elkins Nesheim (Eds.). *Supporting graduate and professional students: The role of student affairs* (New Directions for Student Services No. 115, pp. 101-105). San Francisco: Jossey-Bass.

Hyun, J., Quinn, B. C., Madon, T., & Lustig, S. (2006). Graduate student mental health: Needs assessment and utilization of counseling services. *Journal of College Student Development, 47*(3), 247-266.

Laanan, F. S. (Ed.). (2006). *Understanding students in transition: Trends and issues* (New Directions for Student Services, No. 114). San Francisco: Jossey-Bass.

Lovitts, B. (2001). *Leaving the ivory tower: The causes and consequences of departure from doctoral study*. Lanham, MD: Roman and Littlefield.

Nonnamaker, J. (2004, March). *A model for graduate student development*. Paper presented at the National Association of Student Personnel Administrators Conference, Denver, CO. Retrieved July 2, 2008, from, http://web.mit.edu/nonnama/www/graduatestudentdevelopmentnaspa2004.pdf

Pontius, J. L., & Harper, S. R. (2006). Principles for good practice in graduate and professional student engagement. In M. Guentzel & B. Elkins Nesheim (Eds.), *Supporting graduate and professional students: The role of student affairs* (New Directions for Student Services No. 115, p. 47–58). San Francisco: Jossey-Bass.

Townsend, B. K., & Wilson, K. B. (2006) "A hand hold for a little bit": Factors facilitating the success of community college transfer students to a large research university. *Journal of College Student Development, 47*(4), 439-456.

University of California, Irvine. (2004, December). *A focus on excellence: A strategy for academic development at UCI through 2014*. Retrieved July 2, 2008, from www.evc.uci.edu/planning/plan1204/draft-1204.pdf

Woodrow Wilson National Fellowship Foundation. (2001). *The responsive Ph.D.* Retrieved March 26, 2008, from http://www.woodrow.org/responsivephd

Chapter Thirteen

Assessing First-Year Residential Programs

Andrew Beckett and John R. Purdie, II

Ssessment. For some, this word conjures up images of statistics and charts. Others might think of evaluation, research, or accountability. Too many of us assume assessment means spending an inordinate amount of time, effort, and money. Upcraft and Schuh (1996) define assessment as "any effort to gather, analyze, and interpret evidence which describes institutional, divisional, or agency effectiveness" (p. 18). While we use this definition in our own work and have selected it as the basis for this chapter, we subscribe to Charles Schroeder's view that "assessment is first and foremost about caring" (personal communication, February 18, 2002). Do we care enough about our students to deeply understand their experience and their needs? Do we care enough about our work to find out how effective our efforts are and make the necessary improvements? We begin with the assumption that most educators possess this level of caring. Thus, this chapter does not advocate for assessment; rather, it seeks to demystify assessment and provide a basic primer on how to develop and implement a comprehensive assessment plan to improve a first-year residential program.

Three Roles of Assessment

Although there are different opinions regarding the definition of assessment, we operate from a very simple and practical perspective: Assessment is intentionally gathering evidence, interpreting that evidence (a process Seymour [1995] describes as turning evidence into useful information), and then using that information (e.g., to improve, inform others, or identify student needs). We use the word "assessment" to refer to both a process and a product. One of the benefits of this simplistic view is that it validates a wide range of assessment activities and recognizes that evidence takes a variety of forms.

The first role of assessment is justifying and informing the creation of a first-year residential program. Why should (or does) this program exist? What is it seeking to accomplish? The answers to these questions are the basis for a program's goals. Ideally, these answers come as the result of an initial and ongoing assessment of the needs of the students, faculty, and institution. Programs that are intentionally designed to meet specific needs are more likely to be successful.

The second role of assessment is measuring a program's outcomes, which requires clearly stating what the program is intended to produce. Are there things students should know or be able to do as a result of participating in the program (i.e., learning outcomes)? First-year residential programs often have goals related to retention and academic performance that take the form of targets or comparative benchmarks. Strategies for measuring these different types of outcomes will be addressed in more detail below.

A third role of assessment is measuring the program's processes (i.e., how well did we do what we wanted to do?), which is different from goal assessment (i.e., did we achieve the desired effect?). This is an important role of assessment because it can suggest where to look if the intended outcomes are not achieved. When programs do what they plan to do but fail to achieve the desired results, it suggests that the program may need to be changed in some way.

A Comprehensive and Systematic Assessment Plan

In order to gain a complete understanding of a first-year residential program, one must do more than simply conduct a year-end survey. A comprehensive and systematic plan must be developed and implemented. This may sound like a daunting and time-consuming task, but with diligence and patience a relatively sophisticated plan can be developed and put into place. The first thing to accept is that it requires a multi-year perspective and to recognize that not every program or every aspect of a program needs to be assessed every year. Further, the plan should be a living document, open to amendment as the plan is implemented. Over time, what needs to be assessed and how to best assess it will become clearer.

Assessment should not be the responsibility of any one individual or office. It is critical to involve a variety of people in developing, implementing, and monitoring the assessment plan. Faculty members can provide a wide range of expertise (e.g., developing outcomes, critically analyzing questions, analyzing data, and presenting results). Senior- and mid-level residence life professionals, as well as, the staff and students directly involved in the program should also be included in the development and monitoring of the plan as each brings a different perspective. Having a broad-based, collaborative team that is still small enough to actually accomplish tasks is an immense help in this process.

Goals and Outcomes

Although it has been convincingly argued that high-quality assessment can have a problem-based foundation (Schuh & Upcraft, 2001), we believe that a comprehensive and systematic assessment plan begins first and foremost with goals and outcomes. The first step to creating an assessment plan is to ensure the goals and intended outcomes of a given first-year residential program are clearly defined and measurable. A conceptual structure that can be very helpful in organizing and clarifying a program's goals and outcomes is a logic model (Frechtling, 2007; W. K. Kellogg Foundation, 2004). A logic model (see Figure 13.1) is a versatile tool that can be used for a variety of purposes such as program planning, identifying how program elements are intended to connect to goals and outcomes, identifying goals or outcomes that are inadequately supported by program elements, and providing an initial idea of what might be needed to create a comprehensive assessment plan. Typically, a logic model is much more complex than the one presented here, with multiple boxes for learning outcomes, program outcomes, and program elements.

Program elements are the specific activities, programs, bulletin boards, and services that make up the overall first-year residential program. Each of these has a long list of tasks and other

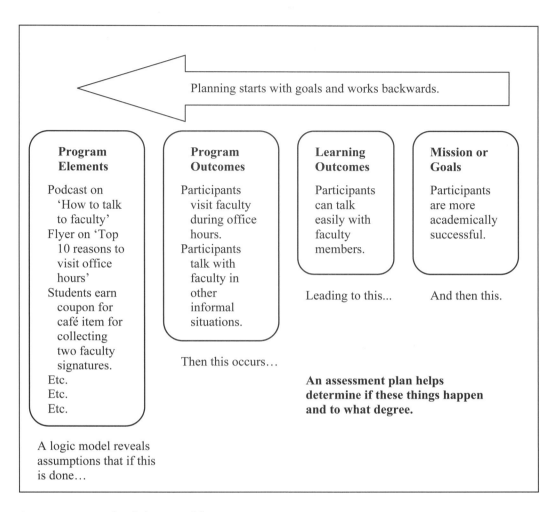

Figure 13.1. Example of a logic model.

activities associated with them, and it is here that the hall staff spend the vast majority of their time. These tasks are done in order that program elements take place because there is an assumption that these tasks and program elements lead to certain outcomes. Bresciani, Zelna, and Anderson (2004) distinguish between program outcomes (i.e., targets or benchmarks) and student learning outcomes, which they define as what a student should be able to know or do as a result of the program element. In our experience, assessment plans often focus primarily on program outcomes (e.g., 85% of program participants visited at least one faculty member during office hours) and remain largely silent on student learning outcomes (e.g., 65% of students are able to list at least 3 reasons for talking with faculty outside of class). A comprehensive assessment plan pays attention to both learning and program outcomes. Examples of measurable goals, program outcomes, and individual student learning outcomes follow.

Goals

Participants will...

◇ Return to the institution (or residence halls) at higher rates than non-participants
◇ Earn higher GPAs than nonparticipants
◇ Be more satisfied than nonparticipants
◇ Earn more credits (and/or drop fewer courses) than nonparticipants
◇ Solidify their selection of a major
◇ Develop short-term and long-term academic goals

Individual Learning Outcomes

Participants will...

◇ Know how to effectively utilize faculty office hours
◇ Know what campus resources exist and when to use them
◇ Be able to articulate their values regarding the purpose of a college education
◇ Be able to determine which notetaking style is most appropriate for them
◇ Know what academic majors they are most interested in

Program Outcomes

Participants will...

◇ Have conversations with faculty outside class
◇ Visit at least two faculty members during their office hours
◇ Explore careers and related majors
◇ Participate in social programming offered

The next step is to determine how each goal and outcome will be measured. Notice that many of the goals above have been defined in such a way as to be quantitatively measured, although some can also be measured qualitatively. Deciding on how one will know the degree to which each goal is being achieved is a critical step, and one that should be regularly revisited. Asking questions such as, "What would it take to convince a skeptic that this goal or outcome had been reached? What might they see, hear, feel, experience, observe, etc. and accept as evidence?" can help focus the process of developing measurements (P. Fabiano, personal communication, October, 17, 2007) to which we now turn.

In addition to both program outcomes and learning outcomes, a comprehensive plan must also assess the degree to which the program's goals are achieved while taking into account the individual student characteristics. Astin's (1993) parsimonious Input-Environment-Output model serves as an excellent reminder that we must take into account students' individual characteristics whenever we seek to assess the impact our programs are having. One of the easiest aspects of any assessment plan is annually collecting demographic data (e.g., high school GPA, SAT/ACT scores, sex, race, ethnicity, in-state/out-of-state), provided effective partnerships with the institutional research or registrar's office have been established.

Quantitative and Qualitative Assessment Methods

Although the debate over the relative merits of quantitative versus qualitative methodologies has raged for years, we join the growing number of researchers who have concluded that both methods are needed in order to gain a complete understanding of student needs and program effectiveness. Here, we offer the pros and cons of each method so that readers can make informed choices about which methods will best serve their needs in particular situations. Both qualitative and quantitative methods should be used as part of a comprehensive assessment plan.

Qualitative Methods

Qualitative assessment has been defined as "the detailed description of the situations, events, people, interactions, and observed behaviors" and is designed to enhance understanding of phenomena or experiences (Upcraft & Schuh, 1996, p. 12). It involves "the use of direct quotations from people about their experiences, attitudes, beliefs, and thoughts; and the analysis of excerpts or entire passages from documents, correspondence, records and case histories" (Upcraft & Schuh, p. 12). The strength of qualitative methods is that they provide rich answers to questions of "why" and "how" and allow for an in-depth understanding of people's experiences. One of the more significant costs associated with qualitative methods is that data collection methods and analysis are extremely time consuming compared to quantitative approaches.

Two of the more commonly used and effective qualitative methods are focus groups and interviews. Both of these allow researchers to ask follow-up questions so a more complete understanding of experience can be gained. Focus groups and interviews are useful tools for assessing what students (or faculty or staff) think about something and why, how they describe their experience, why they describe it in this way, and what they value and believe is important.

Quantitative Methods

Whereas qualitative methods are about understanding why, quantitative methods are frequently about making comparisons (e.g., between points in time, between participants and nonparticipants) and identifying relationships (e.g., between a given outcome and those participating in the program). People commonly assume that quantitative methods are more objective. However, just as with qualitative data, the results of quantitative methods must also be interpreted. The process of discerning "what the numbers mean" is a subjective process.

Surveys are perhaps the most commonly used quantitative method. Other frequently used methods include examining institutional data (e.g., GPAs, retention and graduation rates, demographic data) and tracking program specific data (e.g., participation rates). Quantitative methods are useful for assessing who is participating, how satisfied participants are and which participants are more satisfied, whether program participants are achieving outcomes such as retention, and which program elements are associated with desired outcomes.

Assessment Tools

This section provides an overview of the various tools educators commonly use to assess first-year residential programs. Both qualitative tools (i.e., focus groups and interviews) and quantitative tools (i.e., nationally normed surveys, home-grown instruments, and other passive techniques) are discussed below. However, we urge the reader to obtain a copy of Schuh and Upcraft's (2001) invaluable handbook *Assessment Practice in Student Affairs: An Application Manual* for a thorough, step-by-step set of instructions for implementing a wider variety of assessment tools. A list of other helpful resources is included in the chapter appendix.

Focus Groups

As with every assessment process, one must first determine what it is he or she wants to know and then develop a set of questions. The major advantage that focus groups have over most assessment techniques is that participants interact with one another and can respond to other participants' views. One participant's response may generate an entire discussion that would not have occurred if the data were collected via a survey or individual interview. However, because participants are interacting with one another, focus groups may not be appropriate for gathering information on topics of a sensitive or highly personal nature. Group membership should also be intentionally determined and can be based on a variety of criteria (e.g., race/ethnicity, gender, distance from home, campus involvement). Since this tool provides perceptions of the group and not the individuals, one should create a variety of homogenous groups.

Most focus groups begin with questions that are broad and open-ended (e.g., What is your general impression of the programs offered in this community?). Such questions prevent the facilitator from "leading" the participants and allow them to describe their experiences in their own words. As the conversation progresses, questions can become more focused to ensure that the participants' views on particular issues are heard (e.g., Have any of you attended any of the dinners in the faculty discussion series? Tell me about those.). Eventually, one can get to the heart of the matter (e.g., In your opinion, has living here helped you become more or less comfortable talking with faculty? Why?). Given the richness of the data generated via this tool it is advisable to create an audio recording of the session and elicit the help of a second person to observe and take notes. After the session is over, the facilitator should record his or her notes and look for emerging themes. Once all the sessions are completed, session tapes or transcripts are reviewed to identify prevailing themes. Generally, participants' names are excluded from reports and are replaced with descriptors such as the participants' gender, ethnicity, or other characteristics related to the assessment. When presenting the results, direct quotes can be useful in illustrating important themes.

Interviews

Similar to focus groups, interviews can provide rich insights into the student experience. The process of conducting an interview is similar to that of a focus group. One should identify what he or she needs to know, develop questions that will help participants provide data, and then set up opportunities to speak with individual students. To be clear, an interview is not about collecting survey data orally; it is more like a focus group of one. The data generated are analyzed in the same way data from focus groups are analyzed. The advantage of interviews over focus groups is that they are a private conversation, so participants may be more willing to share their views, particularly regarding topics that may be sensitive in nature. The obvious disadvantage is that they take more time to gather data from the same number of participants.

Nationally Normed Instruments

A common tool for residence educators interested in assessment is the use of a nationally normed instrument. There are several benefits for using such a tool. First, it is convenient. One does not have to spend time creating questions, distributing the survey, or analyzing the results, which means more time can be devoted to interpreting the results and applying them. Second, nationally normed surveys typically provide data from a pooled sample of students at similar institutions, making benchmarking or comparison against other programs or institutions possible. Such comparisons can provide one with information regarding a program's strengths and areas for improvement. Finally, using nationally normed instruments on a regular basis allows one to track how student responses change over time.

One of the primary disadvantages to using such surveys is cost. Depending on the instrument and the number of students surveyed, the cost for one administration can range from $1000 to more than $10,000. Since the questions used on such surveys are designed for a national audience, they may not be helpful in assessing issues on a particular campus. Finally, the nature of the survey design may mean that the responses are difficult or impossible to merge with other data already available at the institution, which precludes the possibility of cross-tabulating the responses with institutional data or with data gathered from other surveys. While certainly not an exhaustive list, the following are common instruments that may be useful for educators in assessing residential programs.

The Resident Assessment. Partnering with the Association of College & University Housing Officers – International (ACUHO-I), Educational Benchmarking Incorporated (EBI) provides three assessment tools for residence educators interested in measuring student perspectives on issues ranging from paraprofessionals to roommates. One of these three surveys, *The Resident Assessment*, is not designed specifically to assess first-year students. However, it is a comprehensive assessment of satisfaction with the residential experience that can be easily disaggregated by a variety of demographic indicators, including class standing, residence, and program participation. Furthermore, EBI will provide the results of six similar but unidentified institutions, so that a campus can compare its results to peer institutions.

Results from *The Resident Assessment* are often used to compare the perceptions of students who live in a first-year experience program setting to those who live in other buildings. The survey asks how satisfied students are with the sense of community on their floor, how easily they have made social connections, how readily they can find someone with whom to study, if they feel respected by their peers, if they have learned how to effectively resolve conflicts, and many other questions that are likely to be closely aligned with the objectives of a first-year residential program.

National Study of Living-Learning Programs (NSLLP). The NSLLP measures the impact of living-learning communities on social and academic outcomes. While not currently available on an annual basis, the NSLLP is the only nationally normed instrument specifically designed to assess residential learning initiatives. Participating institutions have the ability to benchmark themed-based communities against those at other institutions. For example, a campus can compare the effectiveness of its science and technology learning community with science and technology communities at similar institutions. A second survey administration took place during the 2006-2007 academic year and data are being analyzed at the time of this writing.

National Survey of Student Engagement (NSSE). The NSSE is designed to measure "student participation in programs and activities that institutions provide for their learning and personal development" (National Survey of Student Engagement, 2007). Fundamentally, NSSE measures the extent to which students focus on their academic work and the type of interactions they have with other students and faculty. It is based on the premise that the more time students spend on academically relevant activities, the more they will learn. Although the NSSE is designed to help institutions measure student engagement, it can also be used as an environmental measure for residence halls. Therefore, residence educators interested in promoting academic success may wish to collaborate with their office of institutional research to review NSSE data for residential students. As long as there is a sufficient sample and return rate, NSSE scores can be disaggregated by first-year residential program participation and compared to more traditional halls to gain insight into which, if any, types of student engagement is being fostered.

Cooperative Institutional Research Program (CIRP) Freshman Survey and *Your First College Year (YFCY) Survey.* Similar to the NSSE, the CIRP Freshman Survey and the YFCY Survey are typically used on an institutional level to benchmark against other institutions. The Freshman Survey is designed to measure student characteristics at college entry. As a stand-alone instrument, the Freshman Survey serves as an effective tool for understanding the values, beliefs, and background of students and their needs. YFCY measures the academic and personal development achieved during the first year of college. Used together, institutions can see how the students change during their first year of college. As with the NSSE, this tool could be used to compare participants in a first-year residential experience to non-participants.

Institutional Surveys

The limitations of nationally normed instruments have been noted earlier. "Home-grown" assessments can provide institutionally specific information and will likely provide a more in-depth understanding of student perceptions of a particular campus environment or initiative. Web-based programs, such as SurveyMonkey and Zoomerang, allow practitioners to design, distribute, and even analyze surveys for a relatively low cost. Many institutions also use web-based instructional sites such as Blackboard and WebCT that have built-in assessment features.

As opposed to nationally normed surveys, the limitation of a home-grown survey is precisely that one must develop the survey questions, pilot the instrument, distribute it, collect the data, and analyze the results oneself. However, every campus possesses a rich and all too often untapped resource to address this limitation, its own faculty and staff. Many articles, books, and courses are also available to teach the intricacies of survey design, sampling, and interpretation. It is not realistic for this chapter to cover such topics in-depth; however, we suggest the following questions to guide survey design:

◇ What are we trying to learn?
◇ Who can provide this information?
◇ What questions would elicit that information?
◇ What are we going to be able to do with the results?

This final question is critical. In our experience a question is often predicated by "wouldn't it be interesting to know…," and there seem to be an infinite number of things people find "interesting." However, the purpose of assessment is being able to use the information. Interesting questions often do not yield useful information. We cannot emphasize enough how important it is to know how the data will be used before it is collected.

Institutional and Secondary Data Sources

Designing a survey or conducting a focus group is a time-intensive process for both the practitioner and students. Often, nonintrusive assessments that use existing institutional data can provide helpful information to residence educators in the design, implementation, and evaluation of residential programs. Basic demographic information can be very helpful (e.g., Who are your students? What are their academic majors? How many are from out of state? What are their socio-economic, religious, and ethnic backgrounds?). Institutional data can also be used to help identify the need for programs (e.g., What first-year courses have high failure rates? Are there particular majors that have high dropout rates?). Some data may provide insight into the effectiveness of programs (e.g., After accounting for entering abilities, do participants have higher grades? Were they retained at a higher rate?).

In addition to data provided by the registrar, there are other secondary sources that could be helpful to practitioners. For example, to better understand student needs and behaviors, one can systematically browse electronic communities such as Facebook or MySpace to learn more about students. Many institutions have also adopted electronic portfolios as a means for helping students organize and make meaning of their collegiate experience. Such portfolios can be used to assess both student needs and outcomes.

Reporting Results

Reporting assessment results is perhaps the most difficult step in the assessment process. As Seymour (1995) notes, "Measurement without feedback is just data" (p. 75). Raw data are seldom of much use; at the very least they must be collated and put into an easy to read format. Determining how the data will be analyzed and with whom it will be shared prior to conducting the assessment will help ensure that the results will be used. Far too often assessments are administered, a brief report is written, and the report is filed and never used. It is not possible to cover all the details of how to report results in this chapter, but the following suggestions may assist program administrators in thinking through this process.

Assessment is always political (Upcraft & Schuh, 1996), and so the intended audience for the assessment results is a primary consideration. What is their connection to, and level of knowledge regarding, the program being assessed? What kind of information will they prefer? Are they more likely to relate to students' personal voices or statistical analysis? If the latter, what is their level of expertise with statistics? Second, what is the best method for displaying the results: a table, graph, direct quotation, concise summary, or detailed description? Should data be presented in disaggregated form, and if so, to whom? For example, if disaggregated data would highlight performance disparities between various programs, one must be thoughtful in how information about low-performing programs is distributed, especially if sharing the results publicly might embarrass individual administrators or instructors. Ensuring those directly responsible for programs are always involved in both developing and reporting assessment results is critical.

Sharing results via a written report will be appropriate for most assessment and audiences. However, ongoing reports of assessment may help create a culture that uses the results. Regularly setting aside 15 minutes in a staff meeting, dedicating a section of a newsletter, offering brown bag lunches, or including results in professional development opportunities will likely be more effective than sending a single, exhaustive report to constituents once a year. Furthermore, such practices remind organizational leaders of the importance of assessment, which, in turn, helps create a culture that makes decisions based on results versus anecdotes.

Developing a Timeline

Moving from episodic, unconnected assessment activities to a comprehensive and systematic assessment plan requires collaboration, patience, and most of all leadership and commitment. Even if a department has a full-time staff member responsible for assessment, he or she cannot possibly do everything. Furthermore, it is more likely to get institutional buy-in if the entire organization becomes invested in the assessment. Determining in advance who will be responsible for the various components of the plan and spreading that responsibility widely will help create an organizational culture that embraces assessment. It will also help the organization take into account the time involved in assessment so that staff are not overburdened with other responsibilities during the process.

For example, if a program would like to know whether a sense of community has developed in a particular residence hall during the first six weeks of the fall term compared to other residence halls, this is one aspect of its overall assessment plan. In this situation, we will assume that a short survey has been developed to assess this outcome. This portion of the assessment plan that focuses on data collection, analysis, and dissemination might look something like this:

Week 5 – Generate a random sample of residents in each community and prepare survey for distribution.
Week 6 – Distribute survey.
Week 7 – Collect and analyze data.
Week 8 – Discuss results at senior staff and resident director staff meetings and make decisions about what actions, if any, need to be taken.
Week 9 – Discuss results and intended actions at resident assistant staff meetings and shared with residents.
Week 10 – Discuss actions (if any were taken) at resident director and senior staff meetings

Providing this level of detail in the plan allows for advanced notice of when data are being collected and discussed. Housing operations are notorious for having staff meetings dominated by urgent, but not always important, issues. Therefore, planning a discussion of the results in advance will help ensure that the topic is deemed a priority for that given week. Furthermore, planning to take action during the ninth week indicates to all staff that there are implications of the results and that assessment drives ongoing program planning and development. Providing details such as 'resident assistants will distribute the survey during the sixth week' and 'hall directors will share the results with their staff the ninth week' will help ensure that members of the organization understand their roles and responsibilities regarding assessment.

As various elements of the assessment plan are developed and put onto an annual timeline, one can begin to see the time involved in collecting, analyzing, and using the results, and how these activities overlap with other obligations of staff. One of the benefits of developing a timeline is that it can be used to drive an iterative conversation regarding what needs to be assessed, and when/how frequently it needs to be assessed (e.g., monthly, quarterly, annually, less than once a year). For example, it might be determined that outcomes like community development need to be assessed every fall, while outcomes related to faculty interaction, major selection, and leadership development might receive a thorough assessment once every couple years. In most departments, there simply is not sufficient time and budget available to assess every aspect of a first-year residential program every year, and even if there were, it takes time to develop and implement program improvements. Feeding assessment results to a program faster than it can reasonably react might lead the staff to create a diffused and less-meaningful array of responses. Additionally, assessing something before there has been adequate time for a program to react is wasted effort, providing data that simply reinforce what was already known.

Getting Started: A Case Study

This chapter was designed to give the reader an overview of the roles of assessment in residential education with a focus on the importance of connecting assessment with learning outcomes as well as highlighting tools, techniques, and considerations for conducting and reporting assessments. However, we offer a hypothetical first-year experience assessment plan as an example of how assessment can be done throughout an organization.

Midwest University is a public institution in southern Iowa serving 15,000 undergraduates, 5,000 of whom live on campus. The hometowns of 80% of the students are within two hours of the campus; however, the university's nationally known business program is a large draw for out-of-state students. The Department of Residence Life at Midwest, which primarily serves first-year and sophomore students, offers 10 living-learning communities designed to integrate curricular experiences into the residential setting.

Each year, the department of residential life partners with institutional research to administer the CIRP Freshman Survey. Because the institution has participated in the CIRP since 1990, it has the ability to analyze how student values and aspirations have changed over time. This information has been particularly helpful in planning programs for students. For example, in the late 1990s, the department noticed a large shift in the number of students who were affiliated with a religious organization and decided to collaborate with local religious organizations to provide opportunities for dialogues on various religious topics. Recently, the data have indicated an increasing percentage of incoming students who have consumed alcohol during high school. The department of residence life shared these data with the health center, and together, they increased programming aimed at curbing binge drinking.

Every other year, the department participates in the YFCY, gaining valuable insight into how students spend their time and how their experience has changed their values and beliefs. Disaggregating the data by residence hall and learning community has allowed the department to assess how various residential environments shape the student experience. During the years when YFCY is not administered, the department identifies different normed surveys to address specific issues it currently faces. For example, it 2003, it used an instrument created by EBI to assess the effectiveness of its paraprofessional positions.

In addition to national surveys, residence educators at Midwest administer a student survey in the fall and spring terms. The survey has helped the staff at Midwest understand their strengths and areas for improvement. The fall survey is administered after the fourth week of class. Students are asked about their satisfaction with facilities, programming, and staff as well as their degree of involvement with both fellow residents and the campus in general. The results are disaggregated by hall and community and given to the hall director one week after the data are collected. The results are then discussed at every level of the department—from the senior administrators to the resident assistants, as well as with the RHA and hall governments. The results are also summarized and posted in each hall; the full results are posted electronically. If some results are unclear, hall staff conduct focus groups with students over dinner to better understand the issues. The students' reactions to the results are also fed back into the staff discussions.

Based upon the results, decisions are made (many of which are directly communicated back to the residents). Items of interest are then reassessed via the spring survey. More importantly, the spring survey serves as the department's mechanism for assessing the seven learning outcomes it has developed for students. Through a series of discussions with faculty associated with the learning communities and colleagues in the college student personnel program from a nearby campus, the department generated three to five questions to measure the degree to which students are achieving the residential learning objectives. Each spring the department measures one or two of the learning objectives using these questions.

In addition to surveys, the department collaborates with colleagues in institutional research to examine the academic achievement and retention of first-year students by hall and learning community. This analysis has been extremely helpful for both the department and the institution at large. For example, several years ago the department began to notice trends in attrition for some of its buildings. It added a question on its spring survey that simply asked students if they planned to return next fall. Taking advantage of the predictable mid-spring lull in the hall directors' conduct load and the completion of the RA selection process, each residence hall director was asked to interview as many of the students who indicated they were leaving as they could during a two-week period to gather information about why the student was leaving. The data were pooled and several trends emerged. These trends were shared with the director of enrollment management, and strategies involving both academic and student affairs were jointly created.

The Midwest assessment plan demonstrates how one may systematically use assessment to measure student needs, experiences, and outcomes in a cost-effective manner. Using national surveys and local assessments, the department monitors student perceptions and outcomes in an effort to continuously improve the college experience. National results are used in staff training and goal development. Institutional data are quickly disseminated to frontline staff so that they can address local issues in a timely manner. Assessment results are shared with campus colleagues who, in turn, are involved in the design and implementation of future assessment projects.

Every Journey Begins With a Single Step

In conclusion, we would like to offer this simple observation: Like so many things, the only way to really learn how to do assessment is to start doing it. We have learned invaluable lessons from respected colleagues like Charles Schroeder, Lee Upcraft, Gary Pike, Trudy Banta, and Greg Blimling, and we have benefited greatly from working alongside many colleagues we cherish deeply. This chapter is a reflection of what we have learned from them, and we hope it is a useful contribution to your learning. However, much of what we have learned about assessment has also come from our own experience, which has often seemed to us as little better than "trial and error." But no one learns how to do anything without making some mistakes along the way. Assessment is no different. Assessment is also an iterative process; one that you will improve upon as you engage in it. Start somewhere. Build on your strengths and expand from there.

References

Astin, A. W. (1993). *Assessment for excellence: The philosophy and practice of assessment and evaluation in higher education.* Westport, CT: American Council on Education, Oryx Press.

Bresciani, M. L., Zelna, C. L., & Anderson, J. A. (2004). *Assessing student learning and development: A handbook for practitioners.* Washington, DC: National Association of Student Personnel Administrators.

Frechtling, J. A. (2007). *Logic modeling: Methods in program evaluation.* San Francisco: John Wiley & Sons.

Seymour, D. (1995). *Once upon a campus: Lessons for improving quality and productivity in higher education.* Phoenix: Oryx Press.

Schuh, J. H., & Upcraft, M. L. (2001). *Assessment practice in student affairs: An application manual.* San Francisco: Jossey-Bass.

Upcraft, M. L., & Schuh, J. H. (1996). *Assessment in student affairs: A guide for practitioners.* San Francisco: Jossey-Bass.

W. K. Kellogg Foundation. (2004). *Logic model development guide.* Retrieved January 15, 2008, from http://www.wkkf.org/pubs/tools/evaluation/pub3669.pdf

Appendix

Suggested Resources

Recommended Readings on Assessment

Krueger, R. A. (1994). *Focus groups: A practical guide for applied research.* Thousand Oaks, CA: Sage.

Astin, A. W., et al. (1996). *Nine principles of good practice for assessing student learning.* Washington, DC: American Association for Higher Education. Retrieved July 2, 2008, from http://www.fctel.uncc.edu/pedagogy/assessment/9Principles.html

Patton, M. Q. (2002). *Qualitative research and evaluation methods.* Thousand Oaks, CA: Sage.

Rea, L .M., & Parker, R. A. (2005). *Designing and conducting survey research: A comprehensive guide* (3rd ed.). San Francisco: Jossey-Bass.

Schuh, J. H., & Upcraft, M. L. (2001). *Assessment practice in student affairs: An application manual.* San Francisco: Jossey-Bass.

Upcraft, M. L., & Schuh, J. H. (1998). Facts and myths about assessment in student affairs. *About Campus, 3*(5), 2-8.

Workshop/Training Opportunities

International Assessment & Retention Conference (National Association of Student Personnel Administrators)
    http://www.assessconf.net/

National Assessment Institute (Indiana University-Purdue University Indianapolis)
    http://www.planning.iupui.edu/conferences/national/nationalconf.html

National Conference on First-Year Assessment (National Resource Center for The First-Year Experience and Students in Transition)
    http://www.sc.edu/fye/events/

Student Affairs Assessment Seminar (American College Personnel Association)
    http://www.myacpa.org/pd/assessment/

Nationally Normed Instruments

Cooperative Institutional Research Program/Higher Education Research Institute
    http://www.gseis.ucla.edu/heri/herisurveys.php

Educational Benchmarking Inc. (EBI)
    http://www.webebi.com/

The National Study of Living-Learning Program
    http://www.livelearnstudy.net/

National Survey of Student Engagement
    http://nsse.iub.edu/index.cfm

Chapter Fourteen

Concluding Thoughts: Residence Life's Impact on the First-Year Experience Today and in the Future

Beth M. McCuskey

As part of my dissertation research (McCuskey, 2003), I asked select practitioners and faculty members to identify current and emerging trends in the housing profession and to forecast a timeline and level of impact to the trends. The data revealed 35 trends important to the profession, which served as the basis for a later edited collection (McCuskey & Dunkel, 2006). This chapter discusses select findings from these two projects with implications for first-year programming. Additionally, a model that ties together many of these findings to support student learning in the residential setting is presented.

Current and Emerging Trends

Our Students: Today and Tomorrow

Popular accounts of today's students often present conflicting pictures of their values, attitudes, and beliefs. For example, Sacks (1996) found Generation X college students to be transitioning toward a postmodern philosophy where they were grounding themselves in entertainment and relativism. His description of students was based on their consumerist attitudes and the general belief that because they paid tuition, students deserved to get "A" grades. Light (2001), on the other hand, seemed genuinely enchanted by students' desire to learn—both in and outside the classroom. Anderson and Payne (2006) note a similar disjuncture in descriptions of Millennial students, described by certain authors as "sheltered, confident, and team oriented" (e.g., Howe and Strauss) and by others as "skeptical, cynical, and self-interested" (e.g., Taylor) (p. 25).

These disjunctures are explained, in part, because writers and researchers try to make sense of generational tendencies prior to, or as, they are occurring. In *Millennials Go to College*, however, Howe and Strauss (2007) ground their generational research in looking at patterns of behavior over time. Their thesis is that emerging generations take on the characteristics of the exiting generation, so by extrapolating the characteristics of today's elderly population, we can see how the current generation is emerging. If they are correct, the Millennial students of today will exhibit characteristics similar to the generation that won WWII. Howe and Strauss demonstrate several characteristics of current students that support this conclusion. These traits include civic-mindedness and the importance these students place upon having families. While it is uncertain exactly when the next generational shift will occur on our campuses, it is likely that we are currently about half-way through the Millennial Generation. If Howe and Strauss' research proves true, this suggests that about in 10 years, the next generation to enroll on our campuses will assume characteristics similar to those of the Silent Generation, born between 1925 and 1942, and who exhibited largely conformist tendencies.

The Role of Parents

Howe and Strauss (2007) predict increasing levels of parental involvement as the generation of the parents with students enrolled in higher education shifts from the Baby Boomers to Gen Xers. In *Generation Me*, Twenge (2006) dubs Generation X parents "stealth fighters," highlighting the sometimes adversarial relationship between parents and institutions. Whatever the character of parental involvement, residence life programs must be prepared to work with more parents and at increasingly deeper levels. In fact, residence life professionals in my study predicted that

> In loco parentis will reemerge in some form. Parents and families will increase their participation and involvement in their students' lives. Housing professionals will commit more resources to working directly with parents of residential students. (McCuskey, 2003, p. 123)

Given the negative tenor of some parent-institution interactions and the amount of resources managing parent relationships could demand, it is easy to understand why faculty, staff, and administrators sometimes resist working with parents. The residence life profession is also grounded in helping students make the transition from adolescence to adulthood, so parental involvement may seem at odds with this philosophical perspective. However, evidence suggests that students want their parents to be involved. The Fall 2007 CIRP Freshman Survey (Higher Education Research Institute, 2008) found that 24% of first-year college students felt their parents had too little involvement in helping them choose college courses, while 22.5% of respondents felt that their parents had too little involvement in helping them select college activities. Similarly, findings from the 2007 National Survey for Student Engagement (NSSE) suggest that 75% of students tend to follow the advice of their parents.

Moreover, survey data suggest that parental involvement is connected with higher levels of engagement. For example, students who have frequent contact with their parents report higher levels of engagement and higher degrees of satisfaction with their college experience. However, these same students also report lower grades than their peers with less involved parents (NSSE, 2007). Whether the increased parental involvement is due to students' lower academic performance is unclear, suggesting the need for more research on the role of parent involvement in student success. Yet, given students' desire for parent involvement and the link to engagement and satisfaction, it makes sense to consider new approaches to involving parents.

One approach would be for a residence life department to "map" all of the formal contact points the department or institution has with parents and look to close the gaps. This includes looking at the communication that is developed for all parents and the nature of communication that takes place with individual parents related to individual student circumstances. Does the department correspond directly with parents to share information about its programs? What information is the department willing to share with parents regarding their individual students? Seeking the help of parents as partners in their children's educational journey at the beginning of the academic year can help mitigate possible problems later in the year.

Safety and Security

As noted in chapter 11, the terrorist attacks on September 11, 2001, and shootings at Virginia Tech and Northern Illinois have heightened concerns about safety on campus, altering the professional landscape and necessitating new approaches to campus security. Since the tragedy, for example, Virginia Tech has upgraded its campus security system, improved its communication processes, and developed strategies to enhance communication about troubled students (Grimes, 2007). Residence life departments will be challenged to find the resources to improve the physical security of their buildings. This may involve the installation of cameras, new and improved door locks, and speaker systems to announce safety messages. All of these enhancements come with a price, which may change the priority of other planned facility or programmatic enhancements. Such changes may also result in developing protocols that conflict with the openness and freedoms typically found on a college campus.

As conversations about campus security take place on the national stage, residence life practitioners can also look to their own training for solutions. Through a focus on building community, possible threats to safety can be identified and mitigated early. Whether it is identifying a stranger who does not belong in a building, or communicating concern for a fellow resident who is acting strangely, residence life professionals can play a vital role in campus safety efforts.

Administration and Operations

The residence life philosophy is frequently enacted through its facility operations, with many decisions being dictated by the mission of the housing department and its connection to the academic mission of the institution (Short & Chisler, 2006). This is particularly true with construction or renovation projects. Privatized residence halls, where a private developer is contracted to build residential accommodations, may be seamlessly managed by the host institution or maintained at arm's length depending on the department and institutional mission. Additionally, Hill and Fotis (2006) suggest that facility managers are responding in new ways to students who exhibit consumerist tendencies by shortening the time to complete work requests and building new facilities to provide more private space for students concerned about sharing a room (quite possibly for the first time in their lives).

Financial considerations are also a primary concern for residence life administrators who must often balance multi-million dollar budgets. Concerns about finances include the impact of aging facilities and deferred maintenance, decreasing state support for higher education, and the impact of "cost of attendance" upon those who can least afford higher education. Addressing these issues calls upon the residence life administrator to seek alternative revenue streams, to literally live the cliché of "doing more with less," and to build a strong case for reinvestment in housing facilities.

In addition to the physical plant, residence life administrators must also manage an ever-changing technological infrastructure, trying to meet students' technology expectations, navigating bandwidth issues, and incorporating technological advancements into administrative processes. Technology is also likely to affect academic course delivery and, in turn, the work of residence life professionals. For example, Zeller (2006) suggests that technology will be used to deliver classroom material, freeing up class time for more meaningful interactions between faculty and students. He envisions a day where the "seamless use of technologies within the physical campus environment will allow for the seamless integration of curricular and co-curricular experiences" (p. 62). Thus, residence life professionals must be poised to become effective partners in the delivery of seamless educational experiences.

Finally, another operational consideration necessary in the delivery of residence life programs and services is the department's human resources. As with other administrative decisions, the organizational structure of a residence life department reflects its philosophy and core values. For example, some new staffing models create paraprofessional positions to support student learning or offer new staff training experiences to address social issues on campus. It is also important to remember that the live-in experiences of current residence life administrators may not reflect reality of live-in experiences of today's staff or the needs of tomorrow's residence life operation (Belch & Kimble, 2006). As live-in roles shift to become more educational, the routine tasks of the position, such as front-line facility management, may need to be delegated to other staff in the department (Belch & Kimble). Thus, departments may wish to explore what tasks fall to their live-in staff and whether reallocating some tasks could free time to focus on educationally purposeful endeavors.

Campus Partnerships

Another research finding suggests that, "Boundaries between academic programs, student affairs, and business services units on campus will become blurred. Partnerships and coalitions will become the preferred strategy for program and service delivery" (McCuskey, 2003, p. 125). This finding is consistent with recommendations identified in *Learning Reconsidered* (Keeling, 2004), which discusses new structures and partnerships that will be necessary to facilitate student learning on campus. In order to support students, practitioners must look at new ways of delivering programs that fall outside the typical silos of academe.

Residential learning communities are an example of programs that may blur typical boundaries. While there are many approaches to structuring learning communities, a typical model involves students living together and taking several courses together. Learning is enhanced in several different areas. Frequently, the courses are linked by a synthesizing seminar that helps students draw connections across different courses. The cocurricular component may include formal activities such as service-learning projects or trips to gain hands-on experiences in the areas being studied. The social component of living together in the same community also helps students make informal connections.

Another consideration that emerged relates to enrollment management and its influence on the work of residence life practitioners. Research findings suggest that residence life will emerge as a partner in recruiting and retaining students (McCuskey, 2003). This is consistent with the literature, which has suggested that residence life plays a role in student retention (Pascarella & Terenzini, 1991; 2005). Additional linkages have been made between the quality of residential facilities and student recruitment. For example in a study of nearly 14,000 American college students, 42% deemed residence halls "extremely important" or "very important" when selecting a college (June, 2006). The same study found that more than a quarter of students rejected an institution because an important facility was inadequate. Delivering programs and services that fulfill institutional enrollment management strategies has become an important role for residence life professionals.

Learning Outcomes of Residence Life Programs

While respondents did not always agree, academic integration, as an overall theme, evolved as the most important programmatic element in my study (McCuskey, 2003). For example, when asked to reflect on residence halls renovations to connect to academic purposes "through classroom space...and other academic support features," one respondent replied, "This will be one of the most important areas for housing in the future. Housing operations that fail to connect with the academic community will fail as an integral part of the campus community." Another respondent commented, "I believe this is a fad that will pass" (McCuskey, 2003, p. 329).

Related to academic integration is the notion that "the residential experience will be linked more directly with the attainment of educational outcomes" (McCuskey, 2003, p. 117). This finding is consistent with recent publications such as *Learning Reconsidered* (Keeling, 2004) and *Learning Reconsidered 2* (Keeling, 2006) that suggest a need for student affairs practitioners to more effectively link their programs to student learning outcomes. Similarly, the regional accrediting agencies for higher education have embraced the assessment of student learning as a significant principle in reaccreditation visits. As the Middle States Commission on Higher Education (2006) notes, "...because student learning is a fundamental component of the mission of most institutions of higher education, the assessment of student learning is an essential component of the assessment of institutional effectiveness" (p. 65). The notion of cocurricular learning supporting institutional accreditation efforts is also emerging as an area where residence life practitioners need to focus their assessment efforts.

Learning outcomes supporting multiculturalism and diversity are another emerging area in residence life (McCuskey, 2003). Research participants suggested, "Diversity issues will continue to create challenges for housing programs. Finding ways to celebrate diversity while creating truly diverse residential experiences will be a high priority for housing administrators" (McCuskey, 2003, p. 124). In this area, efforts to educate residence life staff may be as important as efforts to educate students. As one respondent suggested,

> I think diversity and related issues are already woven into the fabric of student housing, and I don't see an increasing impact in this area. My sense is that students coming to campus these days may be more sophisticated in, and tolerant of, these changing demographics than many of us in the housing profession are. (McCuskey, p. 283)

Howard-Hamilton and Johnson (2006) identify several theoretical foundations of multiculturalism and review several ways that housing administrators can deliver training and programming to enhance their campuses. They also suggest that administrators explore their own identities as a part of this process to understand any biases that they may incorporate into their own value systems. Finally, they suggest that multiculturalism be explored as a topic within specialized learning communities. As the demographics in our country and on our campuses change, strategies to build inclusive communities will continue to be an important consideration for the residence life profession.

A Model That Ties it Together

The first part of this chapter highlighted trends affecting the residence life profession as identified by a doctoral research study. This section ties many of these elements together in a model developed to discuss strategies for overlaying a student learning framework onto an existing residence life program (McCuskey, 2005). Because residence life involves significant operational considerations as well as programmatic ones, the model addresses both elements. Additionally, the model asks practitioners to look at their existing work within a learning framework containing three critical elements: (a) effective environments, (b) systems of support, and (c) learning linkages. Since its original publication, the model has been updated to demonstrate the importance of assessment and evaluation as tools to further improve residence life programs (Figure 1).

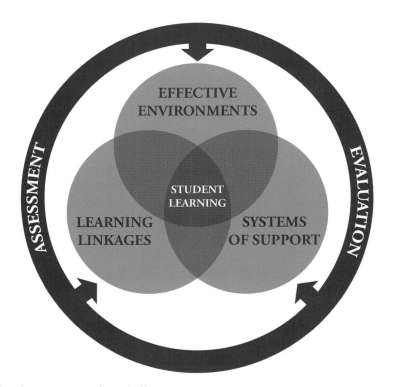

Figure 1. Student learning in residence halls.

Creating Effective Environments

Residence life programs naturally focus on the environment. Unlike most campus departments, residence life supports both physical facilities and educational culture. From a "Maslowian" (1987) perspective, residence life environments provide basic food and shelter and promote safety initiatives, provide social opportunities to residents, and support higher-level functions (i.e., self-esteem and self-actualization) that can arguably be more directly associated with learning. This basic approach to program development suggests that the environments we create support physical needs, social development, and intellectual attainment. Thus, as discussed in the first section, the environment is an overarching construct—enveloping physical space and cultural considerations.

From a practical perspective, this involves taking a critical look at our programs. Are facilities cleaned and maintained appropriately? Do students respect the facilities or is vandalism rampant? Do students feel safe in their residence halls? For those departments that manage dining services, are meals nutritious and served at times convenient to student schedules?

While Maslow may not have been thinking of today's college students when he conceptualized his hierarchy, it is important to put these basic needs in the current context. Howe and Strauss (2000) note that today's generation of college students is comfortable with a certain level of affluence. As a result, students want the basic needs—food and shelter—provided by residence life programs to reflect their prior experiences and expectations. Because the definition of "basic needs" is contextual, residence life departments must determine to what extent they will allow student context to define and drive the living-learning environments they create.

Social and intellectual development are also elements of successful learning environments. Does the residence life program support social development by providing opportunities to interact? Are students treated fairly in the disciplinary process? Do programs support developing self-understanding concurrent with developing an understanding of other cultures? Does the student culture in the residence hall support academic success? This attention to the environment—both physical and programmatic—can be the foundation for student learning to take place.

Building Systems of Support

Students arrive on campus from a variety of backgrounds with varying levels of ability. No matter how successful the student has been in high school, the college environment has far greater expectations. Upcraft and Gardner (1989) drew attention to the transitions experienced by first-year students in *The Freshman Year Experience*, where they suggested that higher education institutions invest in their first-year students by developing support systems to enhance the student experience. Residence life programs are poised to offer such support in both the cognitive and affective domains. While cognitive development is most frequently associated with the curriculum, it may be supported in the residence halls. Some ideas of support programs include tutoring services and intentionally designed study groups. Cognitive development may also be enhanced through developing program learning outcomes and assessing whether learning has taken place. For example, simple pre- and posttests can be an effective way to measure whether learning took place in an alcohol education seminar. Assessments can also be created to determine the depth of learning that occurred in a volunteer opportunity.

The affective domain is more closely linked to student affairs work, and there are many examples of the ways that residence life can build support structures to promote affective development. Some programming considerations include conflict resolution skills, multicultural awareness, and even the educational components of a disciplinary system. When cognitive and affective learning take place simultaneously, the results can lead to profound student growth.

Support systems also exist outside residence life. Units such as counseling centers, student health centers, and alcohol intervention programs all provide specialized support for students. Student learning will clearly be impeded if a student is in crisis, has physical health issues, or is making poor choices about alcohol use. Developing an understanding of the support systems on campus and how to refer students to them has always been included in the repertoire of residence life responsibilities. Because they intentionally oppose the "sink or swim" mentality that is often associated with higher education, such systems will remain an important part of residence life work.

Constructing Learning Linkages

A major component of the learning community movement focuses on building intentional linkages across the curriculum. Student learning is enhanced when connections are made across their courses. Learning is also enhanced when students build connections with each other. This peer support is an important element of learning communities. As Love (1999) suggests, "The collaborative nature of learning communities, therefore, encourages students to become integrated both socially and academically at the same time" (Love, p. 2). Residential learning communities can heighten the effects of traditional curricular learning communities because students take courses together and live together. This approach focuses on both cognitive and affective development as students are learning coursework while building the personal relationships that can further assist them in the learning process.

Residence life also is a natural venue for supporting learning linkages through leadership development. Leadership theory may be taught as part of a student course or through RA training, but learning is enhanced through serving in leadership roles. Students can study psychology in their classes, but the RA who is able to defuse a volatile situation or to encourage floor participation at events is putting theory into action.

Creating intentional linkages across academic disciplines or between academic disciplines and personal experiences help solidify the student learning experience. Residence life programs are in a key position to support curricular programs through cocurricular strategies.

Assessment and Evaluation

When this model was originally published, it did not address the key issues of assessment and evaluation. During the 1990s, as it became increasingly important to understand the impact of our work, the term "assessment" was used to broadly define attempts to measure success (or failure) in achieving program objectives. Recently, the term has evolved to focus more narrowly on the "assessment of student learning," while the term "evaluation" has become a standard term for measuring things not directly associated with student learning. In order for this model to be effective, it must be grounded in both assessment and evaluation. While chapter 13 discusses assessment and evaluation thoroughly, these concepts will continue to become such a critical component of residence life work that they deserve further discussion.

First, residence life administrators will be called upon to determine the impact of their environments. It will not be enough to say that we create effective environments, we must demonstrate it. Evaluating environments may run the gamut from simply determining whether student rooms have enough lighting to determining whether it makes sense to spend millions of dollars to renovate facilities. Can we determine that students who live in the new facility are learning more than those who live in the old one? These are the types of questions professionals must begin to ponder.

Assessment will also become the norm in administering systems of support. Does the alcohol intervention program work and how do we know? Do students who participate in tutoring services earn higher grades than those who do not (when controlling for other variables)? Simply stating that these programs are available is not enough. Counting participants in these programs does not measure whether learning has taken place.

Finally, residence life departments must assess whether their learning linkages are making a difference. Do students who participate in a learning community have higher levels of engagement? Are participants in an alternative spring break program learning? Developing learning outcomes for residence life programs, and measuring whether learning is truly taking place, moves residence life work to a much higher level of intentionality.

Assessment and evaluation will affect many residence life decisions in the coming decade. It is a direction being driven by many forces including the K-12 accountability movement, pressures from the federal and state governments, financial concerns about the rising cost of higher education, and employers who want college graduates with marketable skills.

Conclusion

Typically, we make predictions about the future by drawing conclusions from current events. In reality, future events are often drastically different from predictions because of intervening circumstances. Crises such as the terrorist attacks of September 11, 2001, or the tragedy at Virginia Tech cause practitioners to rethink how they approach their work. Economic conditions like a booming economy, or a depressed housing market, can lead to financial conditions conducive to, or restrictive of, construction and renovation plans. Residence life has always supported first-year students and their transitions to higher education. The future suggests that this trend will continue with even more intentionality than in the past. What remains unclear are the intervening circumstances of the next decades that will shape that intentionality.

References

Anderson, C. M., & Payne, R. W. (2006). Understanding students today and tomorrow. In B. M. McCuskey & N. W. Dunkel. (Eds.), *Foundations: Strategies for the future of collegiate housing* (pp. 22-40). Columbus, OH: Association of College and University Housing Officers-International.

Belch, H., & Kimble, G. (2006). Human resources in residence life. In B. M. McCuskey & N. W. Dunkel. (Eds.), *Foundations: Strategies for the future of collegiate housing* (pp. 69-95). Columbus, OH: Association of College and University Housing Officers-International.

Grimes, C. (2007, August 23). Virginia Tech panels urge safety changes. *Daily Press*. Retrieved August 28, 2007, from http://www.dailypress.com/news/dp-09964sy0aug,0,556004.story

Higher Education Research Institute. (2008, January). *The American freshman: National norms for fall 2007: Habits of mind, parental involvement & diversity*. Los Angeles: University of California, Author. Retrieved March 25, 2008, from http://www.gseis.ucla.edu/heri/PDFs/pubs/briefs/brief-012408-07FreshmanNorms.pdf

Hill, M. D., & Fotis, F. (2006). Managing construction and renovation in residential facilities. In B. M. McCuskey & N. W. Dunkel. (Eds.), *Foundations: Strategies for the future of collegiate housing* (pp. 109-120). Columbus, OH: Association of College and University Housing Officers-International.

Howard-Hamilton, M. F., & Johnson, S. D. (2006). Diversity and multiculturalism on college campuses. In B. M. McCuskey & N. W. Dunkel. (Eds.), *Foundations: Strategies for the future of collegiate housing* (pp. 41-58). Columbus, OH: Association of College and University Housing Officers-International.

Howe, N., & Strauss, W. (2000). *Millennials rising: The next generation*. New York: Random House.

Howe, N., & Strauss, W. (2007). *Millennials go to college* (2nd ed.). Great Falls, VA: Lifecourse.

June, A. W. (2006, May 30). Facilities can play a key role in students' enrollment decisions, study finds. *The Chronicle of Higher Education*. Retrieved September 14, 2007, from http://chronicle.com/weekly/v52/i40/40a02701.htm

Keeling, R. P. (Ed.). (2004). *Learning reconsidered: A campus-wide focus on the student experience*. Washington, DC: National Association of Student Personnel Administrators and American College Personnel Association.

Keeling, R. P. (Ed.). (2006). *Learning reconsidered 2: A practical guide to implementing a campus-wide focus on the student experience*. Washington, DC: ACPA, ACUHO-I, NACADA, NACA, & NASPA.

Light, R. J. (2001). *Making the most of college: Students speak their minds*. Cambridge, MA: Harvard University Press.

Love, A. G. (1999). What are learning communities? In J. H. Levine (Ed.), *Learning communities: New structures, new partnerships for learning*. (Monograph No. 26, pp. 1-8). Columbia SC: University of South Carolina. National Resource Center for The First-Year Experience and Students in Transition.

Maslow, A. H. (1987). *Motivation and personality* (3rd ed.). New York: Harper & Row.

McCuskey, B. (2005, September-October). Fitting student learning into residence life: A framework. *Talking Stick*, 19-20, 48.

McCuskey, B. M. (2003). The future of the university housing profession and implications for practitioners: A Delphi study. (Doctoral dissertation, West Virginia University, 2003). *Dissertation Abstracts International 64*, 1999.

McCuskey, B. M., & Dunkel, N. W. (Eds.). (2006). *Foundations: Strategies for the future of collegiate housing.* Columbus, OH: Association of College and University Housing Officers-International.

Middle States Commission on Education. (2006). *Characteristics of excellence in higher education: Eligibility requirements and standards for accreditation* (12th ed.). Philadelphia: Author.

National Survey for Student Engagement (NSSE). (2007). *Experiences that matter: Enhancing student learning and success, Annual report.* Retrieved March 25, 2008, from http://nsse.iub.edu/NSSE_2007_Annual_Report/docs/withhold/NSSE_2007_Annual_Report.pdf

Pascarella, E. T., & Terenzini, P. T. (1991). *How college affects students.* San Francisco: Jossey-Bass.

Pascarella, E. T., & Terenzini, P. T. (2005). *How college affects students* (Vol. 2). San Francisco: Jossey-Bass.

Sacks, P. (1996). *Generation X goes to college: An eye-opening account of teaching in postmodern America.* Chicago: Open Court.

Short, J., & Chisler, C. R. (2006). Privatized and off-campus housing relationships. In B. M. McCuskey & N. W. Dunkel. (Eds.), *Foundations: Strategies for the future of collegiate housing* (pp. 121-133). Columbus, OH: Association of College and University Housing Officers-International.

Twenge, J. M. (2006). *Generation me: Why today's young Americans are more confident, assertive, entitled—and miserable than ever before.* New York: Free Press.

Upcraft, M. L., & Gardner, J. N. (1989). *The freshman year experience.* San Francisco: Jossey-Bass.

Zeller, W. J. (2006). Academic integration and campus transformation. In B. M. McCuskey & N. W. Dunkel. (Eds.), *Foundations: Strategies for the future of collegiate housing* (pp. 59-66). Columbus, OH: Association of College and University Housing Officers-International.

About the Contributors

Bradford L. Angelini is a licensed architect in the states of Michigan, Illinois, Iowa, and Texas. Angelini has completed residence life and housing master plans for Idaho State University and Northern Arizona University, a housing feasibility study for the University of Michigan-Flint, various studies for living-learning communities at the University of Michigan, and the campus master planning of Spring Arbor College. Angelini also completed the design of the Union Drive Dining and Community Center at Iowa State University and the design of the CrossRoads MarketPlace and Dining Center at Eastern Michigan University. Angelini received a Masters of Architecture from Notre Dame in 1989, a Masters of Architecture from the University of Illinois at Chicago in 1983, and a Bachelor of Science in Architecture from The Ohio State University in 1981. Angelini is a partner at Angelini & Associates Architects in Ann Arbor, Michigan.

Leslie Atchley serves as coordinator of assessment and staff development for the Division of Student Affairs at the University of Georgia (UGA). She has previously worked with the student government association at UGA and Colonial Inauguration at The George Washington University. She holds a B.A. in English Literature from the University of Virginia and a M.Ed. in College Student Affairs Administration from UGA. Her professional interests include assessment, staff development, student self-governance, alcohol and other drugs on campus, and general education curricula.

Andrew Beckett serves as the associate dean of students at Miami University (Ohio) and is a directorate member for ACPA's Commission for Assessment and Evaluation. He previously served as the coordinator for freshman interest groups (FIGS) at the University of Missouri-Columbia. Beckett holds a Ph.D. in Educational Leadership and Policy Analysis from the University of Missouri-Columbia, an M.A. in Higher Education from the University of Arizona, and a B.S. in Mathematics from Truman State University.

Mimi Benjamin is the associate director for faculty programs in residential communities at Cornell University. She formerly served as the assistant to the vice president for student affairs and an adjunct faculty member in the Educational Leadership and Policy Studies Program at Iowa State University. She received her Ph.D. in Educational Leadership and Policy Studies from Iowa State University in 2004, M.A. in English from Clarion University of Pennsylvania in 1996, M.Ed. in Educational Leadership from Ohio University in 1994, and B.S. in Secondary Education (English) from Clarion University of Pennsylvania in 1985. Benjamin was a coordinator of residence life at Iowa State University, the assistant director of residential life at Plymouth State College (now University), and a hall director at Plymouth State College before joining the Vice President's Office staff. A member of ACPA, ASHE, and NASPA, Benjamin has served on the editorial board for the "Research in Brief" and "On the Campus" sections of the *Journal of College Student Development*. She was awarded the NASPA Region IV-East Mid-Level Professional award in 2005 and the national Mid-Level Professional Award from NASPA in 2006. She also was the 2007 recipient of the Betty Harrah Manuscript of the Year Award from ACUHO-I. Her research interests include learning communities, student affairs administration, undergraduate student experiences, graduate student development, and ethics.

Calvin J. Bergman is the associate director of residence life at the University of Wisconsin (UW)-Madison. In 1995, Bergman was the first program director of the Bradley Learning Community for first-year students at UW-Madison. Currently, Bergman provides oversight for the Chadbourne Residential College for liberal education and the Entrepreneurial Residential Learning Community (launched in fall 2008 and supported by a five-year grant from the Kauffman Foundation). Bergman continues to lead the integration of academic initiatives across all university residence halls through satellite academic advising offices, which align academic advising and residence hall assignments for one third of the first-year students; residence hall class sections and classrooms, which align course enrollment and residence hall assignment for one third of the first-year students; as well as Technology Learning Centers, tutoring, study group formation, and math supplemental instruction, among other initiatives. Bergman is currently a doctoral candidate with the Educational Leadership and Policy Analysis Department at UW-Madison.

Aaron M. Brower is vice provost for teaching and learning and professor of social work at the University of Wisconsin (UW)-Madison. Brower has published widely in areas of college student success and culture, high-risk drinking, residential learning communities, social work practice theory and research, group work, and social cognition. His work focuses on student success and persistence in higher education and how to "pre-structure" college environments to assure student success. For the past 20 years, he has been developing "integrative learning" programs that help students join their interests and passions within the classroom to those outside of them. In 2006, Brower completed a 10-year project funded by the Robert Wood Johnson Foundation addressing high-risk college student drinking. Brower was also the co-principal investigator for a $10 million, NSF-funded national higher education center that is infusing learning community principles into the training of graduate students in the sciences. He is the co-principal investigator for the National Study of Living-Learning Programs. In 2001, Brower won the Chancellor's Award for Distinguished Teaching from UW-Madison and, in 2006, was named one of the nation's Outstanding First-Year Student Advocates by Houghton Mifflin and the National Resource Center for The First-Year Experience and Students in Transition.

Mary Kay Schneider Carodine is the senior associate dean of students at the University of Florida (UF) with responsibilities for multicultural and diversity affairs, new student programs, Center for Leadership and Service, student legal services, and medical withdrawals. Prior to her tenure at UF, she worked as the director of student programs at Georgetown University. She earned her doctorate from the University of Maryland and worked with leadership development as well as with the U.S. House of Representatives Page Program during that time. Her professional involvement with the American College Personnel Association includes several national convention committees and commission directorate.

Craig M. Chatriand is the interim assistant director for the Academic Success Center at Iowa State University. He has formerly served as a residence hall director at Iowa State University and the University of Northern Colorado. He is currently a doctoral student in the Educational Leadership and Policy Studies Program at Iowa State with research interests in the areas of undergraduate student experiences, student expectations prior to arriving on campus, and issues of student retention. He received an M.A. in Educational Leadership and Policy Studies from the University of Northern Colorado in 2004 and a B.S. in Secondary Education (History, English) from the University of Montana-Western in 2002.

Jim Day was honored to be invited to revise chapter 11, which was originally authored by James C. Grimm. Grimm was chief housing officer at the University of Miami when Jim Day matriculated as a first-year student, and over time they developed a professional relationship and friendship that flourished until Grimm's death. Day has 36 years experience managing and leading college housing programs. He served for 16 years as executive director of university housing at the University of Georgia, where he held a concurrent appointment as adjunct assistant professor in the Counseling and Human Development Department. Day was previously the assistant director of residence and director of Richardson Court Residence Halls at Iowa State University where he earned a Ph.D. in Professional Studies in Education/Higher Education Administration. He spent four years at the University of Wisconsin-Oshkosh as director of housing and was co-founder of the Oshkosh Placement Exchange. He held the position of director of campus residential facilities at Ball State University for four years. He began his professional career at the University of Miami in 1970 as a residence hall director and area coordinator. Day has published numerous articles and chapters on topics germane to campus housing administration. He originated and hosts the international housing facilities officers Internet discussion group – "HOUSWORK." The SEC Housing Benchmarking Survey was conducted, compiled, and published under Day's leadership for 12 years. Day has provided consulting services to housing programs on 18 campuses and is a principle investigator in a biennial survey of student housing construction and renovation projects in the U.S.

Norbert W. Dunkel is the assistant vice president and director of housing and residence education at the University of Florida. He arrived at the University of Florida in 1988 after previously holding administrative positions at South Dakota State University and the University of Northern Iowa. His primary responsibilities include serving as chief housing officer for 10,000 students and family members in an operation with 750 employees and an operating budget of $40 million. Dunkel currently serves as the president of the Association of College & Housing Officers – International. Dunkel has authored/edited 10 books and monographs and more than 40 chapters or articles on various aspects of campus housing. He has served as a consultant to more than 20 universities and colleges and has testified before congressional committees on two occasions. He co-developed and then co-directed the ACUHO-I James C. Grimm National Housing Training Institute for 10 years.

Merrily S. Dunn is an associate professor and program coordinator for the College Student Affairs Administration program, in the Department of Counseling and Human Development Services at the University of Georgia. Prior to her appointment at UGA, Dunn taught at Mississippi State University for eight years. She holds a Ph.D. in Higher Education Administration from The Ohio State University and an M.S. in Higher Education Administration from Iowa State University as well as an undergraduate degree in political science from the University of Nebraska. Her work as a student affairs professional included positions in student housing, judicial affairs, and women student services. Dunn's research interests concentrate primarily on the preparation of student affairs professionals, living-learning environments, and gender issues in higher education.

Brad V. Harmon is associate director of residence life at Furman University, where he has responsibility initiatives that promote student learning and success through the management of the residence life program and supervision of residence life staff. He provides general oversight, leadership, and direction for the Engaged Living Learning communities program, directs the Freshman Advisor program, and coordinates the assessment of student learning and development programming for residence halls and apartments. He has substantial experience with the development and assessment of peer educator programs and has conducted research on peer educator learning processes and outcomes. His professional experience also includes work in academic advising, first-year experience programming, orientation, and residence life. Harmon received his Ph.D. in counseling and student personnel services from the University of Georgia, an M.Ed. in higher education administration from the University of South Carolina, where he worked as a graduate assistant for the National Resource Center for The First-Year Experience and Students in Transition. He holds a B.A. in history from Furman University.

Richard Holeton is associate director of Academic Computing, and head of Student Computing, at Stanford University, where previously he taught in the first-year writing program and English Department for 11 years and coordinated the Computers and Writing Project. While teaching, he served as Resident Fellow in a first-year residence hall for seven years. Prior to working at Stanford, he taught composition and creative writing at Canada Community College and San Francisco State University. He earned his B.A. from Stanford University and M.A. and M.F.A. degrees from San Francisco State University. Holeton is the author of college writing textbooks including *Composing Cyberspace: Identity, Community, and Knowledge in the Electronic Age* and a frequent contributor of articles, scholarship, and presentations about technology in higher education. Also a fiction writer, he is the author of short stories in numerous literary journals, the "classic hypertext" novel *Figurski at Findhorn on Acid*, and other works of electronic literature. His literary work has been anthologized in the *Electronic Literature Collection, Volume 1* (Electronic Literature Organization) and *The Rosetta Screen*, permanent installation at the Martin Luther King, Jr., Public and University Library, San Jose, California.

Mary L. Hummel, is director of housing and residence life at the University of North Carolina at Greensboro. Prior to this position, she served as associate director of university housing and director of residence education at the University of Michigan. Among her responsibilities at the University of Michigan, she directed the living-learning programs. She was the founding director of two of the living-learning programs, specifically in the areas of access for women and underrepresented students. Hummel has consulted, written publications, and conducted numerous presentations in the area of residentially based academic programs on a national level. She has hosted the International Living Learning Program Conference in Ann Arbor. She received her Ph.D. from the Center for the Study of Higher and Postsecondary Education at the University of Michigan. Her master's degree and undergraduate degree are both from the Pennsylvania State University.

Karen Kurotsuchi Inkelas is an associate professor in the College Student Personnel Program, Department of Counseling & Personnel Services at the University of Maryland. Inkelas is the principal investigator for the National Study of Living-Learning Programs (NSLLP). In addition to her work with living-learning programs, Inkelas's other research interests include the Asian Pacific American college student experience and assessments of campus racial climates. Inkelas obtained her B.A. and M.S. from Northwestern University and her Ph.D. from the Center for the Study of Higher & Postsecondary Education (CSHPE) at the University of Michigan. Prior to her appointment at the University of Maryland, she developed and directed the Housing Research Office for University Housing at the University of Michigan from 1998 to 2001.

Joel Johnson currently serves as the director of the College of Engineering Student Programs and Services at Iowa State University. He holds a masters degree in College Student Personnel from Western Illinois University. Previous work experience includes serving from 2000 to 2008, as director for the Office of First Year Experience at Minnesota State University, Mankato. Responsibilities included oversight for campus retention efforts and supervision for the programmatic areas of new student orientation, undeclared academic advising, and learning communities. He also served as administrative chair for the first-year seminar course. Additional higher education experience includes work in residential life, both at Minnesota State, Mankato and the University of Nebraska-Lincoln.

Gene Luna currently serves as associate vice president for student affairs/director of student development and university housing at the University of South Carolina, where he also holds a clinical faculty appointment in the College of Education, teaching in the Higher Education and Student Affairs Administration graduate program. He has direct responsibility for university housing and residence education, student judicial affairs, academic integrity, the National Student Exchange Program, student health center, university counseling center, student disability services, sexual health and violence prevention, student engagement, and a campus initiative to promote health and wellness—Healthy Carolina. Luna has published more than 30 articles and made more than 100 presentations on a variety of higher education subjects. In 2008, he completed a monograph, *Learning Initiatives in the Residential Setting* (with Jimmie Gahagan), published by the National Resource Center for The First-Year Experience and Students in Transition. He has served as a consultant for numerous colleges and universities with his most recent projects focusing on the areas of master planning for student housing, academic and student affairs partnerships, initiatives for first-year students, and environmental sustainability practices.

Beth M. McCuskey is the executive director of residence life, dining services, and the Wyoming Union at the University of Wyoming in Laramie. In addition to overseeing the three departments, she also coordinates the student learning assessment functions for the Division of Student Affairs. Prior to her position in Wyoming, she held a variety of administrative roles in the housing and residence life department at West Virginia University. McCuskey has a B.S. in Economics, an M.A. in Higher Education, an M.S. in Industrial and Labor Relations, and an Ed.D. in Higher Education Leadership—all from West Virginia University. She has served as a faculty member for ACUHO-I's Chief Housing Officer Training Institute and National Housing Training Institute, and helped to conceptualize the AIMHO College, an institute for new housing professionals in the intermountain region. She has been active in NASPA and ACUHO-I, and currently serves as chair-elect for the ACUHO-I Foundation. She has published several articles and co-edited a book, *Foundations: Strategies for the Future of Collegiate Housing*, published by ACUHO-I in 2006.

James Parker is associate director for residence life at St. Louis University. He holds a master's degree in Higher Education Administration from the University of Kansas and a bachelor's degree in history/political science from Southwest Baptist University. Prior to his current position, he was coordinator of the Graduate Student First Year Initiative at the University of California, Irvine (UCI), a new living-learning program for residential graduate students. Prior to UCI, he worked in residential life at the University of Southern California, The University of Maryland-College Park, Michigan State University, and the University of Nebraska-Lincoln. He also served as the assistant director for academic initiatives in the First Year Experience Office at Minnesota State University, Mankato. He is currently co-editing a monograph on personal and professional transformation through organizational change.

John R. Purdie, II earned a B.A. in Speech-Communication in 1991 from Western Washington University (WWU), an M.A. in Higher, Adult and Lifelong Education from Michigan State University in 1994, and a Ph.D. in Educational Leadership and Policy Analysis from the University of Missouri – Columbia in 2007. Purdie's work at these schools, as well as University of Nevada - Las

Vegas and Arizona State University, has given him experience with living-learning communities, community standards, assessment, collaborating with faculty, and occasionally teaching graduate-level courses and first-year seminars. Purdie is proud to serve as the associate director of university residences for residence life at WWU.

Matthew Soldner is the National Study of Living-Learning Program's ACUHO-I/NASPA doctoral research fellow and a doctoral candidate at the University of Maryland. Before returning to doctoral studies, Soldner was associate director of residential life at University of Maryland Baltimore County, in Baltimore, MD, where he worked with living-learning programs and directed the Shriver Living-Learning Center, a program honoring Sargent Shriver and his vision of service and civic engagement. His research has been published in *Research in Higher Education, Journal of College Student Development, NASPA Journal*, and *Journal of College and University Student Housing*.

Katalin Szelényi is a postdoctoral research associate on the National Study of Living-Learning Programs at the University of Maryland, College Park. She received her Ph.D. and M.A. degrees in Higher Education at UCLA's Graduate School of Education and a B.A. degree in Applied Linguistics at Eötvös Loránd University in Budapest, Hungary. Her research focuses on doctoral student socialization in the sciences and engineering, undergraduate women's experiences in science, technology, engineering, and mathematics (STEM) fields, and issues of globalization and citizenship in higher education. In fall 2008, she will join the University of Massachusetts, Boston's College of Education as an assistant professor of Higher Education.

William J. Zeller currently serves as the director of the graduate student center at the University of California, Irvine, where he has also served as assistant vice chancellor. He was formerly the director of university housing at the University of Michigan and has held similar positions at Washington State University and Southeast Missouri State University. He earned his bachelor's degree from Northern Illinois University, his master's in College Student Personnel Administration from Western Illinois University, and his Ph.D. in Higher Education Administration from Iowa State University. He is the author of numerous articles and book chapters with particular concentration on the first-year experience and living-learning programs. He has served as a consultant to many campuses to assist them in the development of new residential learning communities and the design of facilities to support them. He has also held several leadership positions in the Association of College & Housing Officers – International (ACUHO-I).